Saints of the Missal

Saints of the Missal

BY

RT. REV. *Benedict Baur*, O.S.B.

TRANSLATED BY

Raymond Meyerpeter, O.S.B.

MONK OF CONCEPTION ABBEY

VOLUME II
July - December

B. HERDER BOOK CO.

15 & 17 South Broadway, St. Louis 2, Mo.
AND 33 Queen Square, London, W.C.

This is a translation of Volume IV of *Werde Licht* by Rt. Rev. Benedict Baur, O.S.B., published by Herder & Co., G.m.b.H., Freiburg, Germany.

Imprimi potest: ✠ Stephen Schappler, O.S.B.
Coadjutor Abbot

Imprimatur: ✠ Joseph E. Ritter, S.T.D.
Archbishop of St. Louis

March 5, 1958

52344

Contents

v

✦✦✦✦✦✦✦✦✦

JULY

✦✦✦✦✦✦✦✦✦

JULY 1

The Most Precious Blood of Our Lord
Jesus Christ

1. The month of July is dedicated to the Precious Blood, the price of our redemption. All the riches of the work of redemption are gathered together in the Precious Blood, and for this reason its feast is one of grateful remembrance of our having been redeemed by Christ.

2. "Out of every tribe, every language, every people, thou hast ransomed us, Lord, with thy blood; thou hast made us a royal race to serve our God" (Introit).

On this feast the liturgy considers us members of the choir of the blessed in heaven, calling to the Lamb: "Thou wast slain in sacrifice; . . . hast ransomed us with thy blood and given us to God" (Apoc. 5:9). Unlike the high priest of the Old Law, who once a year entered the Holy of Holies, where the Ark of the Covenant was kept and sprinkled it with the blood of sacrificial animals, Christ, our high Priest, has entered into His sanctuary (heaven) and "the ransom he has won lasts for ever" (Epistle). This ransom, this redemption, is effective for all time: it is different from the sacrifices of the Old Law, for it has power to "purify our consciences" and to give us a share in the promised eternal inheritance (cf. Epistle).

"We have found justification through his blood" (Rom. 5:9), and have been rescued from God's wrath and from the danger of exclusion from His Kingdom. By virtue of the blood of Jesus we have the firm hope of entering into the sanctuary of heaven. "He has opened up for us a new, a living approach, by way of the veil, I mean, his mortality" (Heb. 10:20), that is, by His death on the Cross. How grateful we should be! Let us remind ourselves frequently that "a great price was paid to ransom" us, and "glorify God by making [our] bodies the shrines of his presence" (cf. I Cor. 6:20).

"It is achieved. Then he [Jesus] bowed his head and yielded up his spirit. . . . And so the soldiers came and broke the legs both of the one and of the other that were crucified with him; but when they came to Jesus, and found him already dead, they did not break his legs, but one of the soldiers opened his side with a spear; and immediately blood and water flowed out" (Gospel). Our Savior shed blood first at His circumcision; a second time in the Garden of Olives; again when the soldiers scourged Him and roughly pressed the crown of thorns upon His head; a fourth time when, on Calvary, they tore the garments from His lacerated body and nailed His hands and feet to the Cross. Then He hung on the Cross, covered with a garment of His own blood; but He still retained a few drops of blood in His lifeless body; this, too, He wished to shed for us. "He still loved those who were his own, whom he was leaving in the world, and he would give them the uttermost proof of his love" (John 13:1). "He who saw it has borne his witness; and his witness is worthy of trust" (Gospel). To this we reply, with the liturgy: *Credo*—I believe.

3. "He it is, Jesus Christ, whose coming has been made known to us by water and blood; water and blood as well, not water alone. We have a threefold warrant in heaven, the Father, the Word, and the Holy Ghost, three who are yet one; and we have a threefold warrant on earth, the Spirit, the water, and the blood, three witnesses that conspire in one [that is, they testify to the same fact]" (Gradual). John wants to tell us that Jesus the Savior became man, and that we have a threefold testimony to prove it: 1) the water,

that is, the Father's words at the baptism of Christ; 2) the blood, that is, the Son's bloody death on the Cross; 3) the Holy Spirit, that is, the Pentecostal grace in the Church and in the hearts of the faithful.

The Precious Blood of Christ is put into our hands as an offertory gift at Holy Mass. We have the vocation and the right to offer up the blood of Christ, the blood of reconciliation, to the Father by the hand of the sacrificing priest. In Holy Communion we receive, under the one form of bread, the whole Christ, His flesh and His blood, which is the pledge of our salvation on the day when our Lord will come to take us home to the Father (cf. Communion).

The chosen people were commanded to slay the Paschal lamb and to sign their doorposts with its blood. Then: "The Lord will pass on his way smiting down the Egyptians, and when he sees the blood on the lintel and the jambs of a doorway he will pass by that house, and will not let the destroying angel enter your homes to do them injury" (Exod. 12:23). This was a figure and a guarantee of the saving power of the blood of the Lamb of God who takes away the sins of the world. We put our trust in this efficacy of the Blood of Christ.

Collect: Eternal, ever-living God, who didst ordain that Thy only-begotten Son should redeem the world and with His blood atone to Thee for man's offenses; grant, we pray Thee, that we may so worship in this festival rite the ransom paid for our salvation, and find in its power such defense against the evils of this earthly life, that we may enjoy its everlasting fruit in heaven. Amen.

JULY 2

Our Lady's Visitation

1. Not long after the feast of John the Baptist's birth, the
Church celebrates Mary's Visitation. The Archangel Gabriel
had said to the Virgin: "She [Elizabeth] is old, yet she too has
conceived a son; she who was reproached with barrenness is
now in her sixth month, to prove that nothing can be impossible with God" (Luke 1:36). Mary understood. Although,
since the unique experience of conceiving God, she was entirely absorbed in, and devoted to Him whom she carried in
her spotless body, nevertheless Mary hurried over the mountains to her cousin Elizabeth, to offer her services during the
last months before the birth of John. Mary's first act after
becoming the Mother of God was a service of charity toward
Elizabeth and John.

2. The Gospel of the feast tells the story: "Mary rose and
went with all haste to a town of Juda, . . . and there entering
in she gave Elizabeth greeting. No sooner had Elizabeth
heard Mary's greeting, than the child leaped in her womb;
and Elizabeth herself was filled with the Holy Ghost; so that
she cried out with a loud voice, Blessed art thou among women,
and blessed is the fruit of thy womb. How have I deserved to
be thus visited by the mother of my Lord? Why, as soon as
ever the voice of thy greeting sounded in my ears, the child
in my womb leaped for joy. Blessed art thou for believing; the
message that was brought to thee from the Lord shall have
fulfilment. And Mary said, My soul magnifies the Lord; my
spirit has found joy in God, who is my Saviour." Mary is Christ-
bearer: she brings Christ, salvation, and grace into the home
of Zachary. At her coming Elizabeth was filled with the Holy
Spirit, and John was cleansed of original sin and sanctified,
even before his birth. It is Christ who brings salvation to men,

but He brings it through Mary, His Mother. Mary, for her part, placed herself completely at the disposal of the Savior living and working in her while she was at the home of Elizabeth. No doubt it would have pleased her best, now that she had become Mother of God, to stay in the quiet solitude of her own home in Nazareth, in order to live entirely for Him whom she was carrying. Still, she had no sooner heard Elizabeth's secret from the Archangel than she forgot her own wishes and hastened to her cousin. Grace does not permit anyone to neglect the charity, justice, courtesy, and good example that he owes his neighbor.

The Lesson of today's Mass indicates the deeper meaning of the historical event. John the Baptist represents mankind, the Church, all of us. Christ visits us and desires to unite us to Himself in bride-like love. Between the Bridegroom and bride stands Mary, the mediatrix of the bond which Christ establishes with His bride. The gospel record of a past event is really a present fact that is being repeated without interruption in the Church and in us. "See where he comes, how he speeds over the mountains, how he spurns the hills. . . . And now he is standing on the other side of this very wall; now he is looking in through each window in turn, peering through every chink. I can hear my beloved calling to me: Rise up, rise up quickly, dear heart, so gentle, so beautiful, rise up and come with me." Our Lord can hardly wait to go to John, to come to us. He wants to cleanse us from our sins, to sanctify us with His grace, to raise us up and unite us with His own life. He wants to be our Savior and to make us sharers in His dignity, the dignity of the children of God; but always, it is only through Mary and through the Church, that we experience the visit of the Bridegroom. In her He stands at the wall, peers through the window, and speaks to us in order to win us to His love and His redemption. We need more of the deep faith that animated the Church in selecting such a Lesson.

3. How fortunate John and Elizabeth were! Through Mary Mediatrix they experienced the grace-bringing visitation of the Lord. Fortunate are we, also; for, as often as we desire, we may experience the visitation of the same Lord by participating in the celebration of the Eucharistic Sacrifice and receiving Holy Communion. Blessed are we for believing, for belonging to Mary and to the Church, for being permitted in Holy Communion to carry the "creator of the world" (Offertory), "the eternal Father's Son" (Communion), the same Jesus whom Mary carried to Elizabeth. We must hold fast to Mary and to the Church, for Mary is the Mediatrix of grace.

This feast is the birthday of that sublime hymn of praise and gratitude, Mary's Magnificat:

"My soul magnifies the Lord;
  my spirit has found joy in God, who is my Saviour
Because he has looked graciously upon the lowliness of
  his handmaid.
Behold, from this day forward all generations will
  count me blessed;
Because he who is mighty, he whose name is holy,
  has wrought for me his wonders.
He has mercy upon those who fear him,
  from generation to generation;
He has done valiantly with the strength of his arm,
    driving the proud astray in the conceit of
        their hearts;
He has put down the mighty from their seat,
  and exalted the lowly;
He has filled the hungry with good things,
  and sent the rich away empty-handed.
He has protected his servant Israel,
  keeping his merciful design in remembrance—
According to the promise which he made to our forefathers,
  Abraham and his posterity for evermore."

Collect: Lord, bestow upon Thy servants the gift of heavenly grace, we pray Thee, so that we for whom the birth of the Blessed Virgin's child meant the beginning of salvation, may find in the worshipful feast of her Visitation, increase of peace. Amen.

JULY 4

St. Ulrich, *Bishop*

1. At the Synod of Rome in 993, Luitbold, Bishop of Augsburg, asked Pope John XV and the assembled cardinals and bishops for permission to speak. He told them about the life and work of his predecessor, Bishop Ulrich, and asked them to say whether it were right to honor this man as a saint. The clergy unanimously agreed that Bishop Ulrich was a saint worthy of veneration and thus enacted the first solemn canonization.

Ulrich was born at Augsburg in 890, to a noble Swabian family. As an infant he was lean and weak, failing to respond to his mother's ardent care; by an unmistakable miracle he suddenly became healthy and strong. Later he was sent for his education to the monastery of St. Gall in Switzerland. At the age of eighteen Ulrich returned to Augsburg and entered the service of Bishop Adalbero there. The news of this bishop's death in 909 forced Ulrich to interrupt a pilgrimage and to return at once to Rome. Shortly after, his father died, and Ulrich went to Dillingen to solace his mother and to manage the family estate. Back in St. Gall in 920, Ulrich asked the recluse Wiborada whether he ought to become a monk there, but was told that God had other work for him. Soon afterward he was elected bishop of Augsburg and was consecrated on the feast of the Holy Innocents, in 923. Being a prince of the realm, he had important duties to the kingdom as well as to the dio-

cese. Accordingly, he spent some time in faithful service at the
court of Henry I. Eventually Ulrich suggested that his court
and army duties be turned over to his nephew, Adalbero; the
king agreed, and Ulrich was then free to devote his time to
his episcopate.

The city and diocese of Augsburg had suffered heavily from
the raids of the Slavs and Hungarians. It was no easy task to
relieve the misery and restore religious living. The first object
of Ulrich's solicitude was the cathedral school, in which the
clergy were to be formed. Then he worked at reviving monasteries and renovating churches in order to foster divine
services. In the meantime he cared for the poor and sick with
touching charity and devoted all available free time to prayer.
At the age of eighty, after returning from a pilgrimage to Rome,
he exchanged his purple robes for a monk's habit and asked
King Otto to accept his resignation of the bishopric. The king
refused. A year later, on July 4, 973, Bishop Ulrich died, having
governed his diocese for fifty years. He was buried by St.
Wolfgang, the bishop of Regensburg, in the Augsburg church
now bearing his name.

2. "Well done, my good and faithful servant; since thou
hast been faithful over little things, I have great things to
commit to thy charge" (Gospel; Mass *Statuit*). St. Ulrich gave
himself generously to the care of his diocese, to prayer, and to
charitable causes. Year by year he would visit some part of his
extensive territory by ox-cart, gathering the parishioners
around him to scrutinize their lives. Particularly concerned
about the young, he labored to provide schools and good teachers. The oppressed found a kind father in him. He would invite
strangers to his table and serve them himself. His love of neighbor would not permit him to send any needy person away
without relief. In spite of all this activity, however, St. Ulrich
was a man of deep prayer and interior life, often celebrating
Mass two or three times a day. When in Augsburg he always

joined the canons in their recitation of the Divine Office. Truly was St. Ulrich a "good and faithful servant."

"Here was a great priest whose life was acceptable to God. . . . The Lord gave him the blessing which should extend to all nations, renewing the covenant in his person . . . such grace he found in the eyes of the Lord" (Lesson). In the year 955 the Hungarian hordes had reappeared, devastating the land. From the country, people fled to Augsburg, and the enemy surrounded the city. Taking recourse to divine weapons, the bishop ordered prayers and a solemn procession of petition. Then, calling the people to arms, St. Ulrich encouraged them to trust God and led them into battle, wearing a stole and spurring his horse where help was needed, with a total disregard for flying arrows. Faced with this, and hearing that Otto was approaching, the Hungarians raised the siege and withdrew to the Lech River to prepare for battle. On August 10 St. Ulrich celebrated the Mass of St. Laurence for the success of the venture, distributed Holy Communion to the king and all his warriors, and sent them off to battle with his blessing. The furious fighting lasted all day, but toward evening the Hungarians took to flight, losing many men in the swollen river. The victory was attributed primarily to St. Ulrich.

3. Chaplain Gerhard, who wrote the Saint's life immediately after it ended, concludes his account with the following words: "To everyone who reads this biography in the love of Christ, the grace of God will be at hand, for the Servant of God will be a strong support to him in this life and will help him to attain to eternal joys."

Joyfully we sing in the Communion song: "He was a faithful and wise servant, one whom his master entrusted with the care of his household, to give them their allowance of food at the appointed time" (Luke 12:42). We thank God for this savior of Europe, and we beg St. Ulrich to obtain the divine protection for us against the enemy that now threatens from the East.

Collect: O God, Thou seest that we are unable to stand steadfast by our own strength; grant us, then, this favor, that the intercession of Thy holy confessor and bishop St. Ulrich may protect us from all evil. Amen.

JULY 5

St. Anthony Mary Zaccaria, *Confessor*

1. Anthony was born in 1502, the only child of a patrician family of Cremona, Italy. Amidst the wealth and pomp of his upbringing, he distinguished himself by deep, serious piety, and a ready, good spirit of helpfulness derived from his very religious mother. As a boy he often gave his clothing to the first beggar he met. In order to help suffering mankind better, he studied medicine at Padua, receiving his degree in 1524. He established a practice in Cremona in order to attend patients during the day, while in the evening he would gather his friends around him in the Church of St. Vitalis to read passages of the New Testament and discuss them, especially the Epistles of St. Paul. He spent much time praying for guidance in the choice of a vocation. Finally he decided to study theology, and was ordained at the age of twenty-six. As the citizens of Cremona had formerly consulted the doctor, so now they came to hear the preacher, who kindled anew the fire of faith and zeal for Christian living. Anthony was also a tireless pastor and confessor. He renewed the face of the city in a few years by his wonder-working example of generous charity. In 1530 Anthony moved to Milan, to be joined by a law student and another young man who had formerly been very worldly. They enthusiastically helped him to found a congregation of priests who would model their whole lives on the ideals of the early Church. Pope Clement VII approved the "Clerks Regular of St. Paul" in 1533. Gradually they were joined by sons of the

best families of Milan. About 1535 Anthony also founded the "Angelic Virgins of St. Paul" with the help of the countess of Guastalla, to be guardian angels for young girls exposed to dangers. Anthony suffered much from calumnies and persecutions in Milan. Yet he was called to Vicenza to work for the religious rehabilitation of the people there. Returning from this mission he fell ill, but went to Guastalla to reconcile its warring citizens. From this journey he returned only as far as Cremona, to die in the arms of his mother, on July 5, 1539. His body was taken to Milan and buried in his Order's Church of St. Barnabas. Because of this his Congregation was called the Barnabites. It now has seven provinces and numbers about four hundred priests.

2. "In one thing . . . thou art still wanting. Go home and sell all that belongs to thee; give it to the poor, and so the treasure thou hast shall be in heaven; then come back and follow me" (Gospel). When the priests of Milan were pulling his preachers out of their pulpits, calling them the "plague of the city" and threatening to burn their home, St. Anthony tried to encourage his brethren by telling them, "We are fools for Christ." The hatred against them came from both clergy and people. Why? Because they had chosen the foolishness of the Cross of Christ and were preaching Christ Crucified by word and example. Why had this popular physician given up worldly goods and position to live a life of renunciation and sincere imitation of our Lord? It did not make sense. And, to make it worse, a countess had associated herself with Anthony and chosen that foolishness also. Was not all this a slap in the face to the superficial world of Renaissance Milan? Many thought that Anthony was overplaying his role by preaching and doing penance in the streets. Even Pope Paul III did not know for a while just what to make of Anthony's undertakings. He soon understood, however, and lent the weight of his protection to the movement, declaring: "It is just such men that the Church needs; she has plenty of scholars and diplomats."

"My preaching, my message depended on no persuasive
language devised by human wisdom, but rather on the proof I
gave you of spiritual power" (I Cor. 2:4). The Introit puts
these words of St. Paul on the lips of Anthony Zaccaria, because from his youth he had so thoroughly saturated his mind
with the thoughts of St. Paul that his life and preaching were
filled with the spirit of the Apostle. This is reflected in the name
of his Congregation. As a priest he undertook the spiritual and
moral reformation of the people with the ardor and force of
St. Paul. In a few years, he and his brothers reformed all Upper
Italy and thus prepared the ground for the later work of St.
Charles Borromeo.

St. Anthony drew strength for this superhuman missionary
activity from prayer, particularly from his devotion to the
Eucharistic Christ. It was his love for the Blessed Sacrament
that moved him to promote the so-called "Forty Hours Devotion." The Offertory of the Mass alludes to this zeal: "Angels
for my witnesses, I sing of thy praises: I bow down in worship
toward thy sanctuary, giving praise to thy name" (Ps. 137:1).
Another source of strength for Anthony's work among souls
was his charity; he desired to be all things to all men, as did
St. Paul: "God knows how I long for you all, with the tenderness of Jesus Christ himself. And this is my prayer for you: may
your love grow richer and richer yet, in the fulness of its
knowledge and the depth of its perception" (Gradual; Phil.
1:8). In the power of this love Anthony consumed himself for
the sake of those who slandered him. He had only one desire:
to save all.

3. "Be content, brethren, to follow my example, and mark
well those who live by the pattern we have given them" (Communion; Phil. 3:17). Anthony shines out as a model of renunciation, brotherly love, and zeal for the salvation of souls. We
are fools for Christ. "So much wiser than men is God's foolishness; so much stronger than men is God's weakness. . . . God
has chosen what the world holds base and contemptible, nay,

has chosen what is nothing, so as to bring to nothing what is now in being" (I Cor. 1:25–28).

Collect: Lord God, enable us to grasp, in the spirit of Thy apostle Paul, that transcendent knowledge of Jesus Christ which in marvelous ways taught blessed Anthony Mary to gather together in Thy Church new religious families of men and women. Amen.

JULY 11

Solemnity of St. Benedict

1. On March 21 we celebrate the death of St. Benedict, his birthday in heaven. Today's feast dwells on the miracles wrought by the Holy Patriarch during his lifetime, by the grace of God. These may be taken as an indication of the great influence he still exercises over the heart of God.

2. "I will make a great people of thee; I will bless thee and make thy name renowned" (Introit; Gen. 12:2). In these words the liturgy places St. Benedict at the side of the great Patriarch Abraham, father of those who believe, father of the chosen race of Israel. Indeed, God made the silent, hidden hermit in the cave of Subiaco a remarkably great man by giving him, as his spiritual progeny, the chosen race of Western monks, and setting him up as the blessed one (Benedictus) in whom all nations were to be blessed. "He stands firm as a tree planted by running water ready to yield its fruit when the season comes" (Offertory; Ps. 1:3). Through the centuries his Order has continued to produce new branches, blossoms, and fruit. "And never shedding a leaf; all that he does will prosper." "Blessed are they who have seen thee," holy Father Benedict, "and who have enjoyed thy friendship" (Lesson; cf. Ecclus. 48). Thou art the blessed dispenser of blessings; thou art Elias, who "appeased the wrath of God in the judgment of the last

times, reconciled the heart of the father with his children, and renewed the tribes of Jacob." Thou wast called by God to save the Christian faith in the nations of the West from the confusion of the migration of nations, after the unhappy time of the Arian heresy. "The Lord granted him blessing for all peoples" (Communion; cf. Ecclus. 44:25). Therefore, "praise the Lord, my soul; may all that is in me sing praise to His holy name" (Introit Psalm). We sing praise to Him who did such great things for St. Benedict that we still experience wonders through him.

"Like a star in the darkness of night, Benedict of Nursia brilliantly shines, a glory not only to Italy but of the whole Church. Whoever considers his celebrated life and studies in the light of the truth of history, the gloomy and stormy times in which he lived, will without doubt realize the truth of the divine promise which Christ made to the Apostles and to the society He founded, 'I am with you all through the days that are coming, until the consummation of the world' (Matt. 28:20). But when enemies assail the Christian faith more fiercely, when the faithful barque of Peter is tossed about more violently and when everything seems to be tottering with no hope of human support, it is then that Christ is present, bondsman, comforter, source of supernatural power, and raises up fresh champions to protect Catholicism, to restore it to its former vigor, and give it ever greater increase under the inspiration and help of heavenly grace.

"Among these champions shines out in resplendent light our Benedict, blessed 'by name and grace' (St. Gregory). In the providential designs of God he emerged from a dark century when the position and fate of civilization as well as of the Church and of civil society was in danger of collapse" (Pius XII Encyclical on St. Benedict, March 21, 1947, N.C.W.C. translation). Further thoughts of the Holy Father: St. Benedict promoted the cause of Christianity in an extraordinary degree by his virtue, his prudence, and his wisdom. By his outstanding activity and his holiness, he demonstrated the perpetually youthful stamina of the Church. Through his teaching and his example, he renewed moral rectitude and hedged in the homes of religious life with firmer and holier rules. Personally, and through his monks, he brought barbarians out of their rough manner of living and trained them in civil and Christian culture; he educated them to virtue, labor, and the peaceful pursuit of art and science, and bound them together in brotherly love and harmony. St. Benedict founded a family of monks and provided all the means for a life of Christian perfection.

Today we thank God for the manifold great graces He granted to St. Benedict, and through him to the Church throughout succeeding centuries. We are grateful to the Saint for his ready and noble cooperation with those graces.

3. The Gospel of the Mass reveals the secret of the Saint's fruitful life and work—work accomplished in his lifetime, as well as that which still continues in souls. "Every man that has forsaken home or brothers, or sisters, or father, or mother . . . for my name's sake, shall receive his reward a hundredfold, and obtain life everlasting" (Matt. 19:29). Decisive for time and eternity is the leaving of all for the sake of Christ, in order to live an undivided life for Him. This is the path on which St. Benedict places everyone who comes to the cloister in which his Holy Rule is observed: "To you who desire to give up your own will my word is directed." It is a question of returning by the labor of obedience to Him from whom we have departed through the sloth of disobedience. No one should enroll in the school of the Lord's service unless he is willing to make the sacrifice of renouncing his own wishes—in a word, to leave all. The way of salvation is necessarily narrow in the beginning. With progress in faithful and virtuous living, however, the heart will expand, and we shall run, with the unspeakable sweetness of love, on the path of God's commandments (cf. *Prologue of Holy Rule*). St. Gregory says that St. Benedict lived as he taught.

Many miracles that St. Benedict wrought are recorded in St. Gregory's "Dialogues." It is a source of joy to recall them, because they strengthen our confidence in the power of St. Benedict's intercession for us. Many Catholics, especially Oblates of St. Benedict, prize the St. Benedict medal as a means of obtaining heavenly favors. God chose this saint to be a blessing for all nations.

Let us admire Father's splendor, as he rises to heaven on a
    luminous path.
In children, numerous offspring made him like Abraham.
The crow that served him in the cave made him like Elias.
Joseph he was by shining goodness; Jacob, by prophetic power
    (cf. Sequence of Mass).

Collect: O God, who didst fill Thy most blessed confessor Benedict with the spirit of all the righteous: grant unto us Thy servants celebrating this solemnity, that being filled with his spirit, we may faithfully accomplish all that we have promised under the inspiration of God's grace. Amen.

JULY 12

St. John Gualbert, *Abbot*

1. John was born of wealthy, noble parents in Florence, about the year 995. His father, a soldier, expecting to make a military man of John, educated him thoroughly in the art of war. It seems that the boy received no comparable preparation for Christian living, for, strongly attracted by the life of the world, he gave little thought to God for many years. Upon reaching the age for military service he was urged by his father to avenge the murder of his brother. It happened very soon that he accidentally encountered the murderer on a narrow

mountain road. It was Good Friday, and the murderer, un-
armed, begged his enemy to spare him for love of Him who on
this day died for sinners. Grace triumphed; John dropped his
sword, raised the man from his knees and gave him the kiss of
peace. Then John hurried away to a nearby church, where he
prayed with deep emotion. Once, raising his eyes to the crucifix, he saw the head of the Savior nod to him.

A changed man, he went to the abbot of the monastery to
which the chapel belonged and begged for admittance to religious life. This step sent John's father into a rage, but the
abbot was able to calm him, and John became a monk. Within
a short time he proved himself a model Benedictine; he felt,
in fact, that the life was not strict enough for him. According
to the ideas of those days, a monk so minded was free to seek
his ideal elsewhere; and so John went, first to the hermits of
Camaldoli, then to the "Shady Vale" near Florence, where he
began to live the life of a hermit. Soon other young men joined
him there, and they founded the monastery of Vallombrosa,
from which this branch of the Benedictine Order, with St. John
as its superior, spread widely. While visiting a newly-organized
house near Siena he fell ill and died on July 12, 1073. Pope
Celestine III numbered St. John Gualbert among the saints in
1193.

2. "At this time: Jesus said to his disciples: You have heard
that it was said, Thou shalt love thy neighbor and hate thy
enemy. But I tell you, Love your enemies, do good to those
who hate you, pray for those who persecute and insult you, that
so you may be true sons of your Father in heaven" (Gospel).
Such was the heroic act of the young John. Having grown up
with the attitude that one was permitted to avenge by murder, the murder of a relative, he had received and used the
grace to forgive a man who appealed to the example of the
Crucified. He had said: "What you ask of me for the love of
Christ I cannot refuse. I forgive you. Pray that God will forgive my sins, too." This was the hour of grace for John, the

time of victory over human nature. Sending his servant home with his horse, the new man experienced in his heart the entirely new happiness of God's peace. This joy sent him to the church, to the crucifix and fervent prayer. When he saw the Savior nod to him he understood the words: "Be merciful, then, as your Father is merciful . . . forgive, and you will be forgiven. Give, and gifts will be yours; . . . the measure you award to others is the measure that will be awarded to you" (Luke 6:36 ff.).

"Well-loved by God, well-loved among men, a benediction rests upon his memory. . . . He made him great in the sight of kings, entrusted commandments to him" (Lesson). Having learned religious life in the monastery, John sought out a lonely place where he might commune with God, doing penance undisturbed. The Order he later founded was a combination of the eremitical and cenobitical types of life. Although John was abbot of this foundation, he was too humble to ask for even minor orders. The fame of his virtue brought so many young men to his Order that in the following century it claimed eighty abbeys and numerous priories, a rich source of blessings to the Church. St. John trained his monks to renounce earthly things, to be humble, to live a life of silence and recollection in the spirit of sacrifice and, above all, to be perfect in love of God and neighbor. His last words were: "My soul is athirst for God. When shall I be permitted to appear before the face of the Lord?" (cf. Ps. 41:3).

3. St. John's life and work, which were so fruitful for himself and the Church, really began when he forgave the murderer of his brother, overcame his natural feelings, and spoke the word of reconciliation. Thus does God reward the Christian love of one's enemies.

"Forgive, and you will be forgiven." From St. John we can learn to forgive, sincerely and fully, anyone who may have offended or injured us. "Forgive us . . . as we forgive . . . !"

Collect: May the intercession of the blessed abbot John gain us Thy favor, we pray Thee, Lord, and may his advocacy win for us that which we do not ourselves deserve. Amen.

JULY 14

St. Bonaventure, *Bishop, Confessor, Doctor of the Church*

1. Bonaventure is a precious gem of the Church; few men have so well understood how to combine harmoniously a profound knowledge with deep piety. Born in 1221 near Viterbo, Italy, he became ill while still a child, and his parents asked St. Francis of Assisi to come and bless him. The Saint did so, and, when told later that the child had recovered, exclaimed: "Buona ventura." This means, "Fortunate outcome," and it became the baby's name. Bonaventure entered the Franciscan Order and took his theological studies in Paris; study meant for him constant praying and meditating. Asked whence he derived his remarkable knowledge, he pointed to his crucifix and said: "That is the source. . . . I have learned Jesus crucified." In order to apply himself properly to sacred science, he kept mind and body under strict discipline.

When he had become a priest he always approached the altar with tears of intense emotion, so deep was his devotion. He soon became famous as a teacher of theology in his monastery, and later, at the University of Paris. In 1257, when only thirty years old, Bonaventure became general of the Franciscan Order, and controlled its destinies successfully until the year 1273, when Pope Gregory IX named him cardinal and commissioned him to preside over the Council of Lyons (1274). The task set the Council was the reunion of the Greek Church with the

Latin See. Bonaventure's striving for this important reconciliation was successful until, during the third session, he suddenly
lost all physical strength. The Holy Father gave him the sacrament of the last anointing and Bonaventure died on July 15,
1274, at the age of fifty-three. A holy religious, a prudent superior, and a renowned preacher, he was, next to St. Thomas
Aquinas, the greatest theologian of Scholasticism. Pope Leo
XIII referred to Bonaventure as the "Prince among the Mys-
tics." He has also been called the second founder of the
Franciscan Order, and with good reason.

2. "The Lord moved him to speak before the assembled
people, filling him with the spirit of wisdom and discernment"
(Introit). This was true of the Saint, first of all as a gifted
teacher of the Order's young members. Later, as superior he
organized successfully, despite the early difficulties of the
Order, and steered a safe course through the dangerous doubts
and tensions that upset the brethren. He saw clearly the
task set for his Order by the Church, and held the friars to
it. Finally, the words of the Introit apply to his work in Paris,
where he attracted attention as a teacher, and also as preacher
and author of numerous works in which he synthesized the
great mass of the religious thinking of his time. This he did
so systematically and succinctly that he may be said to have
been filled by the spirit of God with a true and profound understanding of divine things. We thank God for having given
His Church so great and holy a teacher. "Sweet it is to praise
the Lord: to sing, most high God, in honor of thy name"
(Introit Psalm), thanking thee for the marvels thou didst effect through, and in, St. Bonaventure. "Glory be to the Father,
and to the Son, and to the Holy Spirit."

"You are the light of the world" (Gospel), the light that
shines in the darkness. A light indeed was this Saint, for his
time as well as for the succeeding centuries. Without sunlight
on the earth, everything would die. Life thrives best where
the sun's rays have full access. In the measure that the light of

faith and grace are active in a soul; in the degree that the spirit of man reaches for and absorbs the eternal light of the triune God, in that degree will man produce sublime spiritual fruit. Surely St. Bonaventure demonstrates this; besides the light of natural knowledge there shone in him with rare brilliance the light of faith, drawing him up into the mysteries of revelation and enabling him to express them attractively. In addition there was in him such an abundance of grace that it filled his heart with a most generous, seraphic love for God and Christ, and urged him to lead souls by his spoken and written word to the source of light. "You are the light of the world. . . . A lamp is not lighted to be put under a bushel measure; it is put on the lamp-stand to give light to all the people of the house; and your light must shine . . . brightly before men" (Gospel).

3. The secret of fruitfulness among the saints lies in the fact that they seek to glorify God, not so much by the restless industry of external activities as by living with Christ in the presence of God. Consequently, in their work they are not self-sold slaves, but freely keep their gaze on God, the one thing necessary. God can use such persons for the execution of His plans, for it is His will and glory alone that they aim at. "He was a faithful and wise servant, one whom his master entrusted with the care of his household, to give them their allowance of food at the appointed time" (Communion).

Collect: O God, who didst give blessed Bonaventure to Thy people as a minister of eternal salvation, grant, we pray Thee, that we may be worthy to have as our advocate in heaven him who on earth taught us the way of life. Amen.

JULY 15

St. Henry, *Emperor and Confessor*

1. Henry II was the last German emperor of the Saxon line.
His father, Duke Henry I of Bavaria, sent the boy, together
with three other children of his, to be educated by the Bishop
of Regensburg. At his father's unexpected death, Henry became Duke of Bavaria and then King of Germany, being
crowned in 1014 by Pope Benedict VIII. Henry possessed a
noble, energetic personality, and was cultured, virtuous, and
devoted to the Church. A thoroughgoing statesman, he managed to serve Empire and Church together, as when he gave
his sister Gisela in marriage to the pagan King of Hungary, on
the condition that Hungary accept Christianity. He thus gained
another nation for Christ; and that pagan king became St.
Stephen. Henry established the bishopric of Bamberg and built
its cathedral, as well as its abbey of Mount St. Michael. At
Monte Cassino he was cured of a severe illness through the
intercession of St. Benedict. He died on July 13 at Gronau near
Göttingen, and was buried in the cathedral of Bamberg. There,
too, lie the remains of his queen, the Empress Cunigunde.

2. "To withstand the attractions of this world" (Collect). As
a young duke and king Henry had the world at his feet; he
might have led a glamorous and pleasure-filled life. The grace
of God, however, enabled him to realize that the world's good
things cannot satisfy the human heart. He was led by a holy
teacher along the path of true wisdom, which is the fear of
the Lord.

"Happy is he that wisdom gains and skill; yet is he no match
for one who fears the Lord. The fear of God, that is a gift beyond all gifts; blessed the man that receives it, he has no equal"
(Ecclus. 25:13–16). The Lesson of the Mass builds on the same

truth: "Blessed is the man who lives unreproved, who has no greed for gold, puts no trust in his store of riches. Show us such a man and we will be loud in his praise. A man so tested and found perfect wins eternal honor; he kept clear of sin, when sinful ways were easy, did no wrong, when wrong lay in his power" (Lesson). The liturgy thus attributes to St. Henry great moral strength and rare heroism. Thou didst prompt him, O Lord, to "withstand the attractions of this world"; Thou gavest him the wisdom and strength, not only courageously to avoid what was forbidden, but also to renounce freely many things he might have enjoyed without sin. A man of prayer, a lover of Mary, St. Henry received from God the rare privilege of having a saint for his wife. They lived together in such a spirit as to verify the words of St. Paul: "The time is drawing to an end; nothing remains, but for those who have wives to behave as though they had none; those who weep must forget their tears, and those who rejoice their rejoicing, and those who buy must renounce possession" (I Cor. 7:29, 30). This is holy, Christian heroism.

"The law of God rules in his heart" (Introit). Henry was in every respect a good ruler. When it became necessary for him to make war, God gave him victory over every enemy. In his immense empire he successfully rooted out existing abuses and strove to protect his people from new injustices and oppression. He succeeded as few rulers do in making his people happy; and this, beyond any doubt, was the result of his union with God, to whom he clung with deep piety and whose commandments he always respected. It was Henry's conviction that one can rule successfully only if his rule is based upon, and helped by, religion; that only Christian faith can make a nation virtuous and happy. Hence St. Henry considered himself as the guardian and promoter of the Christian religion in his provinces. He worked hand in hand with the Church, using all the means at his command; above all, he stood out before his subjects as an example of virtuous, Christian living. In truth, "the law of God ruled in his heart," determining his thinking and doing.

3. "Everything is for you, whether it be . . . the world, or life, or death, or the present, or the future; it is all for you, and you for Christ, and Christ for God" (I Cor. 3:22). Everything belongs to man, to serve him. He is above all, the master of all things; but he belongs to Christ and to God. Man's task is to go to God, using creatures as a bridge to this goal. He may and should use the joys of life, yet in such wise as tools for serving God and rendering Him perfect praise. That is Christian wisdom; it was St. Henry's principle of thinking and acting. We beg his intercession that we too may obtain that grace.

Collect: O God, who on this day didst remove Thy confessor, blessed Henry, from the summit of imperial dignity on earth to an everlasting kingdom, we humbly beseech Thee that, as Thou didst fore-arm him with Thy abundant grace to withstand the attractions of this world, so Thou wilt enable us to put aside the allurements of this life, after his example, and to come in purity of heart to Thee. Amen.

JULY 16

Commemoration of Our Lady of

Mount Carmel

1. This feast of the Blessed Virgin was first celebrated in the Carmelite Order in 1376; it was extended to the entire Church by Pope Benedict XIII in 1726. The introduction of the feast was the natural outcome of the Order's great devotion to the Mother of God from its very beginning. Tradition has it that Mary appeared to Simon Stock, general of the Carmelites, at Cambridge, England, on July 15, 1251; she gave him the scapu-

lar, promising that all who should wear it would be saved. Various popes since the sixteenth century have approved the preaching of this vision and promise. Catholics who wear the scapular celebrate today's feast with sentiments of great gratitude toward Mary, and trust in her help. They are happy to possess in her scapular a pledge of eternal salvation.

2. "Rejoice we all in the Lord, as we keep holiday in Mary's honor" (Introit). We recall today the marvelous election and grace of Mary, the Mother of God, who, as Mother of Christ, became also our mother. We think of the unnumbered graces and supernatural gifts that we have obtained through her intercession from the day of our baptism to the present moment, but, particularly, since our enrollment in the Confraternity of the Scapular. The liturgy lets Mary speak to us in the Lesson: "No vine every yielded fruit so fragrant. . . . It is I that give birth to all noble loving, all reverence, all true knowledge, and the holy gift of hope. From me comes every grace of faithful observance, from me all promise of life and vigor. Hither turn your steps, all you that learned to long for me; take your fill of the increase I yield. Never was honey so sweet as the influence I inspire, never honey-comb as the gift I bring." We know Mary; we possess her, just as a child has its mother and is happy in this possession. It is with holy joy, then, that we celebrate the Commemoration of the Virgin Mother and of all the favors she has obtained for us in the past, as well as the future gifts that she has promised those who wear her scapular. "Alleluia. Through thee, Mother of God, the life we had forfeited has been regained; heaven quickened thy womb, and from it there came forth into the world a Savior. Alleluia."

"Maiden, Mother of God, do not forget us; plead for us, there where thou standest in God's presence, to avert his anger from us" (Offertory). These are our words as we make our offering in today's Mass. When we appear with our gifts, our Mother, full of grace and beloved of God, puts in a good word for us. This is a consoling thought, for we realize that since yesterday's

Holy Sacrifice we have again failed in the service of God; we
have not corresponded with His graces; we have not been
properly grateful for the gifts of His love. He has reason to
reject our offering out of dissatisfaction with us; but Mary steps
in as mediatrix, to "avert his anger from us." After this we may
dare to appear before the majesty of the holy God, and we
entrust our gifts to Mary. In the Secret Prayer that follows we
ask that, "at the saving intercession of God's blessed mother,
Mary . . . those offerings may further our salvation." We
have great confidence in Mary's intercession, and cannot ade-
quately thank her for devoting herself always to our interests
before God and channeling His graces to us. How fortunate
we are to be her children.

3. Those who wear the scapular have a special claim on
Mary's aid during their lifetime as well as at the hour of death.
The scapular is, as it were, the garment of the Mother of God;
we are permitted to wear it as an assurance of her motherly
protection. Anyone who wears the Mount Carmel scapular
should frequently recall her promise that his soul will be freed
from purgatory soon after death. It is understood, naturally,
that he will wear it in the right spirit, manifested by Christian
living.

Collect: God, who hast honored the Order of Carmel by giving
Thy most blessed Mother Mary, ever-virgin, that special title, grant
us this grace, that we who are today commemorating her with
solemn observance may be counted worthy, under the shield of her
protection, to attain everlasting happiness. Amen.

JULY 17

St. Alexius, *Confessor*

1. Alexius was a heroic young man who understood perfectly
our Lord's words, "Blessed are the poor in spirit." The only son
of the wealthy and respected Senator Euphemian of Rome, he

was urged by the grace of God on his wedding-day to forsake
father, mother, and bride, and go into a strange land to live as
a poor, despised beggar. He thus spent seven years in Edessa,
Syria, until his mortification began to attract attention. Leaving
Edessa, he planned to take up the same life at Tarsus in Cilicia,
the home of St. Paul the Apostle, but his ship was driven instead to the coast of Italy. Alexius visited his father, who failed
to recognize him but gave him permission to occupy a closet
under the stairway in his home; here Alexius spent the next
seven years in poverty, despised and insulted by the servants
of his unwitting parents. It was not until his death, in 417, that
his father and mother discovered he was the son they had sadly
missed for thirty-four years.

2. "The love of money is a root from which every kind of
evil springs. . . . It is for thee . . . to shun all this: to aim at
right living, holiness, and faith, and love, and endurance, and
kind forbearance" (Epistle). This is God's way; He rarely finds
men who exemplify the Christian ideal. He therefore raises up
from time to time heroic souls who demonstrate a certain as-
pect of virtue, even to the point of exaggerating it, in order
that their lives may serve rather for admiration than for imitation. Such a one was Alexius. All his thoughts were set on serving God in poverty and in hiddenness, even when the road to
earthly wealth, honors, and family joys was open to him! Other
Christians would have thought nothing of having these normal
pleasures and legitimate liberties, and would have found them
no hindrance to saving their souls. Alexius was, however, spe-
cially called to give a heroic example of self-denial and humility; he renounced everything to possess God. It must have required almost superhuman fortitude to make these sacrifices
continually for thirty-four years, and it must have pained him
to conceal his identity from his parents. "Blessed is he who
endures under trials; when he has proved his worth, he will
win the crown of life" (Alleluia verse).

"And what of us who have forsaken all, and followed thee;
what is left for us? Jesus said to them, I promise you . . .

every man that has forsaken home . . . or father, or mother
. . . for my name's sake, shall receive his reward a hundredfold, and obtain everlasting life" (Gospel). Alexius left all
things. Even if he seems to have revealed a perverted sense of
values; even if his conduct would be disapproved by most men;
still we cannot doubt that his intentions were holy. He forsook
riches and pleasures because he was certain they could not give
him peace of heart; he left father and mother so he could become a perfect disciple of Christ; he deserted his bride because
a higher love had captured his heart. Nor was this renunciation
merely external, for he spent his last years in his parents' home
and depended on their charity, yet never told them he was
their own. When they inquired about his origin he would answer that his home was beyond the stars and that he had no
name. He had, indeed, dropped the name that men had given
him, and he still had to earn one from God. This conduct exposed him to ill-treatment and neglect from servants whom he
had a right to command. Alexius bore all in silence and patience, for with the other sacrificial gifts he had also given himself. Like Peter, then, he might have asked: "What is left for
us?" His hundredfold came in the form of grace and virtue;
with the possession of God would come everlasting life, for
God would "give him charge of all his goods" (Communion).

3. "Religion is ample provision for life, though no more than
a bare sufficiency goes with it. Empty-handed we come into
the world, and empty-handed, beyond question, we must leave
it; why then, if we have food and clothing to last us out, let
us be content with that. Those who would be rich fall into
temptation, the devil's trap for them; all those useless and
dangerous appetites which sink men into ruin here and perdition hereafter. The love of money is the root from which every
kind of evil springs" (Epistle).

It is futile to ask whether Alexius was justified in leaving
his bride and his parents, thereby causing great grief. The
Church has declared him a saint. His actions can be evaluated

only as the fruit of the gifts of the Holy Spirit. In virtue of such gifts, the soul impelled by God does things that lie beyond the boundaries of virtue and prudence set by reason and faith. We simply do not understand such actions and are inclined to look upon them as aberrations. Certainly, it is true that we may not imitate the saints in such cases, since special grace is required for such a special vocation. Yet we may feel certain that Alexius' life was a work of God's grace beyond our understanding; this fact is attested by the Church's canonization of him.

Collect: O God, who dost gladden our hearts on each recurring festival of Thy blessed confessor Alexius, grant in Thy goodness that we who are celebrating his birthday, may also follow his example. Amen.

JULY 18

St. Camillus de Lellis, *Confessor*

1. Camillus was born in Italy in 1550 of noble family, his father being an officer in the army of Emperor Charles V. His mother died while he was still a child, and for lack of guidance he fell into evil ways, gambling and gadding until his father induced him to become a soldier in the service of Venice. While on their way there both fell ill at Ancona, and his father died. Camillus himself developed painful ulcers on his feet, which lamed him the rest of his life. As he struggled homeward he was received by the Franciscans at Fermo with such charity that he resolved to enter their Order. Once in his homeland he applied at the monastery at Aquila, but was refused because of his foot ailment.

The young Camillus then went to Rome to obtain medical care and served as a nurse in the hospital of St. James, the so-called "resort" of incurables. Here his wounds were healed, but new ones broke out and he reverted to his former careless state of mind. Dismissed from service in the hospital because he could not get along with his fellow nurses, Camillus entered the Venetian army in 1570 and fought against the Turks. After that he went to Tunis with the Spanish army, and was almost shipwrecked on his return from Africa. Back in Naples, he gambled away everything he owned and then wandered aimlessly into the south of Italy. In Manfredonia he took a laborer's job at the construction of the Capuchin monastery. Again he asked for admission and again was rejected on account of his ulcers. He even went a second time to St. James in Rome, tried monastic life, and had to give it up.

It was now evident to Camillus that he was not meant for the cloister, and he decided to devote his life entirely to the care of the sick. St. Philip Neri took pity on him and led him into better ways. The sight of so many sick people, neglected by nurses and doctors, furnished the final impetus to his vocation. With several companions he undertook to serve the sick out of genuine charity. It soon became clear to him, however, that he must become a priest if the project was to succeed; and so, at the age of thirty-two, he studied Latin in a class of boys. In 1574 he was ordained. He opened his own hospital, thus laying the foundation for the Order of Camillians approved by Pope Sixtus V in 1586. In the year 1604 Camillus resigned his office as superior in order to spend more time in the actual serving of the sick. He died on July 14, 1614, in Rome. In 1742 he was beatified; in 1746, canonized; in 1886 Pope Leo XIII named him patron of the sick; and in 1930, Pope Pius XI made him the patron of nurses. At the time of the Saint's death his Order comprised five provinces with three hundred members. In the year 1600 it was changed into an Order for priests who would spend their time exclusively in corporal and spiritual works of mercy. The Order began to flourish again in the nineteenth century.

2. "Remember that we have changed over from death to life,

in loving the brethren as we do" (Epistle). When, after his years of undisciplined living, Camillus was so impressed by the charity of the Franciscans that he wanted to join them, a Guardian who happened to be his uncle advised: "Be discreet; let your sudden emotion blow over and your blood cool down. First, try to find a cure for your feet; then it may become evident whether you are called to religious life." As events proved, the desire was merely a straw fire, for Camillus soon returned to his former way of life. When this nobly born youth found himself at length in Rome and in the deepest misery, God's grace came to him in the form of heartfelt sympathy for the sick and dying. Heroic love reclaimed him from the deadly illness of passion and vice to a life of grace, so that he became a blessing not only for the sick but for the entire Church as well. God's grace indeed worked wonders in the heart of this onetime derelict.

"Loving the brethren," Camillus formed a society of male nurses. With the help of a benefactor he was able to open his own hospital. The number of members increased chiefly because of its Founder's holy example. During a Roman epidemic Camillus hurried from house to house with four of his brethren supplying medicine and nourishment, providing jobs for patients and watching over their business affairs. When Camillus heard that almost three thousand deaths had occurred in the hospital of San Sisto in Rome, he rushed there with eight brethren. Indescribable misery prevailed, and to make matters worse, he lost five of his companions within a short time. Helpers became fewer and Camillus had to redouble his exertions for the sick. When night came he did not rest, but made preparations for the next day's labors: straw-sacks he filled for beds, and then mended bed-coverings and gathered up the laundry.

The great heart of this Saint had room for other charities, too. He visited and helped prisoners and poor people everywhere, always leading the way for his brethren, always the most zealous and tireless of all. During the pestilence in Nola,

Camillus and his brethren exhibited marvelous devotion in
their work. When famine followed, he was a rescuing angel.
This spirit of love that gives everything, even life, for the salvation of fellow men, Camillus bequeathed to his Order. Many
of his men died heroic deaths in the service of charity. During
the pestilence of 1656, all but four of his sixty priests died, and
of the lay brothers only one survived. That was the way St.
Camillus understood how the word of the Lord was to be
lived: "This is my commandment, that you love one another, as
I have loved you. This is the greatest love a man can show, that
he should lay down his life for his friends" (Gospel).

3. With Holy Church, we pray that, through the merits of
St. Camillus, God may grant us this spirit of charity. "If a man
is without love, he holds fast to death. . . . God has proved
his love to us by laying down his life for our sakes; we too must
be ready to lay down our lives for the sake of our brethren"
(Epistle).

Collect: God, who didst adorn St. Camillus with an especial gift
of charity to help the dying in their last agony, inspire us, we pray
Thee, through his merits, with the love of Thee, so that in the hour
of our death we may be found worthy to vanquish the enemy and
obtain a heavenly crown. Amen.

JULY 19

St. Vincent de Paul, *Confessor*

1. "Right thou shalt do and with love, and carry thyself humbly in the presence of thy God" (Mich. 6:8). In these words
one has a thumbnail description of the life of Vincent de Paul.
At a time when Europe was harassed by various heresies, God
raised up this remarkable man in southern France—powerful
in word and deed, a saint whom even kings consulted, a main-
spring of every great movement in the France of his day.

Vincent was born in 1576 to poor, simple, God-fearing parents.
As a boy he watched his father's sheep until he found an opportunity for studies, first with the Franciscans at Asar, and
later in Toulouse. Ordained in the year 1600, he spent his time
between 1605 and 1607 in cruel captivity in Tunis. Having escaped to Avignon and then to Paris, he experienced an interior
conversion, in 1609, and promised God to spend the rest of his
life in works of charity. The years 1615 to 1625 he passed as
private chaplain and tutor in the home of Count Condy, General of the Galleys. In 1617 he founded the Congregation of the
Lazarists for home mission work, and later the Sisters of Charity. He opened foundling homes in Paris in which, to this day,
the sisters harbor and educate more than ten thousand orphan
children. His society of Young Ladies of the Holy Cross provides education for girls who live in dangerous surroundings
or are without homes. Vincent, the tireless worker driven by
love of God and of immortal souls, died on September 27, 1660.

2. "The innocent man will flourish as the palm-tree flourishes: he will grow to greatness as the cedars grow on Lebanon: planted in the temple of the Lord, growing up in the
very courts of our God's house" (Introit). We marvel at the
almost limitless range of St. Vincent's activity and at the many
institutions that he originated to support and promote the
kingdom of God on earth. He recognized the evils of his time:
the ignorance, the religious poverty, the moral degradation of
the people, as well as the inactivity of the clergy. He therefore
preached zealously and encouraged missions as an opportunity
for works of mercy. He became poor in order to help the poor.
On a trip to Marseilles, he learned about the sad lot of the galley slaves. In his desire to help them, he gladly accepted the
post of Almoner General of the Galleys offered him by King
Louis XIII. As such he was the chief pastor of these unfortu-
nates. On one occasion he begged so persistently for the freedom of a slave that the overseer finally yielded; but Vincent
had to accept the chains and oar himself. It was only after a

considerable lapse of time that he was recognized and set free. He used every available means that his inexhaustible mercy could find or devise to alleviate physical and spiritual misery.

In collaboration with Louise Marillac, whose love of neighbor matched his own, St. Vincent founded the Sisters of Charity, of whom he wrote: "They had only the homes of the sick for cloister; a poorly furnished room served as cell; their chapel was the parish church; their corridors were the streets of the city; their enclosure was obedience, their grate, the fear of God; and their veil, holy modesty." The whole world loves these angels of mercy, whom Vincent advised: "Let us love God; but at the price of our hands and the sweat of our face." He promoted retreats for lay people. Under Queen Mary Anne he defended the rights and welfare of the Church with frankness and with ultimate success, saving whole regions from death by starvation; he organized the war charity in Lorraine, Picardy, and Champagne, as well as the caring for refugees. Vincent was a powerful opponent of Jansenism, which was just beginning to spread. In addition to these interests inaugurated by himself, he was superior of the Visitation Order, founded by St. Francis de Sales, and acted as spiritual director of St. Francis de Chantal. His was a life of remarkable versatility. Truly, he flourished like a palm tree.

"The harvest . . . is plentiful enough, but the laborers are few" (Gospel). At the time of St. Vincent there were many bishops and priests in France, but workers like himself were few, and sorely needed. "I am sending you out to be like lambs among wolves. You are not to carry purse, or wallet, or shoes; you are to give no one greeting on the way." Workers of apostolic simplicity, with minimum requirements and maximum trust in God, who would apply themselves with a total devotion that would allow nothing to drag them from their places, no one to draw them into other interests, unless these, too, served their cause; who would live only to bring the kingdom of God into erring hearts, only to search out and tirelessly lead back souls to Christ: these were the workers needed.

St. Vincent was such a man. He saw Christ in sinners, in the poor, in the distressed and captive, and never forgot the truth, "When you did it to one of the least of my brethren here, you did it to me" (Matt. 25:40), or St. Paul's, "With us, Christ's love is a compelling motive, and this is the conviction we have reached; if one man died on behalf of all, then all thereby became dead men; Christ died for us all, so that being alive should no longer mean living with our own life, but with his life who died for us and has risen again" (II Cor. 5:14, 15). Vincent was on fire with love for Christ and for His needy brothers and sisters. "The harvest is plentiful enough . . . you must ask the Lord . . . to send laborers out for the harvesting," workers filled with the faith and sacrificing courage of St. Vincent de Paul.

3. How rich in blessings and many-sided was the activity of this saint! Whence did he receive the strength and energy for such vast expenditure of himself in his vocation? Profound interior life was at the bottom of all. Filled with humility, he saw himself as a wretched instrument, and his ready retort to praise was, "God does it." He was a man of much prayer, and he considered it an offense against God's providence to worry unduly. Above all, love of God consumed him and made him love his fellow man so deeply that he would himself become a galley slave if only he could liberate souls from the captivity of Satan.

In the religious houses of St. Vincent there is frequently found this inscription: "God sees thee." Always and everywhere he lived with God, gazing on this intimate friend enthroned in his heart. "The kingdom of God is close upon you" (Gospel).

Collect: O God, who in order that the gospel might be preached to the poor and the dignity of the ecclesiastical state enhanced, didst endow blessed Vincent with the zeal and power of an apostle, grant, we pray Thee, that we may not only revere his godly merits but also conform to the pattern of his virtues. Amen.

JULY 20

St. Jerome Emiliani, *Confessor*

1. Jerome, "Father of Orphans," was a hero of brotherly love. Born in 1481 of a prominent Venetian family, he was brought up entirely for the world and for an illustrious career in the service of the Republic of Venice. He became a bold young officer, filled with lust for battle, and performed many a brilliant feat of arms. Into the wild and easy ways of his frivolous camp-comrades Jerome entered freely. Once, when he was a commandant, he was forced to surrender his fortress Castelnuovo and was taken captive. Loaded with chains, he was thrown into a deep dungeon, where time and darkness forced him to think. In the light of God's grace he began to see the foolhardiness of his former way of life. One evening a veiled lady entered his cell, loosed his chains, gave him the key to the door and left. By following her he was able to evade the guards and slip through the night to Treviso. Here he hung up his prison chains at the altar of the Blessed Virgin: he was a new man, a man of prayer and human pity, of love of God and neighbor.

During the famine of 1518 Jerome gathered the poor orphan children of Venice around him and cared for them; he took the sick ones to a hospital. Often ridiculed as a deceiver and fanatic, he was frequently abused even when he meekly begged for gifts. But he did not let this discourage him. He founded hospitals and orphan homes in nearly all the cities of Lombardy; all his thinking and planning revolved around orphans. In order to give permanence to his work, the Saint gathered around himself some like-minded men and trained them in a house in the remote valley of Somasco, near Bergamo. With this source of helpers and companions, his Institute for the care of the poor, sick, orphans, mentally ill, and needy of all sorts prospered widely. To this day the Somaschi do immense good. Jerome spent his last years in prayer and penance in a quiet cell on a height near Somasco. He died on February 8, 1537, a victim of his zeal in the practice of charity.

2. "My heart lies trampled in the dust, to see the desolation of my countrywomen; no child left, no baby at the breast, in all the streets of the city" (Introit). In these words of the prophet Jeremias the liturgy allows the Saint of this day to pour out his heart. He had lived through the horror-filled days and months of famine and pestilence in Venice when hundreds of fathers and mothers were snatched away by death. Their forsaken children dragged themselves through the streets, starved and half-naked, wild and confused. No one really took the matter in hand until the heart of this noble ex-officer was moved to practical pity. He stooped to the misery that faced him everywhere, with a charity that spread like an overflowing brook enlivening a parched valley. To the parents who were unable to rear their children properly, he cried out: "For the love of Christ, let the little ones come to me; I will give them an earthly father who will teach them about their heavenly Father." The Lesson says: "Share thy bread with the hungry, give the poor and the vagrant a welcome to thy house; if thou shouldst meet one that goes naked, clothe him, do not turn away from thy own flesh and blood." This was St. Jerome's policy, for he believed the promise of our Lord: "If thou hast a mind to be perfect, go home and sell all that belongs to thee; give it to the poor, and so the treasure thou hast shall be in heaven" (Gospel). St. Paul expressed the virtue of Christian charity thus: "If a man is to offer service pure and unblemished in the sight of God, who is our Father, he must take care of

orphans and widows in their need, and keep himself untainted by the world" (Communion). Do we understand Christian love of neighbor as St. Jerome did?

"Then, sudden as the dawn, the light thou longest for will break upon thee. . . . Then the Lord will listen to thee when thou callest on him; thy cry will bring his answer, I am here at thy side . . . then light shall spring up for thee in the darkness . . . and the Lord will give thee rest continually, satisfying thy soul with comfort and thy body with ease. Thou wilt be as secure as a well-watered garden, as a spring whose waters never fail" (Lesson). That will be the reward of Christian charity as St. Jerome practiced it—for the sake of Christ and God. As wholeheartedly as Jerome went about his works of charity, it was not in external activities that he saw his real responsibility, but in interior, unbroken union with God. In the midst of his labors he was prompted by the desire to serve God's interests, and so preserved his liberty of spirit, fixing his gaze always on the one thing necessary.

3. In St. Jerome we recognize the wonderful power of love, and the wisdom of God's providence. If Jerome had not been compelled to drink deeply of the cup of suffering during his imprisonment, he might never have come to his senses and changed his manner of living. What if God had left him to his own selfish ambitions? What if Jerome had not corresponded with the promptings of grace? In either case, those holy undertakings of his would not have brightened the pages of history. There is always something noble about fidelity to God's grace.

It has been continually the practice of the saints not only to pray in the secluded silence of a cell, but also to work creatively with complete devotion to a cause. Their one ambition is to please Him to whom they have given their lives; love of Him motivates all their endeavors. It is easy to see why they bring forth fruit, thirtyfold, sixtyfold, and a hundredfold, and always, as it were, without foreseeing, sometimes even without recognizing the results. They need more imitators.

Collect: By the merits and pleading of blessed Jerome, whom Thou, God, Father of all mercy, didst ordain to be the father and helper of orphans, grant that we may faithfully keep the spirit of adoption whereby we are, in name and in fact, Thy children. Amen.

JULY 22

St. Mary Magdalen, *Penitent*

1. Opinions differ regarding the identity of Mary Magdalen. Recent commentators on Holy Scripture distinguish three Marys: the first, mentioned as living in Bethania, is called the sister of Lazarus and Martha, and is reported as kneeling at the feet of Jesus: "She has chosen the best part" (cf. Luke 10:39). She anointed His head and feet before the Passion (cf. John 12:3; Matt. 26:7). The second Mary of the Gospel is the one out of whom our Lord drove seven evil spirits and who then, out of gratitude, joined the other women of Galilee who accompanied Him; she was present at Christ's death and burial, saw Him at the sepulcher and was there commanded to announce His rising to the rest of the disciples. The third Mary entered the house of Simon the Pharisee to anoint the feet of Jesus, and she is called by St. Luke "the sinner." The liturgy does not, however, count three Mary's, but considers the sinner (Gospel) to be one with the other two. Our meditation will follow the liturgy.

2. "And there was then a sinful woman in the city, who, hearing that he [Jesus] was at table in the Pharisee's house, brought a pot of ointment with her, and took her place behind him at his feet, weeping; then she began washing his feet with her tears and drying them with her hair, kissing his feet, and anointing them with the ointment" (Gospel). St. Augustine offers this comment: "You see a woman of ill repute in the city, who entered the house where her Physician was and earnestly

begged for health [of soul]. She knew that her ailment was
serious. She approached not the face, but the feet of the Lord.
Feet that had trod evil ways hurried to feet that knew only
right ways. She shed tears of contrition, washed His feet with
tears of confession. . . . She spoke by her silence of her devotion." For his part, Simon the Pharisee watched the penitent
and his guest and then proceeded to pass judgment: "If this
man were a prophet, he would know who this woman is that
is touching him." But our Lord took the sinner's part: "Thy
sins are forgiven. . . . Thy faith has saved thee; go in peace."
Mary had found healing for her soul; from then on her life
would be wholly given to love for Jesus, who in His mercy had
banished her guilt and filled her with new and noble ideals.
She left what she had previously loved and joined the holy
women who followed Jesus closely on His last journey from
Galilee to Jerusalem. She continued on to the place where He
was crucified: "And meanwhile his mother, and his mother's
sister, Mary the wife of Cleophas, and Mary Magdalen, had
taken their stand beside the cross of Jesus" (John 19:25).

"But for all my search I could not find him. I met the watch-
men who go the city rounds and asked them whether they had
seen my love" (Lesson). The Church proposes the thoughts of
Pope St. Gregory for our consideration: "Formerly Mary remained cold in her sin, but now she was all ardor, all love. The
disciples had left the grave of the Lord; Mary stayed. She was
seeking Him whom she had not found. She wept while she
searched, and she was on fire with longing for Him who she
thought had been stolen. Thus it happened that she, she alone,
who had stayed back to seek Him, saw Him. She first sought
but did not find Him; she persevered in searching and she
found Him." Thus occurred what the bride, that is, the Church,
sings of in the Song of Songs: "Then I found him, so tenderly
loved" (Lesson). Mary Magdalen hastened along the streets
of Jerusalem early in the morning, to the place where they had
crucified Jesus. There she found the angels who were keeping

watch at the tomb. "Why art thou weeping?" they asked. She spoke to a man whom she took to be the gardener: "If it is thou, Sir, that hast carried him off, tell me where thou hast put him, and I will take him away. Jesus said to her, Mary. And she turned and said to him, Rabboni!" (John 20:15, 16.) She had found Him whom her soul loved, and He gave her a charge: "Return . . . and tell them . . . I am going up to him who is my Father and your Father, who is my God and your God" (John 20:17). Obediently she ran to the Apostles with the news. We rejoice with the fortunate one who has found her All.

3. To the mind of the liturgy, we are Magdalen today. With sincere contrition we throw ourselves at the feet of Jesus, confessing our many sins and negligences. With tearful Magdalen we await the word: "Thy sins are forgiven; go in peace" with God, with yourself, with your surroundings and your work.

"If great sins have been forgiven her, she has also greatly loved." Simon has only contempt for the "sinful woman." God preserve us from the self-righteousness of the Pharisees! It is not without reason that the angels of heaven rejoice over one sinner who does penance more than over ninety-nine self-styled "just" who need not repentance (cf. Matt. 18:13). Like Magdalen, the greatest sinners sometimes become most ardent lovers of God. Under God's mercy, sin may become an occasion for special grace. With confidence, then, we pray for unfortunate souls living in sin.

Although the Apostles left, Mary remained at the tomb. "A good deed is only then perfect when it is matched by perseverance and steadfastness" (St. Gregory the Great).

Collect: Lord, we pray that we may find help in the intercession of blessed Mary Magdalen, whose prayers moved Thee to restore her brother Lazarus to life when he had been dead four days. Amen.

JULY 25

St. James the Elder, *Apostle*

1. James the Elder was a son of Zebedee and Salome of Bethsaida, and so a brother to the Beloved Disciple, St. John. After the Savior had called Peter and Andrew "he went further on, and saw two others that were brethren, James . . . and his brother John; they were in the boat with their father . . . repairing their nets, and he called them to him; whereupon they dropped the nets and left their father immediately, and followed him" (Matt. 4:21 ff.). On account of their impetuous nature, our Lord named them "Sons of Thunder." Together with Peter they were the favored apostles, being the Master's only companions at the raising to life of the daughter of Jairus, at the Transfiguration, and in the Garden of Olives (cf. Matt. 9:18; 17:1; 26:37). James was the first of the apostles to suffer martyrdom, and this occurred in Eastertide of 42 or 44, at the hands of Herod Agrippa. According to an ancient Spanish tradition, his body was taken to Santiago de Compostela for burial, and was rediscovered there in the ninth century. Pilgrimages to his tomb were much in vogue in the Middle Ages. James was highly honored also as the protecting patron of the Spanish in battle against the Moors, and of the whole land of Spain, and of pilgrims.

2. "Have you the strength to drink of the cup I am to drink of?" (Gospel.) This question our Lord directed to James and John after their mother requested: "Here are my two sons; grant that in thy kingdom one may take his place on thy right hand and the other on the left." She, like many others, could envision no other Messias than the wielder of political power who would found an earthly kingdom. Her sons had similar ideas, but our Lord quickly disillusioned them: "You do not know what it is you ask." Jesus made it clear that there is no

other way to exaltation than that of humble obedience to God's will. Their affirmative reply did not necessarily prove, however, that they knew the full implication of His question.

After the first Pentecost James remained in Jerusalem. King Herod wanted to win favor with the Jews, and for this reason he now began to persecute the Christians. "James, the brother of John, he beheaded" (Acts 12:2). This was the fulfillment of the promise: "You shall indeed drink of my cup." But James also now realized the truth of the other promise: "You who have followed me shall sit on thrones, judging the twelve tribes of Israel" (Communion). No longer desiring an earthly throne, he now realized that God often grants our petitions in a way that is quite different from what we had expected, and always in an infinitely better way.

"We have been made a spectacle to the whole creation, men and angels alike. We are fools for Christ's sake; you are so wise; we are so helpless, you so stout of heart; you are held in honor, while we are despised. Still, as I write, we go hungry and thirsty and naked. . . . We are hard put to it, working with our own hands" (Epistle). That is the life of Christ's apostle. He must drink the cup of suffering, taste the enmity and hatred of the world. He cannot be the rich and well-fed head of a human oligarchy, as the immature Christians of Corinth had expected. A fool in the eyes of the world, the apostle bears silently all day the humiliating contempt of the world, patiently repaying with charity. Strong in the strength of Christ, he can ignore calumnies and even bless those who ill-treat him, announcing the gospel to those who make him suffer. And if he has to correct them, then he does it to snatch the guilty from error and to communicate the life of Christ to them. The true apostle cannot act otherwise.

3. Our Lord addresses the same question to each of us: "Have you the strength to drink of the cup I am to drink of?" Can we reply, with James and John, "We have"?

When the other apostles heard about the mother's petition

to Jesus, "the ten others were angry with the two brethren . . .
but Jesus called them to him, and said, You know that among
the Gentiles, those who bear rule lord it over them, and great
men vaunt their power over them; with you it must be otherwise; whoever has a mind to be first among you must be your
slave. So it is that the Son of Man did not come to have service
done him; he came to serve others, and to give his life as a
ransom for the lives of many" (Matt. 20:24 ff.). This is our
Lord's example for us.

Collect: Let Thy people find in Thee a giver of holiness and a
protector, Lord, and may they be fortified by the aid of Thy apostle
James, to please Thee by the conduct of their lives and to serve
Thee in peace of mind. Amen.

JULY 26

St. Anne, *Mother of Our Lady*

1. Chosen by God to be the mother of the virgin Mother of
God, Anne presented to mankind her from whom the Light of
the world would come. Holy Scripture does not mention Mary's
mother, but already in the second century her name had become widely known from the "proto-gospel of St. James." The
name Anne means "rich in grace" and it is so firmly established
as the name of Mary's mother in the tradition and usage of
the Church that there can be no real doubt about it. Concerning Anne's life we have only legendary, unauthenticated details. She is said to have been married to Joachim, a man of
outstanding virtue and piety, and to have become a mother late
in life. The veneration of St. Anne goes back to the eighth century in the East. About 1350 her feast was celebrated everywhere in the West as well; in 1584 Pope Gregory XIII ordered
it to be celebrated by the whole Church. St. Anne is the heavenly patron of mothers, of marriage, of widows, and of orphans.

2. "Rejoice we all in the Lord, as we keep holiday in honor of blessed Anne" (Introit). Even if we know nothing more about St. Anne than that she was the mother of Mary, that is enough to make us rejoice and thank God. One of the responsories at Matins praises her thus: "Exalted and wonderfully salutary, venerable Anne, is the fruit of thy womb, the Virgin Mary, Mother of the Lord, consolation of the world, place of rest for the weary, hope of the sorrowing. Rejoice and be glad, happy mother, for the fruit of thy womb is Mary, mother of the Lord." Whoever loves Mary must necessarily honor her in whose womb God prepared this sublime sanctuary. We must contemplate with reverence her to whom God entrusted the Mother of His Son; we praise the mother of the Mother of God for her unique greatness; it is proof that her holy and just life of faithful service was pleasing to God. With proper admiration do we sing of her virtue in the Lesson: "Unrivaled art thou among all the women that have enriched their homes. Vain are the winning ways, beauty is a snare; it is the woman who fears the Lord that will achieve renown. Work such as hers claims its reward; let her be spoken of with praise at the city gates."

"The kingdom of heaven is like a treasure hidden in a field; a man has found it and hidden it again, and now, for the joy it gives him, is going home to sell all that he has and buy that field" (Gospel). St. Anne discovered that treasure: loving fear of God. Busily engaged as she was in household affairs (cf. Lesson) her mind nevertheless steadily dwelt on higher things, on the God she loved and lived for. It is a truly wise woman who evaluates so shrewdly, in order to serve God unhindered. Only to such a conscientious woman, with her wealth of interior life, could God entrust the one whom the whole Church greets in the words of an angel: "Hail, full of grace; the Lord is with thee." In the womb of St. Anne was Mary conceived without sin, filled with grace, and wholly pleasing to God. Anne was privileged to nourish this child, to live with her and teach her, and to be a witness to the plenitude of her child's grace. Mary is Anne's treasure, the precious pearl of which the Gospel speaks; the reward, humanly speaking, the supremely delightful fruit of her many years of petitioning God with prayers and with confident service.

3. St. Anne was chosen by God to cooperate in the redemption of mankind. But she had to make herself worthy of this holy life. God demands cooperation. Thus, the liturgy can sing of St. Anne: "Thou hast been a friend to right, an enemy to wrong. And God, thy own God, has given thee an unction to bring thee pride" (Gradual). God anointed her with the joy of becoming the mother of Mary. One whom God honors thus, we too must honor. We beg her to obtain for us the grace to carry out our God-given vocation with the same perfect fidelity which led to her renown. "Vain are the winning ways, beauty is a snare; it is the woman who fears the Lord that will achieve renown" (Lesson).

Collect: O God, who wast pleased to bestow Thy grace upon blessed Anne, so that she might fitly become the mother of her who was to bear Thy only-begotten Son, grant us this boon, that we who keep her feast may be helped by her protection. Amen.

JULY 29

St. Martha, *Virgin*

1. Today's feast takes us in spirit to that highly-favored home in Bethania, near Jerusalem, where Lazarus lived with his two sisters, Mary and Martha. Jesus sometimes visited these friends, and it was here, too, that on a memorable occasion He raised Lazarus to life after he had lain four days dead (cf. John, chap. 11). Finally, six days before the feast and only a few days before His own immolation, Jesus came here, "and a feast was made for him there, at which Martha was waiting at

table, while Lazarus was one of his fellow-guests. And now Mary brought in a pound of pure spikenard ointment, which was very precious, and poured it over Jesus' feet, wiping his feet with her hair; the whole house was scented with the ointment" (John 12:1 ff.). Further details about these friends at Bethania are legendary; for example, that they moved to Marseilles and died there.

2. "In one of the villages he entered during his journey, a woman called Martha entertained him in her house. She had a sister called Mary; and Mary took her place at the Lord's feet, and listened to his words. Martha was distracted by waiting on many needs; so she came to his side and asked, Lord, art thou content that my sister should leave me to do the serving alone? Come, bid her help me. Jesus answered her, Martha, Martha, how many cares and troubles thou hast! But only one thing is necessary; and Mary has chosen for herself the best part of all, that which shall never be taken from her" (Luke 10:38–42). Martha was the energetic, busy, observant housewife; when our Lord came to raise Lazarus to life, it was she who ran to meet Him, while Mary stayed in the house, unaware of His presence. "Martha said to Jesus, Lord, if thou hadst been here, my brother would not have died; . . . she went back and called her sister Mary aside; The Master is here, she said, and bids thee come." Then Mary hurried to the grave of her brother and repeated her sister's words. Martha is the emotional, active housewife. She meets Jesus; she sends Mary to Him; then she hastens to the tomb.

"Martha was distracted by waiting on many needs." She appreciated the honor and happiness of having Jesus as a guest; He must take a rest and renew His strength; He would find love and understanding in her house, in contrast to the blind opposition and rejection He met elsewhere. Martha, therefore, did everything in her power to make their beloved Guest feel at home. Her sister, on the contrary, simply sat at the Master's feet and listened to His words, oblivious of

Martha's hustling. When the busy sister complained, Jesus made a pointed reply, not, however, giving her reason to believe that He disapproved of the energetic, active type of woman. He knew that Martha's zeal resulted from her love for Him. Yet, as necessary as solicitous activity is to true hospitality, it is not the most important quality in a host. Only one thing is necessary, and Mary was doing that: "Seek first the kingdom of God"; be busy about God; be solicitous about fostering deep, interior union with God. Only in this way will work and worry be seen in their proper perspective; concentration on God will make work a worship, a service, a glorification of Him. Most important is the life of prayer; the work of external service must not, however, be performed in haste and recklessness, for it would then disturb the interior communing. Active labor should rather support and promote recollection. Both Mary and Martha have a place in Christian living; prayer and work, contemplation and activity, interior rest and faithful performance of external tasks. Mary is our model; Martha is our model; each in her own way.

3. Martha had the joy of receiving our Lord as a guest in her home, and she cared for him with loving enthusiasm. Are we not similarly privileged to receive Christ as our guest whenever a brother or sister calls? "I was a stranger, and you brought me home . . . when you did it to one of the least of my brethren here, you did it to me" (Matt. 25:35 ff.).

"How many cares and troubles thou hast! But only one thing is necessary." In our day there is much restlessness, nervous haste and carelessness, even in specifically religious matters; one rushes from this act to the next; one has time for nothing—not for prayer nor even for Mass; not for thanksgiving after Holy Communion, nor for a quiet, peaceful visit before the tabernacle. Nothing but work; always work! How much more reasonable and salutary for body and soul it would be if we not only earned our pay by energetic labor, but also concentrated on God's service, without letting eye and mind flit away from either our work or God's glory. The one thing necessary is that we do His will, live for Him. Let us ask both Martha and Mary to help us every day!

Collect: Listen to us, God our Savior, so that we who find joy in the festival of Thy blessed virgin Martha may learn from her the spirit of godly service. Amen.

JULY 31

St. Ignatius Loyola, *Confessor*

1. Ignatius filled a definite, desperate need in the Church. While Luther was declaring at the Diet of Worms: "Here I stand; I cannot act otherwise"; and employing every means at his disposal to tear the German Church away from the Holy See, there was taking shape in the mind of the Spanish noble-man Ignatius the decision to dedicate all his powers to the defense of the Church. Born in 1491 in the castle of Loyola, Ignatius was sent to the court of King Ferdinand V, where his interest centered on the military profession. Wounded at the siege of Pamplona by the French, he was brought to his father's castle, and during the time of his painful recuperation there he happened to read a "Life of Christ" and a collection of "Lives of the Saints." Little by little he became interested in these books. It became apparent to him that, measured by super-natural standards, his previous life had been wasted. A new world opened up before him.

When he had fully recovered, Ignatius went to the monas-tery of Montserrat, made his confession, kept a "guard of honor" one whole night before the miraculous image of the Virgin, and then hung his sword and dagger on her altar. He left then, to live for a while in poverty and penance at Man-resa, where he composed his famous "Exercises." At the age

of thirty-two he took his place among the school boys of
Barcelona in order to learn Latin. In Alcalá he found several
men who favored his plans, and with these he pronounced
vows in Paris in 1534. Four years later Ignatius called these
companions to Rome, and there the Society of Jesus came into
being. For fifteen years the Founder held the position of general of the Society and labored with remarkable spiritual success. The Church owes an immense debt of gratitude to Ignatius for his "Spiritual Exercises" and for his Society's activity in
the care of souls, in the missions, and in Catholic scholarship.
When age and work began to tell on his physical strength, the
Saint used to shed tears of joy at the thought of soon finding
his longing for the heavenly home satisfied. He died in Rome
on July 31, 1556, with the holy name of Jesus on his lips. His
motto and that of the Society he founded is: "Everything for
the greater glory of God."

2. "For its sake [the word of God] I am ready to undergo
anything; for love of the elect, that they, like us, may win salvation in Jesus Christ, and eternal glory with it. But thou hast
closely followed the schooling, the guidance, thou hast from
me; in firm resolve, in faith, in patience, in love, in endurance;
all my persecutions and suffering. . . . What persecutions I
underwent! . . . And indeed, all those who are resolved to live
a holy life in Christ Jesus will meet with persecution" (Epistle). In this reading, taken from the common of a martyr, St.
Ignatius and his sons are placed side by side with the heroes of
Christ who shed their blood for His sake. "They will persecute
you just as they have persecuted me" (John 15:20). But it is
exactly in this participation in the sufferings of Christ that the
divine approbation lies, promising that Ignatius and his entire
Society will faithfully stand with Christ and His Church to
serve the interests of God. The Church congratulates St. Ignatius on the grace given him so that he might follow our Lord
with energetic labor and suffering. The Saint used to say: "A
full cup of sufferings is a guarantee that God wishes to make

one great." And again: "Persecution is nothing but the winnow-
ing fan that blows the chaff out of virtue." For Christ said: "If
any man has a mind to come my way, let him renounce self,
and take up his cross, and follow me" (Matt. 16:24). There is
no other road on which to follow Christ.

"It is fire that I have come to spread over the earth, and what
better wish can I have than that it should be kindled?" (Communion.) Ignatius was what his name means, a man of fire.
His whole being was aglow with love of God and souls. His
intention was to organize a society whose principal purpose
would be to give glory to God and to save souls for God. To the
usual three vows of religion he added a fourth which bound
his sons to obey the Holy Father willingly and promptly in all
things, and to permit themselves to be employed anywhere in
carrying out the intentions of the head of the Church. He
taught his companions to master themselves in all things, to
die to the world, and to live, suffer, and die for God's glory.

St. Ignatius was often seen to look heavenward with glowing
countenance while uttering the words: "How disgusted I am
with earth when I contemplate heaven!" A frequent remark of
his was: "What do I wish, what can I wish, besides Thee, my
God?" He usually concluded his instructions with the words:
"Love God with your whole heart, with your whole soul, and
with all your strength." No sacrifice was too great or laborious
for him when there was question of the salvation of even a single soul. He would say: "If I were able to die a thousand times,
I should want to die a thousand times for the sake of one soul."
The love of Christ consumed him. He sent St. Francis Xavier to
India; he was especially concerned about rescuing the German
people from the so-called reformers, ordering all his priests to
offer a holy Mass for that intention; he founded the German
College in Rome, as well as a number of charitable institutions;
and all this to promote the Kingdom of Christ. Truly, a man of
fire!

3. "The innocent man will flourish as the palm tree flour-

ishes; in the house of the Lord he will grow to greatness"
(Gradual). It cost the young officer Inigo no small sacrifice to
choose the life he felt called to; he wavered a long time, but
the dreadful conflict finally ended in the triumph of grace:
He swore eternal allegiance to Mary and to her Son. What he
had promised, he carried out to the letter. St. Ignatius was a
man of the highest integrity. We thank God for having given
this great saint such singular graces. May St. Ignatius be for
us an example, a teacher, and an intercessor with God!

Collect: O God, who, to promote the greater glory of Thy name,
didst reinforce the Church militant with a new army by means of
blessed Ignatius, grant that we who do battle here on earth, with
his help and after his example, may deserve to be crowned with him
in heaven. Amen.

****

AUGUST

****

AUGUST 1

St. Peter in Chains

1. According to ancient records Empress Eudoxia received from Bishop Juvenal of Jerusalem, in the year 439, the chains which had bound St. Peter in that city (cf. Acts 12:1–18). The Empress was said to have sent one of these chains to her daughter Eudoxia, wife of the Roman Emperor Valentinian III, who died in 445. The daughter had a church built in Rome bearing the name, *St. Petri ad Vincula*. In this church were also preserved the chains which St. Peter had worn in his Roman prison. Eudoxia brought the Jerusalem chain to Pope Sixtus III, who touched it to the Roman chain with the miraculous result that the two chains were united into one. So much is legend; historically certain, however, is the fact that the Church of St. Peter *Ad Vincula* became known very early as the Church of the Apostle, probably because it stood on the spot where Peter had been imprisoned and miraculously released. This church was reconstructed by Pope Sixtus III between 432 and 440. Today's celebration was thus originally a dedication feast. Except for the orations and two texts, the Mass is the same as that for the feast of Sts. Peter and Paul on June 29, stressing today the imprisonment and wonderful liberation of the Apostle Peter.

2. After Herod had beheaded the Apostle James and had seen that the Jews approved, he had St. Peter imprisoned (cf. Lesson). When Herod, an apostate Jew, came to rule over Palestine, he wanted to give the Jews the impression that he had remained faithful to the law and worship of Israel. He therefore upheld quite strictly the customs of the people and

also began a persecution of the Christians, shrewdly intensify-
ing it at the time when Jews gathered from every part of the
country to celebrate the Passover in Jerusalem. True to expectation, the beheading of James made the people feel something
of their old national pride, and they extolled their new king,
transferring to him some of their dreams about reviving their
former glory. To encourage this attitude toward himself,
Herod took Peter into custody, even though he could hold no
trial nor shed any blood until after the feast. In this state of
affairs the infant Church had no recourse except to prayer,
and the faithful prayed without interruption for their imprisoned bishop. After the feast, and during the night preced-
ing Peter's scheduled trial, an angel struck off his chains and
led him out of prison. This may prove the power of the
Church's prayer; but it shows as well that man can serve the
will of God even when intending evil. Providence rules wonderfully.

"The chains fell from his hands . . . and as soon as they had
passed on up one street, the angel left him. At this, Peter came
to himself. Now I can tell for certain, he said, that the Lord
has sent his angel, to deliver me out of Herod's hands, and
from all that the people of the Jews hoped to see" (Lesson).
The power of Herod was helpless against the power of God;
neither chains nor prison doors could detain Peter after God
had ordered his release. Christ, at His Church's unrelenting
petition, had wrought victory. This story is repeated today in
much the same way in the so-called Iron Curtain countries,
where cardinals, bishops, and thousands of priests and religious of both sexes have been imprisoned and sent to concentration camps. In China the story is similar—the power
of Herod again. Will this conspiracy of hell and its helpers
not have to give way eventually to the power of God, repeating the miracle of Peter? No doubt; but there must be first a
Church praying this petition without interruption—praying
for forgiveness of sins, offering atonement, doing penance,

daily sanctifying itself. To this Church I belong; am I doing
these things, as is my duty?

3. Let us hear St. Augustine's comment on today's mystery:
"Of St. Peter, we read: They brought their sick so that his
shadow might fall on them when he passed by. If Peter's
shadow could cure bodies in those days, how much more can
his present plenitude of power effect! If the very air set in mo-
tion by his passing could benefit petitioners then, how much
more the favor of the stable Rock! It is proper that, in certain
ancient churches, the iron of those chains should be held more
precious than gold. If the shadow of Peter passing by could
heal, all the more can the chains of his captivity do so. If
the empty shadow had such power to cure, so much the more
should the bonds of suffering bring health, for the weight of
the iron had pressed into Peter's flesh. If Peter could do so
much for the sick before his martyrdom, he can do much more
since his triumph. Hail to those bonds that made a martyr of
the Apostle whom they touched!"

In one of the Vesper Antiphons we pray: "Free us, O Peter,
from the chains that bind us to earthly things—thou who dost
cause the gates of heaven to stand open for those who enter
bliss." It is our earnest plea to the Apostle today, that we, too,
may be loosed from the chains that bind us to anything besides
God, His commandments, and His will.

Collect: God, who didst release the blessed apostle Peter from his
chains and send him forth unharmed: loosen the bonds of our sins,
we pray Thee, and in Thy mercy keep us from all evils. Amen.

AUGUST 2

St. Alphonsus Mary de Liguori, *Bishop,*
Confessor, Doctor of the Church

1. St. Alphonsus is one of the most prominent figures in
the Church of the eighteenth century; he stands out as a messenger of God in that period of rationalism, freethinking and
unbelief. Armed with a plenitude of the spirit and strength
from above, he was able to awaken and fortify the religious
life of his time. Born in 1696 of a noble family in Naples, he
was so richly talented that he obtained his doctorate of law at
seventeen. Practicing law, he won many cases. Once, however,
he overlooked an important word in the minutes of a trial, and
when his opponent pointed out that he had used a wrong
word he gave up law for good.

In spite of his father's opposition, Alphonsus then entered
the clerical state and was ordained at the age of thirty. Simple sermons and pity for the poor characterized the apostolic
career he now inaugurated. At length, after mature delibera-
tion, much prayer and seeking of advice, he founded the "Congregation of the Most Holy Redeemer," or "Redemptorists,"
in 1749. It was to be their task to go out in the spirit of the
gospel to preach missions in both city and country, leading
souls to Christ by instruction. As superior of the Congregation, Alphonsus was always at the disposal of his subjects. In
his learned works, he took up the fight in behalf of the sound
doctrine of the Church against Jansenism and the laxity of the
time. In obedience to Pope Clement XIII he accepted consecration as bishop of St. Agatha, near Naples, in 1762. In
spite of age and infirmity he devoted himself to the new task
with tireless energy. After several vain requests for release
from this office, he finally gained the consent of Pope Pius VI
in 1775. He then returned to the Redemptorist house at Pagani

and lived, patient and cheerful to the last, amid severe ailments of various kinds. His death occurred on August 1, 1784. In 1839 he was canonized, and in 1871, the title of Doctor of the Church was conferred upon him. On his feast the liturgy has him declare: "Gracious comfort, Lord, is the memory of thy just dealings in times long past: I am shaken when I see wrong-doers abandoning thy law" (Gradual). His divine mission is expressed in the words: "God sent him to convert a nation, and sweep away foul traces of sin: he kept his heart steadfastly fixed on the Lord, a bulwark of piety in days when sinners abounded" (Alleluia verse).

2. "The spirit of the Lord is upon me; he has anointed me and sent me out to preach the gospel to the poor and to restore the broken-hearted" (Introit). These words of the prophet Isaias (61:1, 2), which our Lord applied to Himself (cf. Luke 4:18), the liturgy puts into the mouth of St. Alphonsus. Prompted by the Spirit of God, this famed lawyer and nobleman devoted himself to the "least of the brethren," the ignorant, uncultured, neglected. He prepared them for the sacraments, comforted them and advised them, visited their sick, and in general, helped wherever he could. The Saint was particularly fond of the poor country people of the Kingdom of Naples; he even visited the half-savage goatherds in the remote gorges of Sorrento and on the cliffs of Amalfi. Everywhere he brought blessings and led the erring back to God. It was for the instruction of these simple ones that he founded his Congregation. As bishop, St. Alphonsus opened missions in all parts of his diocese, preached every Sunday, and held instructions in Christian doctrine. He compiled a special catechism for the common people and wrote a number of treatises to deepen Christian faith and life among the people. Truly, as the Introit says, the Spirit of the Lord was upon him.

"The soldier on service, if he would please the captain who enlisted him, will refuse to be entangled in the business of daily life" (Epistle). This passage may be taken as an allusion to that moment in the courtroom when Alphonsus, pale with horror on account of his error, cried out: "Deceitful world, now I recognize you for what you are! I should rather be the lowest servant in the Church than the first lord in the courtroom." With that he left the room; his father and relatives saw their high hopes destroyed; they opposed his determination to enter the service of the Church with every means at their disposal. Alphonsus gave only one answer: "God is calling me and I must obey." The whole circle of his acquaintances ridiculed this idea, certain that he had suddenly lost his mind; but he calmly went his way, seeking only God.

Naturally Alphonsus had to worry about many things as a superior and bishop; he had to listen to the requests and complaints of his men; he had to provide for the education of novices and for the material needs of the Congregation; he had to treat with officials about all manner of things; he had to carry on a vast correspondence. Yet all these duties did not hinder him from fostering an interior life in himself and from considering the will and honor of God in every circumstance. Above all things he was concerned about perfectly conforming his will to the will of God; that really characterizes his spirit to perfection: he wanted to please Him alone to whom he was consecrated as priest, religious, and bishop. St. Alphonsus, in a word, took his "share of hardship . . . like a good soldier of Christ Jesus," driven by that love of Christ which made him want to become all things to all men, and to consume all his strength in this cause.

3. St. Alphonsus wrote: "All holiness consists in loving God. All love of God expresses itself in fulfilling the divine will, that is, in complete conformity with God's will." It is his conviction that "it is better and safer to act with the intention of doing God's will than with the intention of giving glory to God; for this is the proper means of avoiding all the snares of self-love. Very often, in pretending to give glory to God, we are really seeking our own will. When we fulfill the will of God and do

what is most pleasing to Him, we cannot be deceived. Let us be convinced that the greatest honor we can render to God is to do His will."

Collect: O God, who didst kindle in Thy blessed confessor bishop Alphonsus Mary a burning zeal for souls, and by his means didst cause Thy Church to bring forth a new offspring, we pray that we may learn from his wholesome teaching and be strengthened by his example to make our way, despite all obstacles, into Thy presence. Amen.

AUGUST 4

St. Dominic, *Confessor and Founder*

1. About the year 1200 the sect of the Albigenses—named for the city of Albi in southern France—was doing great harm in the Church. It denied the basic mysteries of Revelation: Trinity, Incarnation, and Redemption. It rejected the sacraments (especially matrimony), divine services, and every form of visible Church. The fanaticism of these heretics extended to the destruction of churches, monasteries, pictures, and crucifixes. They abolished all relations between Church and State.

In this hour of need God called St. Dominic into the field. Born of devout parents in Catholic Spain, he became a priest and a canon. On a journey through southern France with his bishop in 1203, Dominic learned about the sad state of affairs and immediately joined the missionary priests already at work there, preaching the word of God to the erring with burning zeal. When six brave companions associated themselves with him, he founded the Order of Preachers for the express purpose of proclaiming the doctrine of the Church and defending it against errors. In 1216 the new Order, known as the Dominicans, was approved by Pope Honorius III. St. Dominic died at Bologna on August 6, 1221, admonishing his brethren: "Have charity, preserve humility, and do not separate yourselves from poverty."

2. "Preach the word, dwelling upon it continually, welcome or unwelcome; bring home wrongdoing . . . with all the patience of a teacher" (Epistle). St. Dominic was an apostle glowing with love for doctrine, charity, and souls. He preached not only with words but with the example of a holy life free from all self-seeking, all avarice. He lived in extreme poverty and associated himself with the poor and the insignificant. His imperturbable meekness enabled him to be a living sermon against the insults and abuse from the Albigenses. His habit of tireless prayer was no less a sermon. A contemporary said of him: "Blessed Dominic burned with boundless loving zeal for souls. Day and night and in every place he preached and spoke only about God. He was extremely strict in his living, nourishing himself only with bread and vegetables. He was a great despiser of self and considered himself as nothing. Wrongs and humiliations he bore with patience and joy. I have never seen a man who prayed so incessantly; he spent the nights in prayer for sinners. He loved the Faith; he loved peace, and he promoted both with all his powers."

As his Order grew St. Dominic had to travel a great deal, visiting the different houses; wherever he stopped he preached, in churches or public squares. So great was his eagerness to spread the word of God that once, when he met a group of German pilgrims, he begged the Lord to let him preach in their language. The favor was granted. It was this zeal for the purity of the Faith that prompted him to found the Order of Preachers. In order that their preaching might bear fruit, he demanded of his sons a life of strict poverty, self-discipline, perfect obedience to superiors, and serious cultivation of the sacred sciences. Everything was to further the preaching of the gospel and leading men to God and His Church. God has done, and still does, great things through St. Dominic's Order. We thank Him for having given His Church this great apostle.

"The innocent will flourish as the palm-tree flourishes: in the house of the Lord he will grow to greatness, as the cedars grow on Lebanon" (Gradual). This is the secret of St. Dominic's tremendous effectiveness and admirable success. The *Imitation* says: "The holy man first plans interiorly the works he wants to carry out exteriorly" (Bk. I, 3, 2). First come living with God in a life of prayer, Christian virtue, faith, and intimate love; then God will bless the work. "Vain is the builder's toil, if the house is not of the Lord's building" (Ps. 126:1). But God builds the house in proportion to the intimacy of man's union with Him by faith, purity, and love. St. Dominic was, first and foremost, a man of prayer, of contemplation. No wonder that he accomplished so much for God in the short space of the fifty-one years of his life.

Dante wrote, in *Paradiso*, Canto XII, of Dominic:

"By doctrine high and mighty will sustained,
   he moved 'neath office apostolic fighting:
   like torrent from a source most lofty veined."

Yes, the Saint's doctrine flowed from the heights of prayerful union with God.

3. "My faithfulness and mercy shall go with him; as my champion he shall rise to greatness" (Offertory). "If a man lives on in me, and I in him, then he will yield abundant fruit: separated from me, you have no power to do anything" (John 15:5).

"Your loins must be girt and your lamps burning" (Gospel). St. Gregory the Great comments on this text as follows: "We gird our loins when we tame the concupiscence of the flesh. We have burning lamps in our hands when we perform good works and thereby give our neighbor a good example." Of these good works, our Lord says: "Your light must shine so brightly before men that they can see your good works, and glorify your Father who is in heaven" (Matt. 5:16).

Collect: O God, whose pleasure it was to enlighten Thy Church by the merits and teaching of Thy blessed confessor Dominic, grant that through his intercession she may not be deprived of temporal help, and may continually advance in spiritual growth. Amen.

AUGUST 5

Dedication of the Basilica of Our Lady of the Snow

1. The Church is celebrating today the dedication of one of the four major Basilicas of Rome, St. Mary Major. Legend says that a certain patrician, John, decided with his wife to bequeath their properties to the Mother of God, since they had no children. During their planning, snow fell on the Esquiline hill in Rome, and both dreamed that they were told to build a church on a spot covered with snow. Pope Liberius had the same dream, and so, according to legend, the church came to be built. History records only the fact that Pope Sixtus III restored, in 440, a church built by Liberius and, to commemorate the Council of Ephesus (431), dedicated it to Mary, Mother of God. It is also called the Liberian Basilica. Pope Liberius died in 366.

2. "Hail, holy Mother, in thy womb there lay a King who bears o'er earth and heaven endless sway" (Introit). The Council of Ephesus, condemning the heresy of Nestorius, had solemnly approved the title of "Mother of God" for Mary the Mother of Jesus. The people had been jubilant over this vindication of their belief and immemorial practice. Because of the connection of the Basilica with the Council's decision, we today greet Mary as Mother of God with special joy. We believe in her singular greatness and cry out to her: "Blessed art thou, and worshipful, Mary, virgin; who without loss of maidenhood wast found to be mother of our Savior. Virgin Mother of God, he whom the entire world cannot hold enclosed himself within

thy womb and was made man" (Gradual). "Blessed be the womb in which the virgin Mary bore the eternal Father's Son" (Communion). And St. Augustine's comment: "Let us rejoice, brethren, because the Virgin Mother brought forth in pure, virginal fruitfulness, Him, who was made visible to us—she, who had been created by Him, the invisible One. As a virgin she conceived, as a virgin she became pregnant, as a virgin she carried her Son in her womb. . . . God had to be borne in the manner in which it pleased Him to become man. Thus, she came into being through Him who was made man out of her."

"Blessed are they who hear the word of God, and keep it." That was our Lord's retort to the acclamation from the woman in the crowd, "Blessed is the womb that bore thee, the breast which thou hast sucked." Mary is our Savior's Mother not only physically, but even spiritually, according to the word of her Christ-Son: "If anyone does the will of my Father who is in heaven, he is my brother, and sister, and mother" (Matt. 12:50). "The fact that one virgin gave birth is the pride of all virgins. They, too, are mothers of Christ if they do the will of His Father. According to the spirit, Mary is the mother of Christ's members; that is, she is our mother, for, by her love, she cooperated in causing the faithful, who are members of the head, to be born in the Church, that is, of Catholic parents. Physically, however, Mary is the mother of the head. For, according to the flesh, our head had to be born of a virgin, so as to indicate that His members according to the spirit were to be born of the virgin that is the Church. Mary alone is, therefore, according to spirit and flesh, mother and virgin, Mother of Christ and Virgin of Christ. On the other hand, the Church, consisting of the saints who will possess the kingdom of Christ, is, according to the spirit, wholly mother of Christ, wholly a virgin of Christ; according to the flesh, however, she is a virgin of Christ only in some individuals" (St. Augustine: *On Virginity,* Chaps. 4–6).

3. "Blessed is the womb that bore thee, the breast which

thou hast sucked. And he answered: Shall we not say, Blessed are they who hear the word of God, and keep it?" Our Lord rejects high esteem of the purely natural motherhood of Mary; from a spiritual standpoint, it is meaningless. Only those deserve to be extolled as blessed who willingly listen to God's revealed word and follow it. Hence, even Mary the Mother of Christ is to be called blessed primarily because she heard the word of God and followed it humbly and obediently; because she said: "Behold the handmaid of the Lord; let it be unto me according to thy word." Happy, too, shall we be if we belong to the number of those who hear the word of God and follow it.

In the Communion antiphon we bless the womb of the Virgin Mary that "bore the eternal Father's Son." In the reception of Holy Communion we experience, every day, a kind of divine conception in a sense similar to the unique conception of God once experienced by the Virgin Mary.

Collect: Grant to us Thy servants, Lord God, we pray Thee, lasting health of mind and body. At the intercession of blessed Mary, the glorious and ever-virgin, may we be delivered from sorrows of this life and enjoy the happiness of life everlasting. Amen.

AUGUST 6

The Transfiguration of Our Lord Jesus Christ

1. "Come, let us adore the supreme King of Glory!" This is the Invitatory of Matins for today's feast of the Transfiguration, which is, as it were, another feast of Christ the King. On Mount Tabor Moses and Elias, representing respectively the patriarchs and prophets, gave testimony of Christ, acknowledging Him to be the Messias promised in the Old Testament. At the same time there sounded the voice of the Father saying: "This is my beloved Son . . . to him, then, listen." The liturgy rec-

ognizes in the story of the Transfiguration a prop for our faith and hope.

2. Jesus is the King of Glory who will come in power and majesty to judge the living and the dead. St. Peter tells his experience on Mount Tabor as follows: "We were not crediting fables of man's invention, when we preached to you about the power of our Lord Jesus Christ, and about his coming; we had been eye witnesses of his exaltation. Such honour, such glory was bestowed by God the Father, that a voice came to him out of the splendour which dazzles human eyes; This, it said, is my beloved Son, in whom I am well pleased; to him, then, listen" (Epistle). The glory in which our Lord revealed Himself on the mountain gave Peter, and all of us as well, certainty that He will one day come again; and that He was taken up into the glory of the Father and is, as man, still the king of glory. "Fame shall record his gracious deeds eternally" (Offertory). He, the Son of God, "dispossessed himself, and took the nature of a slave . . . and then he lowered his dignity, accepted an obedience which brought him to death, death on a cross. That is why God has raised him to such a height, given him that name which is greater than any other name; so that everything in heaven and on earth and under the earth must bend the knee before the name of Jesus, and every tongue must confess Jesus Christ as the Lord, dwelling in the glory of God the Father" (Phil. 2:6 ff.). "All the prophets bear him this testimony" (Acts 10:43), and we accept it, worshipping the King of Glory. "A King's honor for my theme" (Gradual), for my thoughts, my wishes, my strength, my love, my sacrifices!

The Transfiguration strengthens our hope, for "it is to heaven that we look expectantly for the coming of our Lord Jesus Christ to save us; he will form this humbled body of ours anew, moulding it into the image of his glorified body" (Phil. 3:20 f.). It is our confident hope that our body will one day become like the body of our Lord glorified on Mount Tabor. In a responsory of Matins the liturgy reminds us: "See how God has shewn his

love towards us; that we should be counted as his sons, be his
sons. . . . But we know that when he comes we shall be like
him" (I John 3:1). In the transfigured Savior we possess a
picture, and also a pledge, of our future transfiguration of body
and soul to glory. In the Transfiguration, the heavenly Father
has signified "the fulfillment of our adoption as . . . children
. . . by the voice speaking out of a bright cloud" (Collect).
The words of the Father, "This is my beloved Son in whom I
am well pleased," apply also to us, who have become living
members of Christ through baptism. Being children of God, we
are also His heirs, co-heirs of Christ, the King of Glory, and
so shall be "sharers in his glory."

3. "Thine is more than mortal beauty, thy lips overflow with
gracious utterance. Joyful are the words that well up from my
heart, a King's honor for my theme. Alleluia, alleluia. Here is
the glow of the uncreated Light, untarnished mirror of his
goodness" (Gradual and Alleluia verse).

"And two men appeared conversing with him, Moses and
Elias, seen now in glory; and they spoke of the death which he
was to achieve at Jerusalem" (Luke 9:30, 31). In His transfiguration on Tabor, our Lord pointed to His crucifixion on Golgotha. He teaches on the one hand that we may not doubt His
promise of heavenly happiness; yet on the other hand we must
know that we "ought to pray, amid the temptations of the
present life, rather for strength to suffer than for glory" (St.
Leo the Great).

"The Spirit himself thus assures our spirit, that we are children of God; and if we are his children, then we are his heirs,
too; heirs of God, sharing the inheritance of Christ" (Rom.
8:16, 17). To be fellow-heirs with Christ of eternal glory—that
is our hope, our promise of future heavenly bliss.

Collect: O God, who in the glorious transfiguration of Thy only-
begotten Son didst confirm, by the witness of the prophets, the truths
revealed to faith, and by the voice speaking out of a bright cloud

didst miraculously signify the fulfilment of our adoption as Thy children; in Thy mercy deign to make us co-heirs of His kingdom and sharers in His glory. Amen.

AUGUST 7

St. Cajetan, *Confessor*

1. Cajetan was one of the first Catholic reformers who opposed the so-called "Reformation" of the sixteenth century by promoting a positive Catholic movement to counteract the reign of doubt, denial, and destruction resulting from the Protestant revolt. He was born in Lombardy, in 1480, and his pious mother offered the infant to God. So well did she plant the seed of Christian virtues that he emerged from youth with innocence intact, despite alluring temptations. Already he felt pity for the poor, and even went hungry himself in order to feed others. He studied law at Padua, attempting to sanctify that profane science by casting on it the clear light of supernatural truths. At the age of twenty-five he began the study of theology and was ordained eleven years later, in 1516. To foster faith and Christian living among the people by leading the clergy to deeper cultivation of the interior life, Cajetan founded, together with Bishop Carafa of Chieti (later Pope Paul IV), the Congregation of the Theatines. The priests of this order aimed against the corruption of the times their genuinely apostolic lives, spent in teaching sound doctrine. They lived in monastic communities with no regular income, depending entirely on unsolicited alms from the faithful for support, for Cajetan believed firmly in the providence of God as set forth in the Gospel of today's Mass. In Venice, Rome, and Naples Cajetan and his brethren developed a charitable activity hitherto unknown. He died on August 7, 1547. His Congre-

gation, once widespread, now has a few houses in Italy. A branch of female Theatines was founded by the Venerable Ursula Benincasa in 1583.

2. "Blessed is the man who lives unreproved, who has no greed for gold, puts no trust in his store of riches. Show us such a man, and we will be loud in his praise; here is a life to wonder at" (Lesson). Cajetan is surely such a man; although wealthy and of noble family he had remained, even as a student of law and theology, a modest and simple person, preferring quiet surroundings to pomp and luxury, ignoring the taunts of his relatives. He could have gained a position at the court of Pope Julius II; but he had come to Rome only as an apostle of charity. Whatever he had or could acquire went to his beloved poor; he kept only his garment and his little room with its table, prie-dieu and straw sack; he never worried about food, and as a result his fare often consisted only of a little bread with fruit or a few beans; but he was no less cheerful for it, nor less grateful to God. Cajetan possessed that precious treasure of interior liberty which fosters the action of divine grace in making saints.

"You must serve God or money; you cannot serve both. I say to you, then, do not fret over your life, how to support it with food and drink; over your body, how to keep it clothed. . . . See how the birds of the air never sow, or reap. . . . See how the wild lilies grow. . . . If God, then, so clothes the grasses of the field, which today live and will feed the oven tomorrow, will he not be much more ready to clothe you, men of little faith? Do not fret, then, asking, What are we to eat? or What are we to drink . . . you have a Father in heaven who knows that you need them all. Make it your first care to find the kingdom, of God, and his approval, and all these things shall be yours without the asking" (Gospel). Cajetan's interest and energy were entirely devoted to the seeking of a supernatural goal: the "approval" of God, the growth of the life of grace in his soul, giving him dominion over the "old man." All other activity had to serve this supernaturally consecrated life. And God, for His part, was faithful to His promise that earthly things should be added.

3. "Seek first the kingdom of God." This does not mean that we should not be concerned about our daily bread, simply sitting with idle hands as if Providence would bring us everything without our effort. It means rather that we should labor to provide ourselves with the necessary physical and social well-being, and to do this always and everywhere in such a way as not to lose sight of our destiny. We may never look upon temporal things as our end; they are only helps to it.

"Seek first the kingdom of God and his justice." There is among men such exaggerated concern about property, money, health, and welfare; it grows even into a slavery to the desire for success; men live and die only for this world.

"You have a Father in heaven who knows that you need" these things. We can learn from Cajetan how wonderfully well a genuine trust in God is rewarded in this life. Our great sin is lack of trust. We live as though everything depended on us; we have lost sight of the fact that God is the decisive and prime factor in our lives. St. Catharine of Siena used to say: "God's help comes to us in the measure that we trust in Him."

Collect: God, who didst give to Thy confessor, blessed Cajetan, the grace to imitate the apostolic way of life, grant that by his intercession and example we may ever put our trust in Thee and desire only the things of heaven. Amen.

AUGUST 9

St. John Mary Vianney, *Confessor*

1. John Vianney was born of simple, pious parents on May 8, 1786, at Dardilly in France, shortly before the outbreak of the French Revolution. Matthew and Mary Vianney's child

understood the meaning of prayer by the time he was three, having already a tender devotion to the Blessed Mother. The boy tended his father's little drove of cattle and sheep until the pastor of Ecully offered to help him get an education. John was a poor student; only the thought of becoming a priest kept him from yielding to discouragement. Called to military service in 1809, he was soon released because of the precarious state of his health. He returned at once to his studies and was ordained to the priesthood on August 9, 1815. After serving as assistant at Ecully for several years he became pastor of Ars in 1818. This parish was in a pitiable condition as to religion and morals, but before many years had passed his prayers and preaching had reformed it. He listened to all who came to him with troubled consciences, and before long people were arriving from every part of France, to the number of twenty thousand a year. The Curé received them all at the cost of heroic mortification and charity; his austere life, amiable disposition, and a supernatural power that went out from him attracted people powerfully. He died on August 4, 1859, and was canonized by Pope Pius XI on May 31, 1925.

2. "Right reason is on the good man's lips; well weighed are all his counsels" (Introit). Men were amazed at the towering wisdom of the simple, unscholarly pastor of Ars. Divine light served him for learning. A saint has said: "What purifies the eye of the heart and disposes one to elevate himself to the true Light is contempt for worldly affairs, mortification of the body, compunction of heart, contemplation of God's admirable being and His pure truth, fervent and trustful prayer, joy in God, ardent longing for heaven." According to this formula St. John Vianney possessed powerful spiritual vision. From his youth he had stayed near the true Light, and it flooded his soul. He opened his heart in prayer, and God filled it with divine light.

Through his transparent personality this light was diffused upon souls, particularly in his catechetical instructions. His

very language seemed to be other than human, and all classes
of hearers found themselves hanging on his words, charmed
by his pleasing voice, the vividness of his picturesque illustra-
tions, the holy fire. How was it that this extremely inept student, who could not pass examinations, eventually became a
master of the word of God? How could he charm the people
so that they believed as he did, loved as he did, and, at his
word, completely changed their lives? "Thou hast hidden all
this from the wise and prudent, and revealed it to little children" (Matt. 11:25). The spirit of God inspired him to know
and to teach; the whole sum of his learning was faith; his book,
Jesus; for, when asked who had taught him theology, he would
say: "The same one who taught St. Peter." The divine wisdom
decreed: "My faithfulness and mercy shall go with him; as my
champion he shall rise to greatness" (Offertory).

"Blessed is the man who lives unreproved, who has no greed
for gold, puts no trust in his store of riches. Show us such a
man, and we will be loud in his praise" (Lesson). Such a man
was St. John Mary: he had neither bag, nor money when he
arrived at Ars in Lent of 1818. He had to store his wood in the
rectory parlor. In his own room were only a poor bed, table and
prie-dieu. The church was his living-room: here he stayed for
hours without moving—bathing, he used to say, in the flames
of love. Reducing his own needs to a minimum, he spent most
of his income and all gifts in repairing and adorning his church.
God and souls were his riches.

St. John spent many hours in the confessional, even late at
night. Whatever time remained at his disposal was devoted to
prayer, by means of which he could effect conversions and
miraculous cures. But he complained: "I see only my sins, and
I do not even see all of them." Repeatedly tortured by this
self-disgust he would cry: "I am drying up with discontent on
this earth," and, "If I had known what it means to be responsible for the welfare of my neighbor, as a priest, I should have
buried myself in a desert." Indeed, "Here is a life to wonder

at. . . . His treasure is safely preserved in the Lord's keeping, and wherever faithful souls are met, his alms-deeds will be remembered" (Lesson).

3. Some sayings of the holy Curé: "Those who make no effort to overcome themselves and bring forth fruits of penance are like trees in winter: they have neither blossoms nor fruit, and yet they are not dead."

"The Cross is a key which will open heaven for those who love and understand it." "Virtue alone has the power to gain for us the most magnificent of all goods, peace of soul and hope of obtaining everlasting life."

Collect: Almightly and merciful God, who didst make blessed John Mary remarkable for priestly zeal and constant fervor in prayer and penance, grant, we pray Thee, that his intercession and example may enable us to win the souls of our brethren for Christ, and with them to attain everlasting glory. Amen.

AUGUST 10

St. Laurence, *Martyr*

1. Laurence is the most celebrated martyr of the Eternal City; as many as forty Roman sanctuaries bore his name during the Middle Ages. He was archdeacon to Pope Sixtus II, with the task of caring for the poor. When the Pope was led away to martyrdom under Emperor Valerian in 258, Laurence expressed sorrow because he was not allowed to accompany him: "Father, where are you going without your deacon? You have never offered the Holy Sacrifice without your deacon. What in me, Father, has displeased you? Try me to see if you have chosen an unfit servant when you entrusted to me the distribution of the blood of the Lord." Pope Sixtus replied: "I am not leaving you, my son; you will have to undergo a bitter struggle. We elders have an easy fight before us. You, the younger, must

triumph over the tyrant with greater glory. Stop complaining; after three days, you will follow me. Go and take care of the treasures of the Church that have been entrusted to you." Laurence obeyed by distributing the possessions of the Church among the poor. Soon he was arrested and ordered to hand over the riches that had been entrusted to him. He called together the poor and presented them to the judge, saying: "These are the treasures of the Church." He was tortured, and the next day he was slowly roasted to death on a hot gridiron. In the midst of his torments he prayed: "Take my spirit, O God, and free me from this mortal existence." Yet he joked with his torturers: "I am done on one side; turn me over." In this manner was fulfilled the promise of his bishop, that he should follow him in three days.

2. "Honor and beauty wait on his presence; worship and magnificence are the attendants of his shrine" (Introit). Thus does today's liturgy praise the splendid church of St. Laurence. In its famous beauty we see reflected the singular holiness of the Saint. So highly was he esteemed by the Fathers that they attributed to his intercession the abolition of paganism from Rome fifteen years after his martyrdom. Surely, St. Laurence presents a picture of rare virtue. He served his bishop by faultless living, preaching, and caring for the poor, even when torturers put his devotion to duty to the severe test of extreme pain. Pope St. Leo the Great in a sermon on this feast exclaimed: "O raging cruelty, thou gainest nothing; thou profitest nothing. That which can die is withdrawn from thy torments, and when Laurence has departed to heaven, thou hast failed with thy flames. The love for Christ could not be overcome by flames; the fire that scorched the exterior was not so vehement as that which burned within" (cf. Breviary). Love for Christ kept St. Laurence from feeling fire and red-hot grill, and carried him to God.

"He who sows sparingly will reap sparingly; he who sows freely will reap freely too" (Epistle). This expresses the policy of St. Laurence in caring for the poor. He gave with joy in his heart, knowing that "God loves a cheerful giver." He who does charity happily with love, wins blessings; God gives the means for more giving: "He who puts grain into the sower's hand, and gives us food to eat, will supply you with seed and multiply it, and enrich the harvest of your charity" (Epistle). Because Laurence was serving Christ in the poor, this promise was fulfilled in him: "If any one serves me, my Father will do him honor" (Gospel). God honored him with the crown of martyrdom; with Christ he became the grain of wheat that fell into the ground and died (cf. Gospel) and then brought forth fruit for itself and for the whole Church. He is a powerful intercessor and a shining example of Christian charity and heroism for all of us.

Weaker was the external fire than the one that burned in the heart of Laurence. What wonderful things the fire of love can do! What can it do in me?

In Matins of this feast, one of the responsories quotes St. Laurence: "I am fortunate to be a sacrificial victim for Christ. Accused, I did not deny Christ; questioned, I confessed Christ; roasted, I thanked God. I offered myself as a sacrifice to God." Must not our sentiments and our speech be the same when we participate in the offering of Holy Mass? The deacon St. Laurence can teach us what it means to offer the Holy Sacrifice properly. The liturgical, unbloody Sacrifice on the altar, if it is also 'our sacrifice,' prompts us to "give unto blood" in daily life, to be willing and happy to assume its labor, duties, and sufferings, and even to give ourselves to martyrdom if called upon.

Collect: Almighty God, who gavest blessed Laurence strength to overcome his fiery torment, we pray Thee grant us grace to extinguish in ourselves the flames of sin. Amen.

AUGUST 12

St. Clare, *Virgin*

1. Clare was born of a noble and distinguished family in
Assisi, Italy, and trained to virtue by her mother. As a child
she was attracted to solitude and prayer, loved the poor, and
gladly went hungry in order to feed beggars. It became her
most ardent wish to be able to speak with St. Francis and learn
from him how to save her soul. The opportunity came; and
after a lengthy consultation with him she made up her mind to
renounce the world altogether, and to follow the Crucified in
poverty and self-denial. Her parents had other plans for her,
but Clare was able to make them understand her motives, and
at the age of eighteen she received a religious garb from the
hands of St. Francis in the Portiuncula Church. When relatives
came to take her from the convent by force, she knelt on the
altar steps showing them her shorn head, and asserted that no
power in the world could dissuade her from carrying out her
purpose. A short time later her sister Agnes joined her, and then
other young women came. St. Francis fitted out a small cloister
for them in San Damiano, near Assisi, and made Clare the first
superior of it. Before long, she became renowned for the power
of her prayer, for her love of the sisters, her humility, and her
penitential practices. On August 11, 1253, she received, in
return for her worn-out life of poverty, the new and eternal
riches of heaven.

2. "Thou hast been a friend to right, an enemy to wrong"
(Introit). With these words we greet and congratulate Clare
today. Her childhood desire for union with God ripened, with
St. Francis' blessing, into a determination to devote her life
entirely to the service of God in voluntary poverty. One evening she left father and mother and with a few companions
went to the Portiuncula, where St. Francis gave her an ash-

colored habit and a rope cincture; the noble young lady had
become a daughter of poverty. She might have had a pleasant,
easy life but she knew the value of goods the world cannot
give, and she ardently desired to be united with Christ's life
of poverty, with its humiliation and suffering. She wanted God
alone—God in all things and above every thing. Her sole motive was love of God, to be exemplified by her total surrender
to His law and His will.

"And God . . . has given thee an unction to bring thee pride,
beyond any of thy fellows" (Introit). It is part of the divine
plan that, the less one possesses of created things, the more
fully one possesses the Creator, and the more powerfully He
works in the soul by filling it with special graces. Clare was
distinguished by her grace of prayer; she lived wholly with
God, in most intimate union with Christ. When her sisters were
exhausted by fasting and night vigils, she would send them to
bed, while she remained all night praying in the choir or preparing everything in church and sacristy for the celebration
of the next day's Mass. Then she would wake the nuns and go
through the exercises of the day as though she had rested all
night. It was from prayer that she drew such strength, joy,
buoyancy, light, and love. Another special grace that God ac-
corded her was love of the cross, suffering for the sake of
Christ.

Twenty-eight of her forty-two years as superior were necessarily spent in bed, in pain so severe that for days and weeks
she could neither sleep nor eat. The thought that she was being
crucified with Christ made her cheerful, however, and she
offered her suffering in atonement for the faults of her sisters.
So powerfully did grace work in her that in 1240, when the
San Damiano convent was stormed by hordes of Saracens fighting with Frederick II against the papacy, Clare went out to
meet them, carrying the Sacred Host in a Monstrance before
her; the attackers, upon seeing this, immediately fled. Another
time, when the enemy had sworn to destroy the town of Assisi,

she saved it simply by lifting her arms in prayer. Truly, "God, thy God . . . has given thee an unction." We thank God for the wonders He worked through the abundant and effective blessings given to Clare, which were graces for the entire Church, for all of us.

3. The less one has of created goods, the greater is one's claim on God. It nearly always amounts to the same thing: to own a thing—to be attached to it. "God alone can satisfy." St. Clare possessed an inner detachment from creatures; she was unaffected by the opinions of men; she was free from selfishness and from all inordinate self-love; this poverty of spirit gave grace its chance to operate freely and richly in her soul.

Collect: Listen to us, God our Savior, so that we who find joy in the festival of Thy blessed virgin Clare may learn from her the spirit of godly service. Amen.

AUGUST 14

Vigil of Our Lady's Assumption

1. The commemoration of Mary's death and bodily assumption into heaven is probably the oldest of all Marian feasts. To solemnize it, Pope Sergius I (687–701) ordered an annual procession for August 15 which would go from the Roman Forum to the Basilica of St. Mary Major. Pope Leo IV, in 847, decreed that the clergy and people of Rome should celebrate a vigil (night service) in St. Mary Major and conclude it with Mass in the early hours of August 15.

2. "All that are rich among the citizens will be courting thy favor. Maidens will follow in her retinue into the King's presence" (Introit). Mary has "gone home," and now, awakened from bodily death to eternal life, as the glorious Queen of the universe she occupies the magnificent throne prepared for her from all eternity by her own divine Son. The Church sings

in the Divine Office: "The holy Mother of God has been lifted up above all the choirs of angels in the kingdom of heaven." "Today Mary has risen into heaven; rejoice; she reigns with Christ." With the Church we lift prayerful hands today, begging, with full confidence in her power, for the favor of her intercession with Him. "Lord, may our offerings be recommended to thy merciful acceptance by the prayer of God's mother, whom thou didst remove from this world for this purpose, that she might confidently plead with thee for the forgiveness of our sins" (Secret). We appeal with faith: on this day of her triumph she will show herself a mother to us in a very special way. We are the "maidens" who "follow in her retinue into the King's presence"; we are her children, who imitate the virtues and holiness of her whom we love, because she promises: "From me comes every grace of faithful observance, from me all promise of life and vigor. Hither turn your steps, all you that have learned to long for me; take your fill of the increase I yield" (Lesson). We, thy children, beg thee to look upon us with favor!

"Blessed art thou, virgin Mary, who didst bear the Creator of the world; thou gavest birth to him who made thee, yet remainest ever virgin" (Offertory). At Matins we read this passage from St. John of Damascus: "How could she taste death, out of whom flowed true life to all? Nevertheless, she submitted to the law given by Him to whom she gave birth. As daughter of the first Adam she was subject to the death sentence effective since the fall; but, as mother of the living God she was, appropriately, taken up to Him. How could death consume her who listened to the word of God, who, by the power of the Holy Spirit, conceived the Son of God in inviolate virginity and consecrated herself entirely to God! How could death claim her! How could that body, in which Life was conceived, fall a prey to corruption! Rather, for this body the straight, level, easy road to heaven was open. If it is true, as Christ the Life and the Truth says, that 'if anyone is to be my servant, he must follow my way' (John 12:26); certainly his Mother ought to be the very first to join Him in heaven, with body and soul." If death and corruption are the consequences of sin, and if the curses that God pronounced on the sin of man brought this death and corruption into the world; and if Mary was conceived without sin and remained so all her life, then the death which she underwent in order to be like her Son could not be expected to hold her fast. Mary's sacred body could not be subject to corruption. Hence, with heartfelt joy we greet her: 'Blessed art thou, virgin Mary, who didst bear the Creator' (Offertory); who, to be worthy to bear Him wast conceived without stain, and consequently, soon after thy holy, happy death, wast raised up and taken by Him, body and soul, to the joys of heaven. 'Hail, full of grace, the Lord is with thee!' "

3. A section of St. Ambrose's homily for the vigil follows: "When you hear that woman say aloud, 'Blessed is the womb that bore thee and the breast that nourished thee'; and when you hear our Lord reply: 'Rather, blessed are they who hear the word of God and follow it,' then you must understand it this way: not as though He despised His Mother; rather, He meant to say that even she would be worthless, if she did not distinguish herself by holiness and virtue. Besides the grace of God, no one can expect anything to insure his salvation except his own efforts and virtue."

Mary's Assumption should excite joyful hope in our hearts. The way she walked during life: the way of firmness in faith; the way of confidence in the Angel's message: "Behold the handmaid of the Lord, let it be unto me according to thy word"; the way of renunciation and of cross-sharing—that way alone will lead to the regions of bliss. Let us walk Mary's way: she is inviting us; she is using her intercessory power to obtain the graces we need to do it; she knows our weakness and carries us in her motherly heart. She is all-powerful!

Collect: O God, whose pleasure it was to choose blessed Mary's virgin womb for Thy dwelling-place; grant, we pray Thee, that

under the strong shield of her protection we may joyfully take part
in her festival: Thou who are God. Amen.

AUGUST 15

The Assumption of Our Lady

1. On October 30, 1950, all the princes of the Church—cardinals, bishops, and other prelates who were in Rome—were
assembled in the Hall of Beatification for a semipublic con-
sistory. Pope Pius XII put the question to them: "Do you,
Venerable Brothers, agree that the bodily assumption of the
Blessed Virgin Mary ought to be announced and declared as a
dogma revealed by God?" There was unanimous approval.
The next afternoon the miraculous picture of Mary, "Salvation
of the Roman People," was carried in solemn procession from
the Basilica of St. Mary Major to that of St. Peter. On the
morning of November 1, while all the bells of Rome were ringing, the Holy Father, speaking from his throne at the entrance
of St. Peter's to a vast throng of the faithful, made the solemn
declaration: "We declare and define this to be a dogma revealed by God, that the immaculate Mother of God, the ever-
virgin Mary, was, after the close of her life on earth, taken up
into the glory of heaven with body and soul." The thousands
in the piazza answered with a powerful "Te Deum." We join
in this hymn of thanksgiving on the beautiful feast of Mary's
assumption.

2. "Now, in heaven, a great portent appeared; a woman that
wore the sun for her mantle, with the moon under her feet,
and a crown of twelve stars about her head" (Introit). This is a
picture of Mary taken into heaven. "Sing the Lord a new song,
a song of wonder at his doings" (Ps. 97:1). Being free from
original sin and from all personal sin, she was also exempt from
the punishment for sin, that is, the necessity of dying. Since her

divine Son, however, had sacrificed Himself by a most painful death, Mary wanted to be like Him in submitting to death. And, just as our Lord, in His glorious resurrection, freed Himself from the power of death and after forty days ascended into heaven with body and soul, so also His Mother, by divine decree, was to be taken into heavenly glory with body and soul.

Again today at Matins the Church reads a sermon of St. John of Damascus, which in part follows here: "Today the immaculate Virgin, who was never desecrated by any inordinate inclination, who moved entirely among heavenly thoughts, was transferred to a heavenly abode. Since Christ, the true life, had sprung from her, how could she be detained by death? She whose ear was ever open to the words of God, and who at the angel's greeting had conceived the Son of God . . . how could this body . . . yield to corruption? If Christ declared: Where I am, there also will he be who serves me, must not His Mother, above all others, be with Him?" Joyfully we accept the doctrine of the Church; we congratulate our heavenly mother on her unique distinction and on her exaltation above the choirs of angels and saints. After Christ she is the only person who has been taken into heaven with body and soul.

"My soul magnifies the Lord; my spirit has found joy in God, who is my Savior, because he has looked graciously upon the lowliness of his handmaid. Behold, from this day forward all generations will count me blessed; because he who is mighty, he whose name is holy, has wrought for me his wonders. He has mercy upon those who fear him, from generation to generation" (Gospel). Elizabeth greeted the youthful Mother of God, who had just entered her home: "Blessed art thou among women. . . . Blessed art thou for thy believing." With Elizabeth we greet Mary taken into heaven. Mary, however, always points at once to Him to whom she owes and ascribes everything of greatness and glory that she had on earth or has in heaven: He "has wrought for me his wonders" and "He has looked graciously upon the lowliness of his handmaid." For the great law of grace is: "He who humbles himself shall be exalted." We do not read of any miracles worked by Mary during her life on earth, nor even of any extraordinary deeds in the natural order. All we know of her life is that she was the handmaid of the Lord (cf. Luke 1:38), who stood in immovable fidelity beside the despised, humiliated, crucified Savior.

Because Mary walked the way of humility, God looked graciously upon her and did great things to her: "From this day forward all generations will count me blessed." Yes, we bless thee, thou humble handmaid of the Lord. We greet thee, exalted above the heavens and crowned as Queen and Mistress of the universe. "Blessing is thine, such as no other woman on earth can claim. . . . Such high renown He has given thee this day, that the praise of thee shall never die on men's lips. . . . Thou art the boast of Jerusalem, the joy of Israel, the pride of our people" (Lesson).

3. "O Immaculate Virgin, Mother of God and mother of men. We believe with all the fervor of our faith in your triumphal assumption, both in body and soul, into heaven, where you are acclaimed as Queen by all the choirs of angels and all the legions of the saints; and we unite with them to praise and bless the Lord who has exalted you above all other pure creatures, and to offer you the tribute of our devotion and our love.

"We know that your gaze, which on earth watched over the humble and suffering humanity of Jesus, in heaven is filled with the vision of that Humanity glorified, and with the vision of uncreated Wisdom, and that the joy of your soul in the direct contemplation of the adorable Trinity causes your heart to throb with overwhelming tenderness.

"We trust that your merciful eyes may deign to glance down upon our miseries and our sorrows; upon our struggles and our weaknesses; that your countenance may smile upon our joys and our victories; that you may hear the voice of Jesus saying to you of each one of us, as He once said to you of His beloved disciple: Behold thy son.

"We believe, finally, that in the glory where you reign, clothed with the sun and crowned with the stars, you are, after Jesus, the joy and gladness of all the angels and of all the saints.

"And from this earth, over which we tread as pilgrims, comforted by our faith in future resurrection, we look to you, our life, our sweetness and our hope; draw us onward with the sweetness of your voice that one day, after exile, you may show us Jesus, the Blessed Fruit of your womb, O Clement, O Sweet Virgin Mary" (Assumption Prayer composed by Pope Pius XII).

Collect: Almighty, ever-living God, by whom Mary, the immaculate Virgin Mother of Thy Son, was taken up, body and soul, into the glory of heaven: grant, we pray Thee, that by keeping our thoughts ever fixed on things above, we may become worthy to share that glory which is hers. Amen.

AUGUST 16

St. Joachim, *Father of Our Lady, Confessor*

1. No mention is made in Scripture of St. Anne's husband, the father of the Blessed Virgin. According to apocryphal writings Joachim was excluded from the privilege of offering sacrifice in Jerusalem, because he was childless. He therefore went to live with shepherds in the desert and there received various revelations from God. He was a man of deep piety and charity. It was only after twenty years that a daughter was born to him and Anne in Jerusalem or Nazareth. The Greeks celebrated his feast in the early centuries; the West began to do so only in the fifteenth century. It was formerly on the Sunday after the Assumption, but Pope St. Pius X transferred it to August 16.

2. "God who . . . didst choose blessed Joachim to be the father of her who bore thy Son . . ." (Collect). The choice of

Joachim is divine assurance of his excellence, for, humanly
speaking, the fruit is the proof of the tree: the immaculate conception of the future mother of God places the unmistakable
stamp of holiness on the marriage of Joachim and Anne. St.
John of Damascus said: "By the fruit of your body are you
known. You lived a pious, holy life and gave life to a daughter
who is more exalted than the angels; indeed, she is mistress of
the angels. Joachim cultivated the interior life and meditated
on the holy word. He nourished his soul with the refreshing
waters of divine grace; in this manner, he turned his mind completely away from things that were not permitted, and directed
it in the path of holiness." It was not sufficient that Joachim be
the husband of the Virgin's saintly mother; in order to be
worthy of the distinction of such fatherhood he had to be holy
himself. If his dignity as father of the Mother of God was great
and unique, so also were his virtues.

"O Joachim, husband of St. Anne, the gentle Virgin's father,
bring thy saving help to all God's household" (Alleluia verse).
Of his traditional charity the liturgy says: "Rich were his alms
to the needy; still, through the years, his good name abides in
memory: the Lord will lift up his head in triumph" (Introit).
As Joachim was generous to the poor on earth, so now in
heaven he distributes spiritual favors to us all. Our certainty
of this prompts us to ask his help in obtaining the gift of salvation. He gave us Mary, Mother of the Redeemer from whom
all salvation must come. His privilege as father of Our Lady
gives him a special task in the Church with regard to those redeemed by Christ. Him "his master entrusted with the care
of his household to give them their allowance of food at the appointed time" (Communion). We claim a special right to his
intercession with God for the grace we need. This flows log-
ically from the consideration that his blood-relationship with
Mary and Jesus places him closer to God than any other saint,
except Anne and Mary.

3. "Thou hast crowned him with glory and honor, bidding

him, Lord, rule over the work of thy hands" (Offertory). St.
Joachim rules over Mary and over Him whom Mary brought
forth for our redemption.

"O Joachim, husband of St. Anne, the gentle Virgin's father,
bring thy saving help to all God's household" (Alleluia verse).

Collect: God, who out of all Thy saints didst choose blessed
Joachim to be the father of her who bore Thy Son, grant, we pray
Thee, that we who pay honor to his festival may feel the power of
his unfailing protection. Amen.

AUGUST 20

St. Bernard, *Abbot and Doctor of the Church*

1. Bernard has many claims to greatness; he was a mighty
reformer of religious life, the second founder of the Cister-
cians, an apostle of the Crusade of 1147, a teacher of the
Church, a wonder-worker, a counsellor of popes and kings, a
peacemaker between nations, a champion of pure doctrine
against error and heresy, a man of personal virtue and holiness,
and an outstanding devotee of the Mother of God. He was
born in the year 1091 in the castle of his noble family near
Dijon, in Burgundy. Equipped with the highest gifts of mind
and heart, well-instructed and carefully trained by his mother,
Bernard stepped out into the world at eighteen and soon came
to realize that snares and entanglements lurked on every side.

To escape these dangers he entered the monastery of Citeaux
in 1113. A few years later his abbot appointed him superior of
a group of monks sent to build the monastery of Clairvaux
(Vale of Light). Here Bernard managed affairs admirably, his
zeal gaining more and more disciples for him until, in a remarkably short time, he was abbot over seven hundred monks.
These included princes, counts, and scholars. He shared the
labors and sacrifices of his brethren, but applied himself during

the night hours to the study of Holy Scripture and theology. A combination of holiness and persuasive eloquence enabled him to dominate the powerful men of his day. A man of prayer, work, and preaching, Bernard also left to the Church a great many writings. Their simplicity and warmth and the beauty of the images in his language merited for him the title "honey-flowing" (Mellifluous) teacher.

After the death of Pope Honorius II in 1130, Innocent was elected to the See, but a group of cardinals set up an antipope. To help clear up this ruinous confusion Bernard traveled throughout France, Italy, and Germany, preaching in behalf of the legitimate pope. People flocked to hear him and to kiss his feet or the hem of his garment. Miracles and healings marked his path; but the real wonder was the man himself, for he could never understand how God could do anything great or good through him. Honor and praise did not affect him in the least, so deeply rooted was his humility. He died at Clairvaux on August 20, 1152.

2. "The faithful man keeps early vigils at the Lord's gates" (Lesson). Bernard's mother sowed the seed of piety in her child's heart. He received good intellectual training in the school at Chatillon and grew to manhood innocent and pure in body and soul. Once, as he lay sick in bed, a woman had come under the pretense of relieving his pain with her harp-playing; but the courageous boy ordered her out. When it came time for Bernard to decide his vocation, he endured a great struggle. Was it to be Christ or the world, pleasure and honors or the serious following of Christ? He prayed, crying out day and night to God for light, and for strength to use it. Then he perceived an interior voice calling: "Come to me, all you that labor and are burdened; I will give you rest. Take my yoke upon yourselves, and learn from me . . . and you shall find rest for your souls" (Matt. 11:28–30). Bernard was seized with a powerful longing to see God in heaven, and his decision was made; the objections of relatives made no difference. In

fact, his victory was so complete that he was able to lead thirty companions to Citeaux. In the monastery Bernard set the pace for all of them by his zeal for prayer, mortification, and humble obedience. Citeaux not only blossomed with new life, but was soon filled to capacity with young men attracted by Bernard; he had come to serve God with all his power.

God gave to His Church in St. Bernard "a minister of eternal salvation" who "taught us the way of life" (cf. Collect). The great and holy monk gave much light for the way that we must travel toward God. The following passage from one of his sermons is particularly illuminating: "Above all, one must remove the abscess of deep-rooted evil habits by opening it with the knife of sorrow and repentance. The pain will be great but it can be lessened by devotion, that is, by the joy that stems from hope of forgiveness and from the victory over sin. The soul gratefully declares, 'Thou hast broken the chains that bound me' (Ps. 115:7). Next comes application of the medicine of penance: fasting, nocturnal vigils, and prayer. For this tedious task the soul needs the nourishment of good works to sustain it; works of piety must be combined with those of penance, for they will confer the needed strength; almsgiving increases our trust in God (cf. Tob. 4:12). Along with the food of good works must go the beverage of prayer to digest the good done and to make it pleasing to God. In prayer one drinks the wine 'that will rejoice man's heart!' (Ps. 103:15), the spiritual wine that intoxicates the soul and makes it forget carnal desires. It penetrates to the very core of the languishing heart; it distributes the nourishing substance of good works to the various members of the soul by strengthening faith and hope, by enlivening and ordering charity and by making life complete. What remains to be done? Now, one should be quiet after the exertion of activity, and give oneself over to contemplation, which will cause the soul to glow with charity. This charity is glowing with zeal. When it has filled the heart it bubbles up and overflows, diffusing itself without danger or disadvantage;

it is the fulfillment of the law and the filling of the heart. Necessary, then, to the perfection of the spiritual life are contrition, devotion, works of penance, works of mercy, love for prayer, the practice of contemplation, and the perfection of charity" (Sermon 18 on the Song of Songs).

3. St. Bernard, although a monk strictly secluded by the walls of his monastery in the rigid framework of monastic discipline, yet became the dominating figure of his time, broad as the world. In him the interior life of contemplation was combined in most wonderful harmony with strenuous activity welling from the depths of that inner life, which made him the "salt of the earth." "Believe me, heaven and earth must disappear sooner than that one jot, one flourish disappear from the law; it must all be accomplished. Whoever, then, sets aside one of these commandments, though it were the least, and teaches men to do the like, will be of least account in the kingdom of heaven; but the man who keeps them and teaches others to keep them will be accounted in the kingdom of heaven as the greatest" (Gospel).

We admire St. Bernard, too, for his deep and tender love of Mary. His writings gave the Catholic Marian cult a powerful impetus in his day; they continue to do so in ours.

It was his love for the Church that induced this strictly observant monk to be often away from his monastery for months at a time, laboring for Christian morality and the true Faith. The Church's interests were those of Christ, in his estimation. May the Great St. Bernard be an example for us, a light to lead us to God!

Collect: O God, who didst give blessed Bernard to Thy people as a minister of eternal salvation, grant, we pray Thee, that we may be worthy to have as our advocate in heaven him who on earth taught us the way of life. Amen.

AUGUST 22

The Immaculate Heart of Our Lady

1. When the Church concludes the cycle of feasts commemorating our redemption with the feast of the Sacred Heart of Jesus, she means to indicate the hidden source from which the redemptive acts of our Lord spring. At the same time she reveals to us in the heart of Jesus an outline, a summary, of all the mysteries of His life. The Church is doing a similar thing today. Our veneration of the heart of Mary has as its first object the person of the Mother of God, with special reference to the heart, the physical heart, as the natural symbol of the whole inner life of Mary. But, especially, we venerate her most pure, most serene, and most ardent love for God and Christ, together with her motherly love for us who were redeemed by the blood of her Son and are bound to Him as living members. Our veneration of the immaculate heart of Mary is inspired by the perfect sanctity of her interior life and by the special relation of her person to that of her divine Son. The Gospels reveal the deepest roots of this veneration (Luke 1:46 ff., Magnificat; 2:19, 51; John 2:3, the wedding-feast at Cana; 19:15 ff., Mary under the Cross). This devotion was propagated by St. John Eudes together with that to the Sacred Heart of Jesus. Liturgically the cult goes back to the approval of Pope Pius VII in 1805. Pope Pius IX gave the feast a proper Mass and Office in 1855. It was the apparitions at Fatima that offered Pope Piux XII an occasion to respond to the appeals of many bishops and faithful by consecrating the whole world to the immaculate heart of Mary on October 25, 1942. He prescribed the feast for the entire Church in 1945.

2. "Joyful are the thoughts that well up from my heart: a King's honor for my theme" (Introit psalm). The liturgy puts David's words into the mouth of Mary. Her heart is fully

turned toward God, "kindled by that divine fire." Her grateful chanting of the Magnificat (Alleluia verse) reveals the depths of her inner life. Elizabeth had just spoken: "Blessed art thou among women, and blessed is the fruit of thy womb"; thou art "the mother of my Lord. . . . Blessed art thou for thy believing" (cf. Luke 1:45). Mary claims no credit for any of the great things that Elizabeth says about her. Instead she humbly turns to God, ascribing every favor to Him: "He who is mighty, he whose name is holy, has wrought for me his wonders" (Luke 1:49). She is merely the "handmaid of the Lord." Mary's heart was most attentive to all that happened during the Holy Night and to the story of the shepherds' vision (cf. Luke 2:19). She continued to keep in her heart all her experiences with the Child, and all His words. After He had been lost and found, she said to Him: "Think, what anguish of mind thy father and I have endured, searching for thee." She was hurt. "But he went down with them on their journey to Nazareth, and lived there in subjection to them, while his mother kept in her heart the memory of all this" (Luke 2:48, 51). During the Passion and utter humiliation of her Son, Mary shared His suffering most intimately: "At this time: Mary, the Mother of Jesus, and his mother's sister . . . had taken their stand beside the cross of Jesus" (Gospel). Then, the prediction of the aged Simeon was fulfilled: "As for thy own soul, it shall have a sword to pierce it" (Luke 2:35). We have here a glimpse into Mary's heart, and we sympathize with her in the torment she suffered under the cross on which her Son was offering Himself to the Father. We see her complete fidelity to Him to whom she has consecrated her entire being; but we could never fathom the vehemence and extent of her faith, nor the incomparable quality of her love. That heart and its secrets belonged to the Redeemer so completely as to exclude every shadow of sin or imperfection. Filled with grace and virtue, it knew and thought of nothing but God; it beat with love for Him alone. Shall we not honor this heart and try to make our hearts like it?

"Let us come boldly before the throne of grace, to meet with mercy and win that grace which will help us in our needs" (Introit). For us, this throne of grace is the immaculate heart of Mary. Under the image of that immaculate heart we recognize her of whom the Gospel says: "And Jesus, seeing his mother there [under the cross], and the disciple, too, whom he loved, standing by, said to his mother, Woman, this is thy son. Then he said to the disciple, This is thy mother." In John, He thought of all of us, and gave us to her whose motherly love and care he had himself experienced for thirty-three years. From this moment on, Mary's heart has glowed with tender and most intimate love for us, the ineffable love with which she consumed herself for Jesus. She recognizes Jesus in us, just as we must recognize Him in the poor: "When you did it to one of the least of my brethren here, you did it to me . . . when you refused it to one of the least of my brethren here, you refused it to me" (Matt. 25:40, 45). We believe in this love of our Mother's heart, as our Lord commanded: "This is thy mother," a "mother of mercy, our life, our sweetness, and our hope." In the image of the most pure heart we recognize her who invites us in the Lesson: "No vine ever yielded fruit so fragrant. . . . It is I that give birth to all noble loving, all reverence, all true knowledge, and the holy gift of hope. From me comes every grace of faithful observance, from me all promise of life and vigor. Hither turn your steps, all you that have learned to long for me, take your fill of the increase I yield" (Ecclus. 24:23 ff.). Mary's is a heart full of treasure ready to be given to us. "Let us come boldly before the throne of grace."

3. In times of great public calamities, such as war, famine, epidemic; in times of serious collapse of faith and morals among the masses; in times when such evil forces as atheistic Communism seek to destroy all religious faith, fearful hearts must ask: "Who will save us?" Certainly the diplomacy of politicians will not, nor the eloquence of intellectuals, nor the

gold of bankers, nor bombs, nor soldiers; God alone can save us. He will rescue us from spiritual catastrophe, at least, if we take refuge in the heart of Mary. She stated at Fatima that she alone could help, by interceding for us at the throne of divine mercy. As a pledge of future victory and peace she promised solemnly: "My immaculate heart will triumph." It is our task to contribute what we can to that victory by a magnanimous response to her announcement. This is the spirit in which we ought to celebrate today's feast; we should continue to celebrate it day after day in our hearts by our trust in Mary's motherly love and by an earnest desire that, through her, holiness and love of God may be more and more fostered in us. Sweet Heart of Mary, be our salvation!

"We pray that our hearts may be kindled by that divine fire which burned so marvelously in the heart of the blessed virgin Mary" (Secret).

Collect: Almighty, everlasting God, who didst prepare a worthy dwelling-place for the Holy Spirit in the heart of the blessed virgin Mary, grant us this grace, that in devoutly keeping the feast of her immaculate heart, we may have strength to live according to Thy heart's desire. Amen.

AUGUST 24

St. Bartholomew, *Apostle*

1. St. Bartholomew (Nathanael) was one of the first disciples of our Lord (cf. Matt. 10:3; John 1:45 and 21:2). "Jesus saw Nathanael coming towards him, and said of him, Here comes one who belongs to the true Israel; there is no falsehood in him. How dost thou know me? Nathanael asked; and Jesus answered him, I saw thee when thou wast under the fig-tree, before Philip called thee. Then Nathanael answered him, Thou, Master, art the Son of God, thou art the King of Israel"

(John 1:47–49). After our Lord's resurrection Bartholomew was with Peter and several other apostles when Jesus appeared at the Lake of Genesareth (cf. John 21:2). According to tradition he preached the gospel in India, Mesopotamia, and Armenia. At the command of Astyages, whose brother Polymius he had gained for Christ, Bartholomew was martyred by flaying. His relics are honored in the Roman church dedicated to him.

2. "God has given us different positions in the church; apostles first, then prophets [i.e., preachers possessed of such eloquence that the working of the Holy Spirit is evident]" (Epistle). In the organization of the Church God gives to each a special grace for the performance of his particular duty. In obedience to this call, and aided by the corresponding grace of God, Bartholomew left Jerusalem after Pentecost and traveled eastward as far as India, laboring tirelessly for the spread of the kingdom of God. As supports for his preaching, God gave him "miraculous powers, then gifts of healing" (Epistle). Bartholomew gained various regions for the Faith, announcing to all his converts: "You are Christ's body" (Epistle). In this unity with the mystical body, the Church, they experience the happiness and riches of divine adoption, of grace, of redemption, of power over sin and hell; they receive the true life that comes only from God.

We owe gratitude for these supernatural gifts, not only to God and to Christ, but also to the apostles. For God established them "as princes over all the lands." The feast of an apostle, then, is a day of grateful rejoicing over the treasure that they brought to the world and to us, personally. We renew our faith in the truths taught us by the apostles and their successors, our ecclesiastical superiors; we persevere in imperturbable fidelity to the body of Christ, and consider ourselves fortunate to belong to this fellowship. St. Paul defines us truly: "You are Christ's body, organs of it depending upon each other" (Epistle).

"You who have followed me . . . shall sit on thrones" (Communion). The apostle follows his master to death in order to bear witness to His teaching and to become like Him. Only he is a true apostle and preacher who lives according to the gospel he preaches and is willing to give his whole life for it. Such an apostle was St. Bartholomew, and therefore he occupies a throne, like a prince; a great one in the kingdom of the glorified Lord, a friend of Christ. On the day of the resurrection of the dead, "when the Son of Man sits on the throne of his glory," this apostle, too, will judge "over the twelve tribes of Israel." He will ratify the sentence of Christ the Judge on the one hand: "Come, you that have received a blessing from my Father, take possession of the kingdom which has been prepared for you since the foundation of the world," and, on the other hand, he will echo Christ's condemnation: "Go far from me, you that are accursed, into that eternal fire which has been prepared for the devil and his angels" (Matt. 25:34, 41). "Holy thou art, O Lord, and wast ever holy, and this is a just award of thine, blood to drink for those who have shed the blood of thy saints and prophets" (Apoc. 16:5). The apostle Bartholomew and all the apostles and saints will, in the judgment, along with Christ condemn all infidelity in the world, all apostasy from His Church, all sins and every injustice of which men are guilty. The holy ones will acknowledge and approve all the good deeds and holy intentions of the just, all the faithfulness to Christ's example, all sacrifices and self-denial undertaken for Christ, all prayer and striving for virtue, in a word, all genuinely Christian conduct. In the judgment they will give testimony of Christ just as they have done in their apostolic life, work, and death. If God thus honors His apostles, should we not honor them too? Yes; "Great reverence I have for thy friends, O God," not only in words, but also in the approval of their teaching and example, which I show forth practically, in my life.

3. "You are Christ's body, organs of it depending on each

other" (Epistle). In this body each member has his proper task and function, whether as teacher, or healer of the sick, or worker of miracles. St. Bartholomew had his special vocation and grace, and he cooperated with God. Each of us has his place in the divine plan. We do not live for ourselves only; we live in and for the whole body of Christ. Our praying, our working, our suffering—everything bears fruit for all mankind, or at least for all who belong to the body of Christ. Must not consciousness of this fact be a powerful incentive to prayer and to the sanctification of all our labors and sufferings?

"Behold, here is a true Israelite in whom there is no guile." High praise, indeed! Happy is he whom the Lord can thus point out.

Collect: Almighty, everlasting God, who hast given us a reverent and holy joy in this day's festival of Thy blessed apostle Bartholomew, grant, we pray Thee, that Thy Church may love what he believed and preach what he taught. Amen.

AUGUST 28

St. Augustine, *Bishop, Confessor,* *Doctor of the Church*

1. Aurelius Augustine was born in Tagaste, North Africa, to the pagan Patricius and his Christian wife Monica, in 354. After completing studies in Carthage he went to Rome in 383, and the next year moved to Milan to be a professor of rhetoric. Up to this time his life had been a colossal struggle to realize truth and moral stability in himself, as his *Confessions* testify. In 374 he joined the Manichaeans, but was not satisfied with their doctrines. Only after years of searching and groping did he come under the influence of St. Ambrose, whose preaching, together with Monica's prayers, enabled him to find his way

into Christianity. He had been particularly impressed by the words of St. Paul: "Let us pass our time honorably, as by the light of day, not in . . . lust and wantonness. . . . Rather, arm yourselves with the Lord Jesus Christ" (Rom. 13:13, 14). Augustine had resigned his teaching position in preparation for baptism, which he received with his son Adeodatus and a friend, from the hands of St. Ambrose at Easter, 387. He then started for Africa with his mother; but Monica died at Ostia, near Rome.

In the year 391 he received ordination to the priesthood, and three years later was consecrated coadjutor to Bishop Valerius of Hippo. In 396 he succeeded to the See and labored in it for thirty-four years in the full ardor and strength of his love for Christ, preaching with untiring zeal, shepherding priests and people, and championing Catholicity against Manichaeans, Arians, Donatists, and Pelagians. His interest and activity embraced the entire Christian West in its unique and fruitful scope. Augustine died on August 28, 430, while the Vandal King Genseric was besieging his episcopal city of Hippo.

2. "The Lord moved him to speak before the assembled people, filling him with the spirit of wisdom and discernment" (Introit). For a number of years Augustine followed devious paths that led him into temptations and sin. Possessed of a natural light of reason far above the average, he still felt unequal to the power of the threefold concupiscence. At the age of thirty-three, when he finally received baptism, the light of faith was kindled in his soul, that light which infinitely surpasses the natural acumen of even the greatest genius. Illumined by faith he attained to true wisdom, to the truth, the interior peace, and the security of spirit that he had hitherto sought in vain. He now cleansed his heart of the evil desires of his previous life, allowing the gifts of the Holy Spirit to flow in unimpeded. "Blessed are the clean of heart; they shall see God" (Matt. 5:8). With his new wisdom he came to grasp ever more clearly the meaning of world events and of the manifold, mysterious

happenings in every day, viewing them from the standpoint of God. More and more he experienced the urging and the action of God within himself, and learned to follow the attractions of grace with a generous heart in order to advance into super- natural light and holiness. The singular fullness of his wisdom has made him teacher and guide to all succeeding generations. Augustine was, in the full sense of the word, "the salt of the earth . . . the light of the world . . . the city . . . built on a mountain top . . . the lamp . . . put on the lamp-stand to give light to all the people of the house" (Gospel). These wonders accomplished in the passionate, erring, sin-ridden Augustine were the work of God's grace, as was also Augus- tine's cooperation in them.

"It is for thee to be on the watch, to accept every hardship, to employ thyself in preaching the gospel, and perform every duty of thy office" (Epistle). St. Augustine was a bishop after Paul's own heart; his zeal for the spiritual and physical welfare of his flock was boundless; his house was open to everyone; he was at the service of anyone who came seeking advice, and the call of the most insignificant man could draw him away from the deepest research; as at home, so was he in the midst of ecclesiastical functions ever the loving father, concerned about everyone and everything. If guilty of neglect or error in any matter, he would make a public confession of it. Once he asked pardon of his parish for having perchance received anyone with a lack of friendliness, or given a harsh answer. His letter to Cajus gives evidence of this humble manner and of his pre- occupation with God: "If you have read anything in my writ- ings and tested it with your own judgments, do not think of this truth as coming from me, but turn rather to Him who gave me the thought and you the ability to judge it. But if you find something erroneous, be convinced that it is from me." Such was his attitude toward his works that have been the marvel of contemporaries and of all posterity. He realized that "all strength rests on humility, for all pride is frail. The

humble souls are like rocks: at the bottom, indeed, but solid
and firm. The arrogant are like smoke: they reach high, but the
least wind moves them. 'Upon whom shall My spirit rest?
Upon the humble and silent man, the one who trembles [with
reverence] at my words' (cf. Isa. 66:2). He [God] does not
fear a shaking house; for it is He who gives the house firmness."

3. There is a remarkable power in the grace of Christ. To
the youthful Augustine it became clear that "the simple and
unlearned snatch the kingdom of heaven courageously for
themselves. And we, with our cold reasoning, wallow like
weaklings in flesh and blood." With the letters of St. Paul in
his hand he seeks out a hidden nook in the garden, and the
decisive battle begins: grace draws him, but the passionate
memory of his former worldly, lustful life holds him back. He
throws himself down under the fig-tree and weeps: grace has
conquered. All bonds of ambition and of sensuality lie severed.
"By God's grace, I am what I am" (I Cor. 15:10). He then sells
his property, giving to the poor all but what he needs to keep
alive. Now he is free for God.

St. Augustine's conversion was a miracle of grace, as was
St. Paul's. What God did for him is for us a source of confidence. It prompts us to ask much of God's goodness, through
the intercession of St. Augustine; for Augustine is a powerful
advocate, an intercessor who can do wonders for us with God.

Significantly, Christian art represents St. Augustine in episcopal vestments, with a flaming heart in his hands as a symbol
of his ardent love of God and his fellowmen. Augustine is all
love: his prayer, his renunciation, and his works serve love;
his preaching and tireless writing serve love. If anyone dared
to utter an uncharitable word in his presence, Augustine would
either reprove the offender on the spot, or else leave the company. He gladly took his priests and others to his own table,
but he would have no unnecessary talking there. Every guest
could read the inscription on the wall of his diningroom: "He
who likes to criticize the conduct of an absent brother should

know that there is no room at this table for him." Where there is genuine love of God, it will prove itself and express itself in universal Christian love of neighbor.

Collect: Give heed to our entreaties, Almighty God, and, at the intercession of the blessed confessor bishop Augustine, graciously bestow the fruits of Thy wonted mercy upon those to whom Thou grantest the confident hope of Thy lovingkindness. Amen.

AUGUST 29

The Beheading of St. John the Baptist

1. The Church celebrates St. John's birthday on June 24; today's feast commemorates his heavenly birthday, the day of his death. As far back as the fourth century this day was kept in Africa, the Orient, Gaul, Spain, and Rome. The story of the beheading is told by all three synoptics (Matt. 14:1; Mark 6:14; Luke 3:19–9:7).

2. "Fearlessly did I talk of thy decrees in the presence of kings, and was never abashed" (Introit). John had told Herod: "It is wrong for thee to take thy brother's wife" (Gospel). Courageously he condemned this adulterous marriage, though he could easily suspect that Herod would retaliate. "Herod had sent and arrested John and put him in prison, in chains, for love of Herodias, his brother Philip's wife, whom he had married." John was not afraid of the mighty, for he recalled the words of God to Jeremias: "Do not be afraid of them, as thou wouldst not have me shame thee before them. I mean to give thee strength this day, strength as of a fortified city, or iron pillar, or brazen wall, to confront the whole land, princes of Juda, and priests, and people. All will be thy adversaries, but they shall not master thee; I will be at thy side, the Lord says, to bring thee deliverance" (Lesson). Like "a flourishing palm

tree" this "innocent man" stands before us, a "cedar of Lebanon that defies every storm" (cf. Gradual). He who fears God as John did need have no fear of men; he is stronger with God's strength than they. "Well may the good man rejoice, Lord, in Thy protection" (Offertory).

"He must become more and more, I must become less and less" (John 3:30). In these words the Baptist outlined his own fate. A short time before people had been coming from all directions to hear him and receive his baptism. Then Jesus began His ministry, for which John had prepared the way. After that the Forerunner stepped back unselfishly; generosity and humility characterized all his labor for the Greater, who was to come. He rejoiced to see some of his disciples turn and follow Jesus. Meanwhile Herodias had conceived an intense hatred for the preacher who dared to condemn her marriage; she was watching for a favorable opportunity to get her revenge. It came at Herod's birthday party, when her daughter ensnared the king with her dancing, so that he swore to give her whatever she might choose to ask of him. Prompted by her mother, the girl replied: "My will is . . . that thou shouldst give me the head of John the Baptist; give it me now, on a dish." Herod reluctantly but slavishly complied. As St. Augustine comments: "The head of John on a dish! An accursed command, because one could not bear the truth. A maiden dances; her mother is in a rage; in the midst of the pleasures of a banquet, a frivolous oath is taken and the godless oath is carried out. And thus was the word fulfilled: He must become more and more, and I must become less and less. John actually did become less when he was beheaded; but Christ was lifted up on the Cross."

3. An ancient preface tells the story in figures: "God, thou didst deign to grant the forerunner of Thy Son the honor of being beheaded in defense of the truth. He who baptized Christ with water was baptized by Him with the Holy Spirit, and for His sake was sprinkled with his own blood. The herald

of the truth who is Christ, because he kept Herod away from his brother's marriage bed, was thrown into the dark prison, where he rejoiced in the light of Thy Godhead."

"The man who humbles himself will be exalted" (Luke 18:14). May the Baptist obtain for us the grace to follow his example and, always and everywhere, to stand up fearlessly for the cause of Christ, who is God; of Christ, whose body is the Church.

Collect: Lord, we pray Thee that the worshipful feast of Thy forerunner and martyr, Saint John the Baptist, may effectually help us to salvation. Amen.

AUGUST 30

St. Rose of Lima, *Virgin*

1. The first blossom of sanctity that the Church put forth in newly discovered America was Rose of Lima, in Peru. Having renewed paradise in her own soul, as it were, she tried to renew it about her. Born on April 20, 1586, of poor parents, she received the name Isabella in baptism; on account of the delicate rose-color of her face, however, she was usually called Rosa. As a child she had already conceived the desire of pleasing Christ alone, the Bridegroom of souls, and she had begun a life of renunciation and prayer. Her mother, proud of the child's beauty, continually tormented her by insisting that she primp and paint, bind her hair with flowers and adorn her neck with coral. Though Rose reluctantly obeyed, she never lost her abhorrence for these things. She worked with tireless diligence at spinning and sewing in order to relieve the poverty of her parents; always amiable, she concerned herself about others, ever ready to fulfill their wishes, encourage them or give them joy. The parents were determined to have her marry a certain rich young man, and her mother even went so far as

to supplement her pleading with threats and maltreatment. Rose suffered intensely but could not be dissuaded from her intention to consecrate her heart entirely to God.

Finally, when she was twenty, Rose obtained permission to enter the Third Order of St. Dominic. As a tertiary she continued to live with her family; she now increased her fasts, nocturnal vigils, and other austerities, despite the fact that this manner of life brought all kinds of insults, abuse, and slights from her acquaintances. But God showered graces upon her, particularly the grace of prayer. At the age of thirty-one she fell seriously ill; her death occurred on August 24, 1617. She was beatified in 1668 and canonized in 1671.

2. "I have betrothed you to Christ, so that no other but he should claim you, his bride without spot" (Epistle). St. Paul found it necessary to defend himself against those in Corinth who were casting suspicion on him by attributing ignoble motives. He therefore had recourse to the argument that zeal for the glory of God working in him was urging him to lead his Christians to the heights of betrothal with Christ. What St. Paul was trying to do for his flock was an accomplished fact in Rose. Even as a child she had grasped the mystery of virginity and of spiritual marriage to Christ, according to the Apostle's words: "There are some eunuchs, who . . . have made themselves so for the love of the kingdom of heaven. . . . That conclusion . . . cannot be taken in by everybody, but only by those who have the gift" (Matt. 19:11, 12); or, again: "He who is unmarried is concerned with God's claim, asking how he is to please God. . . . So a woman who is free of wedlock, or a virgin, is concerned with the Lord's claim, intent on holiness, bodily and spiritual; whereas the married woman is concerned with the world's claim, asking how she is to please her husband" (I Cor. 7:32, 34). Rose chose virginity in its highest form, that is, betrothal with Christ. She knew no earthly lover, and for Christ's love she had to endure bitter accusations and hard, cutting remarks, even from her own

mother. All through the years of trial her one thought was to be a pure, worthy spouse of her Lord the Savior. He had called her to this: "Rose of my heart, you are to be my bride." And she responded; "Behold the handmaid of the Lord; let it be unto me according to thy word" (Luke 1:38).

"Behold, the bridegroom is on his way; go out to meet him" (Gospel). "You are to be my bride." That is why our Lord put her in the school of suffering and humiliation of every sort. Her withdrawal from the world, her mysterious abstention from food and drink, her frequent raptures and ecstasies, all were declared by many to be hypocrisy, hysteria, or the work of the devil. In addition to the sufferings from without, Rose had to endure all kinds of painful physical ailments: lameness, fainting spells, attacks of weakness. She bore these ills patiently, recognizing in them the hand of God punishing her for sins. She considered herself unworthy to live and breathe, and continually cried to God for mercy. Her most painful trial in this process of preparing for the sublime privilege of betrothal with Christ came in the form of spiritual dryness; for years she was subject to hours of frightening emptiness of spirit and aridity of heart, during which she had no inclination to prayer, no consolation, no ability to conceive pious thoughts and aspirations, no perception of the nearness of God. She was oppressed by the thought that God had rejected her on account of her sins, had excluded her from the bliss of heaven, doomed her to join the damned in hell. Such thoughts tormented her day and night.

Thus she reached the maturity required of a spouse of Christ. Suddenly there was light in her soul; the refreshing dew of grace fell on her in abundance; the peace of God flooded her heart. The ardor of her love grew so strong, that nothing was ever able to separate her from Christ again. The Lord now blessed her with a wonderful prayer-life, so that, at all times, whether she was asleep or awake, always and everywhere God was present to her spirit. In spite of all these favors, Rose went about her work and associated with other people in such a normal way that nobody suspected the enraptured state of her soul. Yet all could detect the force of her love for God in her many-sided, active charity, and in her desire to suffer with Christ and for His sake. Her union with Him was so intimate that she shared His life more and more and became ever more fruitful in good works. The words of Isaias were fulfilled in her: "The Lord will give thee rest continually, fill thy soul with comfort, thy body with ease. Not more secure the well-watered garden, the spring whose waters never fail" (58:10–11). "Behold, the bridegroom is on his way; go out to meet him" (Gospel). A holy death perfected Rose's betrothal with Christ. It was for her the ardently longed-for homecoming of the beloved to the heavenly bridal chamber. "Rose of my heart, you shall be my bride."

3. We congratulate St. Rose today on the holy union to which our Lord so graciously called her and so wonderfully led her. All her sacrifices and conflicts were a part of her vocation to divine espousals. She was a rose among thorns, indeed.

We praise the heroic fortitude with which she endured the numerous trials at the hands of men and God until she was ready for complete oneness with Him. As always, the struggle to preserve purity and to acquire the treasures of Christian virginity, the sacrifices demanded in the entire dedication to love of God, brought their reward.

May St. Rose be our model and our intercessor with God, so that we may acquire the strength to follow her example and be true to the vocation which He has given us in the Church. St. Rose, draw us in your path toward Christ!

Collect: Almighty God, giver of all good gifts, who didst will that blessed Rose, a flower of purity and patience, nourished betimes with the dew of Thy grace, should blossom in the Indies, grant, that we, Thy servants, may hasten to follow where the fragrance of her passage beckons us, and so deserve to become a perfume offered to the Father by Christ, who is God. Amen.

SEPTEMBER

SEPTEMBER 3

St. Pius X, *Pope and Confessor*

1. On August 20 the Roman Martyrology announces the death of Pope Pius X in these words: "At Rome, the death of the holy Pius X, pope and confessor, victorious champion of the faith and freedom of the Church, outstanding for his zeal for religion." Born in the village of Riesi, Joseph Sarto was the second of ten children. His father was a messenger, and his mother a seamstress. It was only at the cost of much labor and thrift that they were able to rear their large family. Both were possessed of deep faith and sincere piety. When "Beppo" expressed the desire to become a priest, the pastor of Riesi gave him instructions in Latin; then the boy walked almost five miles to Castelfranco to school every day, summer and winter. After four years he went to the seminary of the diocese in Padua, where he pursued his theological studies with success. On September 18, 1858, he was ordained in Castelfranco and celebrated his first solemn Mass at Riesi. In October of that year the bishop appointed him assistant at Tombolo. From 1867 to 1876 he labored as pastor in Salzano, whereupon he was made a canon and appointed spiritual director of the seminary, as well as chancellor, at Treviso. On June 11, 1884, Father Sarto became bishop of Mantua. In 1893 he was created cardinal by Pope Leo XIII, and three days later, named Patriarch of Venice, where he remained until his elevation to the Chair of Peter on August 4, 1903. His acceptance of the tiara was expressed in these words: "If it is God's will that this chalice should not pass from me, His will be done. I accept the election as a cross." Pius X took up the reins of Church government

with courage and confidence; in both public and private life
he proved himself a holy priest and pope. On August 20, 1914,
soon after the outbreak of the First World War, he offered his
life for the peace of the world. Beatified on June 3, 1951, he
was canonized on May 29, 1954.

2. "I have lifted up a chosen one from among the people
and anointed him with my oil, so that my hand may be always with him and my arm impart strength to him" (Introit).
As a boy and student Joseph Sarto bore many hardships; but
he loved poverty and the poor. In his last will he wrote: "I was
born poor; I have lived poor; I want to die poor." Whatever
he earned in his various positions found its way to the poor,
except for the pittance that sufficed to feed him and his sisters.
After he became pope millions of lira passed through his hands
to poor churches, institutions, and private persons. The Lord
lifted this poor boy up wonderfully; for in spite of poverty he
was able to become a priest and to advance quickly in the ecclesiastical offices. "With my oil, I have anointed him, so that
my hand may be always with him and my arm impart strength
to him." Indeed, the blessing of God accompanied him on his
rise from assistant pastor to bishop, to pope. Wherever he
went new Christian life blossomed forth in parish, diocese and
universal Church. His sole ambition was to "restore all things
in Christ," especially the priesthood. On August 4, 1908, he
issued his "Admonition to the Catholic Clergy." In every phase
of his papal activity he proved himself worthy of that dignity
which the cardinals had had such difficulty in persuading him
to accept. When asked what name he wished to assume as
pope, he had answered. "I choose to be called Pius, in view of
the fact that the popes who bore this name in the past century suffered most for the Church." The Lord visibly chose
this man.

"He filled him with heavenly wisdom and apostolic fortitude" (Collect). One characteristic trait of Pope Pius X was
his artless, natural modesty. He certainly shattered precedent

when, in the beginning of his pontificate, he entered the Basilica of St. Peter walking among the faithful, instead of allowing himself to be carried on the "Sedia Gestatoria." He never put himself forward, but was always the humble, unassuming, priest and pastor, always self-forgetful, and kind; it was precisely this humble manner, however, which gave him his inflexible firmness when there was question of God's cause, such as the rights and freedom of the Church or the salvation of souls.

Pope Pius had an unusually clear understanding of his time and its needs. His first encyclical of October 3, 1903, "pronounced a masterful diagnosis of the evils of that time and their remedies," declared Pope Pius XII. He opposed so-called modernism with firm courage; he was especially concerned with the renewal of the Christian spirit, with the becoming celebration of divine services, the Christian instruction of children and youth, the chastity and sanctity of priests, the early admission of children to Holy Communion, and the promotion of frequent, even daily, Communion for all, the scientific training of the clergy, and the more profound study of Holy Scripture. All these interests and efforts bear witness to his "heavenly wisdom and apostolic fortitude." The Epistle of today's Mass characterizes St. Pius X admirably: "We have passed God's scrutiny, and he has seen fit to entrust us with the work of preaching; when we speak, it is with this in view; we would earn God's good opinion, not man's, since it is God who scrutinizes our hearts . . . you found us innocent as babes in your company; no nursing mother ever cherished her children more; in our great longing for you, we desired nothing better than to offer you our own lives, as well as God's gospel, so greatly had we learned to love you" (I Thess. 2:4 ff.).

3. In the Communion prayer we beg God to grant us, through the intercession of St. Pius X, the grace to be strong in faith and united in His love.

We thank God for having given us so holy a pope during

the unusually difficult days at the opening of this century. May his image remain vividly present to us as a shining example of genuinely Christian and priestly living! May he be our powerful intercessor at the throne of God!

Collect: O God, who for the defense of Catholic faith and the restoration of all things in Christ didst fill blessed Pius X, Pope, with heavenly wisdom and apostolic fortitude, grant graciously that we, following his directions and example, may obtain an eternal reward. Amen.

SEPTEMBER 8

The Birthday of Our Lady

"Let us solemnly celebrate today the birth of the ever-virginal Mother of God. From her came forth He who sits on the high throne" (Benedictus antiphon). The liturgy of this feast repeatedly calls upon us to rejoice: "Joyfully let us celebrate the birth of Mary, so that she will make intercession for us with Jesus Christ" (Vesper antiphon). "Let us celebrate the exalted birth of the glorious Virgin Mary; she was found worthy to be the Mother of God but did not thereby suffer the loss of virginal chastity" (Magnificat antiphon). Mary's birth is a day of jubilation, the Aurora which announces the coming of the Sun, Christ the redeemer.

2. "The Lord made me his when first he went about his work, at the birth of time, before his creation began. Long, long ago, before earth was fashioned, I held my course. Already I lay in the womb, when the depths were not yet in being, when no springs of water had yet broken. I was there . . . when he poised the foundations of the world . . . I made play before him all the while . . . with the sons of Adam for my play-fellows" (Lesson). What is said here about the infinite

and unfathomable wisdom of God, the Church applies to Mary. She was the fruit of wisdom of God's eternal thought; she was the unique product of God's wisdom, sublime above everything else; she was singled out by nature and grace and vocation to cooperate in the work of redemption, becoming the "Mother of all the living." As Mother of Christ, she was the throne of God's incarnate wisdom. All her thinking and willing were so intimately one with His, that her whole being and life were a radiation of the wisdom of Him "in whom the whole treasury of wisdom and knowledge is stored up" (Col. 2:3).

"The sons of Adam for my play-fellows." This is a consoling word of Mary to us, banished children of Eve, on the day of her birth. She longs to be near us in order to bring us to Christ and to stand by us as a helpful mother and mediatrix of grace. It is true that the God-man is the only mediator through whom we can gain entrance to the sanctuary of the Godhead, and in whom God has descended to the lowliness of man. This Incarnation of God was accomplished, on one hand by the action of the Holy Spirit, and on the other, through the cooperation of the Virgin. She stands closest to the Godhead, high above all the angels and saints in her nearness to Him. She has thus become for all mankind the cause of salvation. Now she exercises the office of mediatrix with her Son. As long as men are in need of salvation; as long as sin and want stalk the earth, she hastens to help, to obtain forgiveness and grace. Her care for us is the fruit of her transcendent maternal love. Indeed, it is her delight to mother us. We believe this firmly; we thank her; we trust her; we greet her with the words: "Hail, Holy Mother, in thy womb there lay a King who bears o'er earth and heaven endless sway" (Introit).

3. "Listen to me, then, you that are my sons, that follow to your happiness in the paths I show you. Listen to the teaching that will make you wise, instead of turning away from it.

Blessed are they who listen to me, keep vigil, day by day, at
my threshold. . . . The man who wins me [Mary] wins life
[that is, Christ] drinks deep of the Lord's favor" (Lesson).

"Happy art thou, sacred virgin Mary . . . for out of thee
arose the sun of righteousness, the Christ, our God" (Alleluia
verse). Thou didst present Him to us in the Holy Night at
Bethlehem; thou givest Him to us again today in the Consecration and in the Holy Communion of this Mass.

Mary was born in humble circumstances but she was exceed-
ingly rich in the eyes of God. Her wealth and greatness are her
Immaculate Conception, her plenitude of divine grace and her
vocation to Motherhood of God. Here again the fundamental
principle of the order of grace is in evidence: "God has chosen
what the world holds base and contemptible, nay, has chosen
what is nothing, so as to bring to nothing what is now in being" (I Cor: 1:28).

Collect: Lord, bestow upon Thy servants the gift of heavenly
grace, we pray Thee, so that we for whom the birth of the blessed
Virgin's child meant the beginning of salvation, may find, in the
worshipful feast of her Birthday, increase of peace. Amen.

SEPTEMBER 12

The Most Holy Name of Mary

1. The feast of the name of Mary is closely connected with
the fearful struggle between the Christian nations and the
Turks. In the thirteenth century the Turks began to encroach
on the West and continued to threaten its Christian culture
for fully four hundred years. It had become an important duty
of the popes to mobilize the Christian nations and to repel
the Turks. In 1453 Constantinople fell into Turkish hands
and, soon after, the entire Balkan peninsula. The Turks gained
access to Hungary in 1526, and three years later were threaten-

ing Vienna but were halted by internal strife. In 1683 they besieged Vienna, but were crushingly defeated by the combined forces of Germany and Poland on September 12. In memory of the liberation of Vienna from the infidel, which he attributed to the invocation of the Holy Name of Mary, Pope Innocent XI extended this feast to the universal Church. It is understood, naturally, that this is a feast of the person of Mary, not merely of her name.

2. Mary is the mother of Jesus, the only-begotten, consubstantial Son of God; she is the Mother of God. Her immaculate conception, her spotless purity, her sinless virginity were graces that fitted her for this role. From this Motherhood all the other graces flow—her bodily Assumption, her dignity as Queen of the universe, and especially her vocation to be our mother and to channel the life of grace to us. As we could not, without Mary, have Christ, the author of our supernatural life, so neither, without Mary, could we have the grace of Christ and participation in His life. Hence, we come to the "Mother of Divine Grace" and confidently invoke her as our intercessor, asking her to turn to us and to show us Jesus. We beg her to take us by the hand and lead us through the storms of earthly life to her Son, for she is the "clement, loving, sweet Virgin Mary." It was in this spirit that the city of Vienna and all the Christian nations prayed to her in 1683, when their very existence was at stake. And Mary rescued them. Therefore, again in our day, when our Christian culture is being threatened from the East, we go to Mary. She will save us, too. "All that are rich among the citizens will be courting thy favor. Maidens will follow in her retinue into the King's presence; all rejoicing, all triumph, those companions of her enter" (Introit). The Church, all of us, are led by our heavenly Mother to Christ the King, rejoicing.

"At this time God sent the angel Gabriel to . . . Nazareth, where a virgin dwelt . . . and the virgin's name was Mary. Into her presence the angel came, and said: Hail, thou art full

of grace; the Lord is with thee . . . thou hast found favor in
the sight of God. And behold, thou shalt conceive in thy womb,
and shalt bear a son, and shalt call him Jesus. . . . The Holy
Spirit will come upon thee, and the power of the Most High
will overshadow thee. Thus this holy offspring of thine shall be
known for the Son of God. . . . And Mary said: Behold the
handmaid of the Lord" (Gospel). "Handmaid of the Lord" is
the name she assumed, though the angel had just addressed her
as "full of grace." We greet her today with the words of the
angel: "Hail, Mary, full of grace: the Lord is with thee: blessed
art thou among women, and blessed is the fruit of thy womb"
(Offertory). The figurative language of the Lesson forms a
fitting background for the tremendous truth uttered by the
angel: "No vine ever yielded fruit so fragrant; the enjoyment
of honor and riches is the fruit I bear. It is I that gave birth
to all noble loving, all reverence, all true knowledge, and the
holy gift of hope. From me comes every grace of faithful observance, from me all promise of life and vigour. . . . He who
listens to me will never be disappointed, he who lives by me
will do no wrong; he who reads my lesson aright will find in
it life eternal" (Ecclus. 24:23 ff.). To this liturgical description of Mary we may add some of the titles given her by a
Catholic hymn: She is the purest rose, all beautiful and chosen:
The maid immaculate whom the Lord takes as His bride. She
is queen of the heavenly host of angels, the delight and honor
of saints, the comforter of men, refuge of sinners, helper of
her children, best mediatrix. All these noble titles harmonize
with that sweet name: Mary.

3. "Such high renown he has given thee this day, that the
praise of thee shall never die on men's lips" (Judith 13:25).
St. Bernard, the great admirer of Mary, will help us to keep her
lovely, powerful name in our hearts. He translates "Mary" as
"Star of the Sea," adding: "If thou wouldst escape destruction
amid the storms of life, turn not your eyes from the brilliance
of the Star. When you are plagued with pride, inclined to

calumny or jealousy, look up to the Star, to Mary. In dangers, needs, and doubts think of Mary, call upon Mary. Let not her holy name leave your lips or go out of your heart. If you follow her, you will tread no false path; if you pray to her, you will never despair; if you think of her, you will not err. If she holds you, you will not fall. If she protects you, you need have no fear; if she is leading you, you will not grow weary; if she smiles on you, you will reach your goal. And thus you learn from experience with what justice it is said: 'And the virgin's name was Mary.'"

St. Bonaventure preaches the same doctrine: "O Mary, how wonderful is your name! It tells us that you are our Mistress (his translation of the word "Mary"), for you are the mistress of angels and men. Through your hands comes every good thing we have. Fortunate are we to have such a mistress, who is so generous and can do so very much for us with her divine Son; we must fly to her with utmost confidence."

Collect: Grant, we pray Thee, Almighty God, that Thy faithful people, who enjoy the protection of the most holy Virgin Mary and delight in her name, may by her dear intercession be delivered from all ills on earth and made worthy to attain everlasting bliss in heaven. Amen.

SEPTEMBER 14

The Exaltation of the Holy Cross

1. The Holy Cross on which our Lord died was carried away from Jerusalem by the Persian King Chosroa II in 614. In 628 it was recovered by Emperor Heraclius, and a year later brought back to Jerusalem. Today's feast commemorates this latter happy occasion, the "exaltation" or glorification of the symbol and instrument of our salvation. The liturgy speaks of the Holy Cross as the "Royal Banner," the "Tree of Life," and

the Redeemer's "Sign of Victory"; but also as the "Wood of Martyrdom" of the suffering Savior. On May 3 we viewed the Cross in the brilliant light of Easter; today, since the Church year points emphatically toward the end of things, this Holy Cross stands as a symbol of the second coming of our Lord on the Last Day, when He will take His Bride, the Church, home with Him. This feast is characterized by the consideration, mentioned in both the Epistle and Gospel, that Christ was "exalted" through, and on, the Cross.

2. "That is why God has raised him to such a height, given him that name which is greater than any other name" (Epistle). The reason that St. Paul refers to is the fact that Christ, the Son of God, "dispossessed" Himself, took the "nature of a slave," and was, externally, "fashioned in the likeness of men." Truly, "He lowered his own dignity, accepted an obedience which brought him to death, death on a cross." On the Cross He experienced His deepest humiliation, but, by the same Cross, He merited exaltation. If He had not humbled Himself before the Father unto death on the Cross, then, according to God's present plans, He would not have received the exaltation. This had to come by way of the Cross. "Humiliating" as the Cross is, it is essentially "exalting." It was the Cross that gave our Lord "a name which is greater than any other name," that of *Kyrios*, Lord. "Everything in heaven and on earth and under the earth must bend the knee before the name of Jesus, and every tongue must confess Jesus as the Lord." The Cross exalted not only Christ, it exalts every one of us who stands by Him, and, like Him, carries the cross of obedience to the Father in heaven. In the Cross there is salvation, life, and resurrection.

"If only I am lifted up from the earth, I will attract all men to myself" (Gospel). The arms of the Crucified are spread wide for a loving embrace; they proclaim that the love of the Good Shepherd is seeking, attracting to Himself, all hearts; "Come to me all you that labor and are burdened" (Matt.

11:28). Love conquers by sacrifice; it does not cast down but lifts up; it does not take, but gives. No one, before or since, has so powerfully influenced the hearts of men and won them to himself as did our Lord from His Cross. He draws us so truly and really to Himself that His passion and death, His resurrection and ascension permeate our lives and become our destiny. In one of his sermons on the passion Pope Leo the Great says: "Among men, there is only one, our Lord Jesus Christ, in whom all are crucified, all die, all are buried and rise again; for He Himself said: 'If only I am lifted up from the earth, I will attract all men to myself.'" It is especially by means of the sacraments that our Lord draws us to His Cross, into the riches of His life and His redemption, so that we may become His members. The sacraments sprang from the Cross of Christ. The Fathers teach that the Church was born on the Cross; they recognize in the blood and water from the Savior's side the fundamental sacraments of baptism and Eucharist, which serve as the principal builders of the body of the Church: They assimilate us into Christ's life to save and sanctify us for eternal happiness in God. "If only I am lifted up . . . I will attract all men to myself." Yes, draw us, Lord!

3. "It is for us to make our boast in the cross of our Lord Jesus Christ: in whom is our salvation . . . our resurrection" (Introit). At our baptism we were signed with the sign of the Cross, exalted with Christ through the Cross, fitted out with power over sin, passions, world, flesh, and Satan. "In this sign thou shalt conquer." That is why we "make our boast in the cross" and cling to it.

"In this sign. . . ." We make it so often upon ourselves and others. If we do so with faith and with the right motive God will give us each time a grace, a light, a special help; and this in proportion to our trust.

Do we fully appreciate the cross, our sufferings, that is, our participation in the passion of Christ? Do we try to escape it? Then we should pray today for the grace to understand aright the Cross of Christ and our vocation to share it; the grace to walk bravely the royal road of suffering.

Collect: O God, who on this day dost gladden us by the yearly feast of the Exaltation of the Holy Cross, we pray Thee grant that we who have known its mystery on earth may be found worthy to enjoy in heaven the bliss it has purchased for us. Amen.

SEPTEMBER 15

The Seven Sorrows of Our Lady

1. Devotion to the Mother of Sorrows found its way into the Church in the thirteenth century, chiefly through the influence of the Order of Servites. The fifth general of the Order, St. Philip Benizi, extended the wearing of the scapular of the Sorrows of Mary to people in the world. Since the seventeenth century there have been two feasts of the Seven Sorrows, one on the Friday after Passion Sunday and the other on September 15. The former was established by Pope Benedict XIII in 1724, the latter by Pope Pius VII in 1814 to commemorate Napoleon's return from imprisonment. The seven sorrows are: 1) the prophecy of Simeon at the presentation of the Child in the Temple, 2) the flight into Egypt, 3) the loss of the Child in the Temple, 4) the meeting of Mary with her divine Son on the road to Calvary, 5) the Crucifixion, 6) the removal of the Body from the Cross, and 7) the burial of Christ.

2. "Woman, this is thy Son" (Gospel). Our Lord had arrived at the goal of His earthly mission and was about to accomplish the reconciliation of man with God. In this, the great, the decisive moment of mankind's history, Mary stood erect at the side of her Son's Cross. She was renewing the offering she first made at the presentation in the Temple. She was offering to the Father, as ransom for the world, the blessed fruit of her womb. Jesus would expire in a few moments; then

the sacrifice would be completed, the salvation of man accomplished. "This is thy mother." Jesus gave Mary to us as our mother in the realm of grace. When He told John she was his mother he was addressing also us, giving us His mother at the moment of His death. His words to her, "Woman, this is thy son," engendered in her heart a most intimate motherly love for us, who are the brothers and sisters of Christ through grace. Surely at that moment, as once in Nazareth, Mary pronounced a *fiat* (be it done), and thus, by a consent prompted by love for us she granted the last wish of her Son. It was in this hour of her deepest sorrow that she became our Mother. We are the children of her sorrows, given to her to replace Jesus, so that she might extend her love of Him to us.

"Joseph of Arimathea took His body down from the Cross." Catholic piety has imagined Joseph as laying the sacred Body into the arms of Mary as she sat near the Cross. It was a moment of fresh sorrow for the loving Mother. We attempt to enter into the depths of her sorrow, for we recognize in the "Pieta" an expression of the intimate communion of hearts between Jesus and Mary. Formerly she had carried Him beneath her warm heart, then in her arms—that child so dear, so lovely. And now she had Him in her arms again, no longer a child, but the powerful conqueror of sin and Satan, the Redeemer of mankind—dead. At that moment, the entire treasure of redemption lay in her hands. Never had she been so rich before: rich for us, for she had just been bequeathed to us as our mother. She had given her all; now, at the foot of the Cross, she had gained all by her participation in the sufferings of Christ. With sympathetic, grateful hearts, we look on her: "This is thy mother."

3. Let us ponder some stanzas of the "Stabat Mater," one of the few sequences left in the Missal:

> Is there one who would not weep,
> Whelmed in miseries so deep
> Christ's dear mother to behold?

Can the human heart refrain
From partaking in her pain,
In that mother's pain untold?

Bruised, derided, cursed, defiled,
She beheld her tender Child
All with bloody scourges rent;

For the sins of his own nation
Saw Him hang in desolation,
Till His spirit forth he sent.

O thou mother, fount of love!
Touch my spirit from above,
Make my heart with thine accord:

Make me feel as thou hast felt;
Make my soul to glow and melt
With the love of Christ my Lord.

Virgin of all virgins best!
Listen to my fond request:
Let me share thy grief divine:

Christ, when thou shalt call me hence,
Be thy mother my defense,
Be thy Cross my victory.

Collect: O God, in whose sufferings, as Simeon foretold, a sword
of sorrow pierced the sweet soul of Mary, Thy august virgin-mother,
grant us this boon: that we, who reverently call to mind her anguish, may secure the happiness which Thy own sufferings have
gained for us. Amen.

SEPTEMBER 16

St. Cornelius, *Pope and Martyr*

St. Cyprian, *Bishop and Martyr*

1. With the feast of St. Cornelius, who died in 253, the Church joins that of St. Cyprian, a famous bishop of Carthage, who was his contemporary. Cyprian was born there about the year 200 and came to be known as the most beautiful ornament of the third century, for he was outstanding as a Christian bishop, writer, and martyr. Diligent application to studies prepared him to become a teacher of eloquence in Carthage, winning respect and even fame by his talent and flawless life. Having learned about the gospel of Christ, he wavered for some time between truth and error, but was baptized in 246. He gave part of his property to the poor and reserved the rest for church use. A year after his conversion he was ordained priest. His complete change of life brought him ridicule from his former associates in Carthage, but the Christians respected him highly and chose him to succeed Bishop Donatus, who died in 248. Consecrated bishop, Cyprian lived wholly for Christ and the flock entrusted to him. During Emperor Decius' persecution of Christians in 250 he fled Carthage and hid, but continued to encourage by letter those confessors of the faith who were languishing in prison. In 251 he was able to return to his people. He worked earnestly to heal the wounds that the persecution had inflicted and to prepare the Christians for further struggles and trials. Under Emperor Valerian a new persecution broke out in 257, and the following year, on September 14, Cyprian heroically suffered the death of a martyr.

2. Quotation from St. Cyprian: "When I was still living the life of a heathen, it seemed hard and tedious for a man,

having been born anew [in baptism] and filled with a new spirit, to lay aside his former ways and, while still in this mortal frame, to become a new and different man. The passions are powerful, tireless tyrants. At every opportunity pride inflates, drink lures, anger rages, avarice urges, cruelty presses, ambition excites, and lust tyrannizes the slave-mind of the man who has given himself over to them. So thought I; and, because at that time I was enslaved by so many evil notions and so firmly enmeshed that I could not hope ever to extricate myself, I willingly surrendered to vices that held me fast. Since I did not believe in the possibility of improvement, I lived in accordance with my old misery.

"When baptism had re-created me, however, and washed away the stains of my former life, and had planted in my heart, now reconciled with heaven, the pure serene light from above; after this second birth through the Holy Spirit had changed me into a new man; then, in a wonderful manner my wavering was turned into firmness, the hidden was revealed, the darkness changed to light; what formerly frightened me began to attract; what formerly seemed impossible now seemed possible. Then it became clear to me that the "old man," born of the flesh and enslaved by sin, had led a merely earthly life, while the "new man," animated by the Holy Spirit, now entered upon a divine life. There is only one way to find a sweet, stable peace for our souls, and to gain a firmly grounded, lasting security, and that is to escape the storms of the restless world by running into the harbor of salvation, to keep one's eye constantly fixed on heaven, and, in communion with our Lord and in intimate union with God, to look upon everything in the world that men consider great as being beneath one's dignity. He who is greater than the world can no longer seek or wish for the things that the world can give. Released from the snares of the world, cleansed from the impurities of earthly life, and become more worthy of the realm of light promised by immortality one finds the security and stability that establishes a bulwark for eternal goods" (Letter to Donatus).

3. "What a great and glorious day it will be when Christ will survey His people and, with divine understanding, decide the worth of each one and confer the reward for faith and holy love. What an honor and joy it will be to behold God, to triumph with Christ our Lord and God, in His kingdom of light, and to enjoy heavenly, unending bliss with all the just, the friends of God. Then we shall enjoy what no eye has seen, no ear heard, no human heart experienced.

" 'Not that I count these present sufferings as the measure of that glory which is to be revealed in us.' (Rom. 8:18). Yes; when this brightness of God shall be revealed in us, then we shall be happy, happy through the Lord, who knows how to honor His servants beyond all human concept. But how will those who have separated themselves from God be able to bear their misery? Dear brethren, let this thought linger in your hearts, let it hover before your minds, day and night: the thought of justice that punishes the godless and rewards the just" (from the same letter).

Let us take to heart what St. Cyprian here proposes for our consideration from his own personal experience.

Collect: May the festival of the blessed martyr-bishops Cornelius and Cyprian gain us Thy protection, we pray Thee, Lord, and may their holy prayers win us Thy favor. Amen.

SEPTEMBER 17

St. Hildegard, *Virgin*

1. Hildegard was born in Germany in 1098. At the age of three she received in her soul a light from heaven which remained with her. As a growing child she exhibited extraordinary purity of heart and piety, and she was so ignorant of worldly inclinations that her parents decided to dedicate her to

the service of God when she was only eight. She was entrusted
to the care of the female recluse Jutta to be educated in the
religious life. Her book-learning never went beyond reading,
writing, and the rudiments of Latin. After Jutta's death in
1136, Hildegard assumed charge of the sisters who had
gathered around Jutta. About 1148 she undertook the foundation of the convent on Mount Rupert, or Rupertsberg, near
Bingen: later, in 1160, she established the convent at Eibingen.
She died on September 17, 1179, having been frail all her life
and thus accustomed to suffering.

St. Hildegard's zeal for the Church induced her to make
long journeys: to Cologne, Treves, Metz, and southern Germany. Her gifts as a visionary sometimes reached great heights,
and an inner voice compelled her to write about what she
had seen. In that way, despite her lack of education, she developed an unusually fruitful activity as a writer. Her most
important work is "Scivias" or "The Ways of God." The forceful
language she used in her books filled her contemporaries with
astonishment and reverence. Kings and princes, bishops and
religious turned to her for advice and help. Thus she kept up
an active correspondence. At the Synod of Treves, in 1147, St.
Bernard successfully used his powerful influence with Pope
Eugene III to have Hildegard's writings approved. Surely, he
argued, the pope would not allow this wonderful light, which
God Himself had set up, to remain hidden.

2. "What to the world is foolishness God has chosen to confound the wise; what the world calls weak God has chosen to
confound the strong, so that no one should boast before Him"
(Epistle). Neither educated nor physically strong, St. Hildegard managed to write some important treatises, to preach
penance and to perform notable acts of charity. How could
she do this? By cooperating faithfully and consistently with the
grace of God from her childhood; by incessant effort in the
purification of her thoughts, her will and her actions, so that
no shadow of sin might retard the flow of grace into her soul.

Thus the supernatural life grew so strong in her that she readily did all her thinking, willing, and acting in God. As a consequence of this oneness of purpose, God was able to dwell in her more and more intimately with the fullness of His light, opening her interior sight to His mysteries, and putting into her hands the power of healing and working miracles. Hildegard remained perfectly calm when people called her a fool and a hypocrite, persecuting her with their hatred. She was undisturbed when some of her sisters misunderstood and deserted her. God had indeed chosen the weak in order to put to shame what the world considered learned, wise, and strong. St. Hildegard came to be considered a prodigy of her sex, of the Benedictine Order and of the Church, and was rated as a prophetess of the world.

"She is a wise virgin, one of the number of the prudent virgins" (Antiphon). "The kingdom of heaven will be like ten virgins, who went to bring the bridegroom to his bride's home. Five of these were foolish and five wise; the five foolish, when they took their lamps, did not provide themselves with oil, but those who were wise took oil in the vessels they carried" (Gospel). St. Augustine sees in the foolish virgins those people who live in continence and perform good works, but do so out of regard for the opinion of others, in order to please them and to be esteemed by them. "Whoever lives according to the opinions of others has no oil in his lamp"; his life is an outward show. When men cease to praise him, his oil gives out. The lamps of the wise virgins burned "on oil from within, on peace of conscience, on sincere love." In the face of death and judgment, the praise of men counts for nothing; only that will count that a man has within himself. "When the just King shall sit in judgment, who will boast of having a chaste heart? Perhaps your conscience does not accuse you; but He, whose eye sees better, whose gaze penetrates everything—He will find something." The prudent virgins enter the wedding-hall; to the foolish, the door is closed—"I know you not." St. Hildegard concentrated her attention on God so as to please Him and live for Him. Her life was interior, not external. Virginity alone is not sufficient, even with lamp in hand, that is, good works. There must be, in addition, an interior living with God, a life of undivided devotion and true love of Him. This is the life of the Christian virgin.

3. God taught St. Hildegard how to become truly great and holy: "I will teach you to despise earthly things, to seek what is eternal, to flee honors, to put all your trust in Me, to desire nothing but Me and to love Me ardently, above all else."

"I am He that in an instant elevateth the humble mind to comprehend more reasons of the eternal truth than if anyone studied ten years in the schools" (*Imitation:* III, 43, 3).

Collect: O God, who didst favor Thy holy virgin Hildegard with heavenly gifts; we beg Thee, grant us the grace to follow in her footsteps and perseveringly practice her teachings, so that we may thus become worthy to find our way out of the darkness of this world into Thy blissful light. Amen.

SEPTEMBER 17

Imprinting of the Sacred Stigmata of St. Francis of Assisi

1. St. Bonaventure tells the story: "When the faithful servant of Christ, Francis, two years before his death, began a forty-day fast in the solitude of Mount Alverno in honor of St. Michael the Archangel, on September 29, 1224, he became flooded more abundantly than usual with the sweetness of heavenly contemplation. About the time of the feast of the Exaltation of the Holy Cross, he saw a seraph coming out of the heights of heaven and hovering over him. When the apparition was gone, a powerful flame of love remained in

the Saint's heart. The vision had left on his body a wonderful image of the passion of Christ, as though the impression of a seal had been left by the previous, melting fire. At once there appeared the marks of the nails in his hands and feet, and his right side seemed to have been pierced by a lance; a red scar formed around the wound, and blood often flowed from it and moistened his garments. As a result of this new, extraordinary miracle, Francis became a different man, decorated with the wounds of the Lord. He came down from the mountain with an image of the Crucified, not on stone or wood formed by man, but with one impressed by the finger of God on his very body."

2. "O God, who didst by manifold revelation show forth in Thy blessed confessor Francis the wondrous mysteries of the Cross . . ." (Postcommunion). This feast of St. Francis fits well into the season of the Exaltation of the Holy Cross and of the Sorrowful Mother. The open wounds on the body of this saint serve to strengthen our faith in Christ, the crucified Savior. This miracle occurred "in a world grown cold" so that "our hearts might be filled with burning love of Christ" (cf. Collect). In Francis the image of the Crucified was brought home to us in a new, human form. This is an indication that our Lord earnestly desires to impress us with the mystery of the Cross which, to the natural man is usually so unintelligible and puzzling that he would like to escape from it; yet our Lord's words are still true: "If any man has a mind to come my way, let him renounce self, and take up his cross, and follow me" (Matt. 16:24). By meditation and prayer St. Francis had steeped his soul so deeply in the mystery of the Cross and with such fervor, that he became a "speaking image" of the Redeemer. He stands before us today as a powerful and impressive preacher of the Cross of Christ. May his preaching draw us closer to the crucified Savior!

"That . . . our hearts might be filled with burning love of Thee" (Collect). Golgotha is the best school of divine love;

there is "revealed the love of God" (I John 4:9). "Here, as if
God meant to prove how well he loves us, it was while we were
still sinners that Christ . . . died for us" (Rom. 5:8). Jesus
could have redeemed us and restored us to that life lost
through sin by shedding a single drop of His blood, or even by
the least of His redemptive acts; but His love compelled Him
to sacrifice everything, even His life, for us, for me, for every
man; and He would do it by death on the Cross, after having
submitted to countless insults, injustices, pains, and tortures.
Must we not say, with the Apostle: "My real life is the faith I
have in the Son of God, who loved me, and gave Himself for
me" (Gal. 2:20). And, again: "With us, Christ's love is a compelling motive, and this is the conviction we have reached; if
one man died on behalf of all, then all thereby became dead
men; Christ died for us all, so that being alive should no longer
mean living with our own life, but with his life who died for us
and has risen again" (II Cor. 5:14 ff.). It was by contemplating
the crucified Savior that St. Francis, the great lover of Christ,
learned to love. He immersed himself so deeply in the abyss of
the love of the Crucified that he became all love, and love
transformed him so that he was crucified with Christ (cf. Gal.
2:19), and shared the wounds of the Redeemer. Golgotha, the
Cross, is the school in which we, too, by contemplating the
love of Christ, may elevate ourselves more and more to a return
of His love and thus become strong enough to accept the trials,
privations, humiliations, and sufferings of daily life. In a certain sense, then, we shall bear the wounds of our Lord in our
bodies and be crucified with Him. May St. Francis obtain this
grace for us, this love for Christ!

3. God "revealed" the secrets of the Cross in St. Francis,
and the crucified Redeemer "renewed" the wounds of His
body in that of the Saint in order that "our hearts might be
filled with burning love" for Him. Love is the goal of all the
commandments: "Thou shalt love the Lord, thy God." That is
the great commandment; all others are concerned with the

formation of love. All will be fulfilled in and through love; but we can learn charity only in the school of the Crucified. For this reason the Church frequently recommends or prescribes the sign of the Cross in our prayers and lives.

Collect: Lord Jesus Christ, who didst reproduce, in the flesh of the most blessed Francis, the sacred marks of Thy own sufferings, so that in a world grown cold our hearts might be filled with burning love of Thee, graciously enable us by his merits and prayers to bear the cross without faltering and to bring forth worthy fruits of penitence. Amen.

SEPTEMBER 18

St. Joseph of Cupertino, *Confessor*

1. Joseph Mary was born in the southern Italian town of Cupertino on June 17, 1603. His parents were sincere Christians, but poor. His mother so accustomed him to discipline that Joseph later remarked that he had no need of a novitiate when he entered religion. The deep piety of the boy of five grew through the years until it often appeared when he was praying that he might be in ecstasy. Along with prayer went a life of mortification and penance, from his earliest years.

At seventeen Joseph was no longer able to repress his desire to become a Franciscan; the friars, however, rejected him because of his lack of education. Then he went to the Capuchins, was given the habit in August, 1620, and dismissed after eight months because it seemed there was nothing he could do. Finally, and with great difficulty, his mother succeeded in having him received as a brother of the Third Order by the Franciscans at Grotella. Here he performed menial tasks in the monastery and among the mules. Little by little Joseph gained the respect of the people and of his brethren until, in 1625, he was placed among the choir-novices. In 1626 he pronounced his vows and two years later was ordained priest. His ecstasies became so frequent that he was excluded from choir service, lest he disturb the others. Father Guardian took him as a companion on his journeys until the people became alarmed at his ecstasies and miracles; then he sent Joseph to the Inquisitors at Naples, who declared the monk free from blame. To avoid further disturbances among the people, however, he was sent from one monastery to another, spending time in Rome and Assisi. He was not permitted to celebrate Mass in public. His last stop was at Osimo, where he died in 1663. He was beatified in 1753 and canonized in 1767.

2. "The wisdom that is worth having is the love of God. When she reveals herself face to face, men come to love her, seeing her beauty and recognizing her wondrous power" (Introit). This love of God burned brightly in Joseph's soul from childhood, preserving him from sin and folly, enkindling in him such fervor of devotion and love of prayer that he sometimes forgot to eat for several days. Most noteworthy in him was the gift of rapture: oftentimes his body was lifted up, especially at the altar. On one occasion a "Calvary" was being erected: two crosses had been set in place, while the third, a much heavier one, lay at some distance from its place. Joseph saw this from the monastery, flew to the cross, picked it up as if it had been a splinter, and dropped it into the hole intended for it. The same love of God caused to grow in him an exact fidelity to his vows, a zeal for acts of self-denial and Christian charity. Indeed, "the wisdom that is worth having is the love of God." It is significant that the epistle of today's Mass places the canticle of love of God and of neighbor on our lips. Love is the secret of our Saint's remarkable life. What value has prayer, sacrifice, and labor if they do not spring from love of God and fellowman? They are nothing but deceit, foolishness, and vanity. "Make charity your aim" (I Cor. 14:1).

"There was once a king, who held a marriage-feast for his

son" (Gospel). Those invited to the feast offered foolish ex-
cuses, and so, "Here is the marriage-feast all ready, and those
who had been invited have proved unworthy of it. You must go
out to the street corners, and invite all whom you find there to
the wedding." In the parallel passage of St. Luke we read
specifically, "the poor, the cripples, the blind, and the lame"
(Luke 14:21). The liturgy means to tell us: Joseph, a poor,
unlettered shoemaker, and impractical young man who was
rejected by one monastery on account of ignorance and by
another on account of his awkwardness—this youth was chosen
and invited to the wedding-feast, to the perfection of virtue
and of sanctity, the most intimate union with God. Already, as
a boy, he had enjoyed special favors, and yet he found difficulty in becoming even a laybrother of the Third Order. Amid
the lowest services he grew in inner union with God, and ultimately was admitted to theology. As a priest he could scarcely
celebrate Mass without becoming wrapt in holy contemplation.
"Blessed are the poor in spirit," the little ones who count for
nothing in the world. They are the ones who are invited to the
banquet of the King.

3. "God looked upon him with an eye of favor, lifted him
up from his low estate, and raised his head high" (Alleluia
verse). We marvel at the power of grace, to bring forth such
rare fruits of virtue and holiness in this Joseph of Cupertino.
But the divine seed found good soil in his heart. Anyone who
understands and practices poverty, who loves self-denial and
renounces his own will, who completely frees himself from
everything that could retard his progress toward God, who out
of humility remains calm under calumny, and persecution—
such a one is ripe for the life of holy love. We have much to
learn from such a saint.

We beg Joseph of Cupertino to obtain for us the grace to
love God ever more perfectly. Love is the highest, most decisive force in our lives.

Collect: O God, under whose providence Thy only-begotten Son was lifted up above the earth so that He might draw all things to himself, accomplish Thy gracious purpose in us, and let the merits and example of Thy seraphic confessor Joseph help us to rise above all earthly desires and make our way into the presence of Him who is God. Amen.

SEPTEMBER 21

St. Matthew, *Apostle and Evangelist*

1. Matthew, also known as Levi, was a tax-collector in Capharnaum, an important town on the Lake of Genesareth. The Jews hated the 'publicans,' as they called the tax-gatherers, because these officials not only exacted money from God's people to give to a pagan ruler, but enriched themselves unjustly in the process. And now, "Jesus saw a man called Matthew sitting at work in the customs-house, and said to him, Follow me; and Matthew rose from his place and followed him" (Matt. 9:9). And "then Levi made a great feast for him in his house" (Luke 5:29). When Jesus "was taking a meal in the house, many publicans and sinners were to be found at table with him" (Gospel). From that time on Matthew lived with the other apostles. After our Lord's ascension, he labored in Palestine, and later, according to tradition, in Ethiopia, where he was martyred. His relics are venerated in the Cathedral of Salerno, near Naples. St. Matthew is the author of the first Gospel, written in the Aramaic language between the years 60 and 70 after Christ. In it he was chiefly concerned with proving that Jesus was the Messias so long awaited, and that His Church was the realization of the Messianic kingdom, which the Jews had envisioned as an earthly power.

2. "Follow me; and Matthew arose from his place and followed him." St. Ambrose comments on this incident as follows:

"Mysterious is this calling of the tax-collector, whom He invites to follow Him, not with bodily steps but with the giving of his heart. But he, called by this brief word . . . leaves his previous, profane business and follows the Lord with complete surrender of spirit. Yes; he even prepares a great feast; for, when once a man has inwardly received Christ, he will be satiated with the greatest measure of overflowing pleasures." In the Introit of the Mass we praise the supernatural wisdom of the publican: "Right reason is on the good man's lips." That is Christian wisdom; it sacrifices the temporal in order to pursue the eternal. Whatever is not Christ, whatever holds us back from Him is not worthy of us. We are amazed at the insight and determination of the tax-collector, who at a moment's notice leaves all and joins the Master in whose company he can expect to find only poverty and renunciation. God's grace can do such things.

"Follow me!" Matthew was condemned by his own people as a sinner, because of his occupation. And yet this was the man whom our Lord called. The Master appeared at Matthew's "great feast" with His disciples and many "publicans and sinners" in order, as St. Jerome says, "to have an opportunity to teach and to satisfy with spiritual nourishment, those who had invited Him." But, alongside these, were the Pharisees, the "just," asking: "How comes it that your master eats with publicans and sinners?" That was the way the zealots, the "pious," judged things. To them Matthew was a sinner with whom they would have nothing to do. Those who look upon themselves as justified will go their way empty-handed, because they do not permit our Lord to draw them. They stand at a distance like strangers ignoring Him who would win them. Jesus says: "It is mercy that wins favor with me, not sacrifice. I have come to call sinners, not the just" (Gospel). The sacrifices and good works of the self-justified are worthless and hollow because they are not motivated by the spirit of merciful love of neighbor, even the sin-hardened neighbor.

3. Just as our Lord called to Matthew, "Follow me," so today He calls us in the sacrifice of the Mass, in His coming in Holy Communion, and in many graces during the day. Do we always respond, leaving all to follow Him?

Matthew gave himself to God and His cause to the extent of writing the first of the four Gospels. He was so deeply concerned about the redemption of his erring brethren that he wanted to prove to them that Jesus was the Messias for whom their fathers had longed through the centuries. A true follower of Christ feels an urgent impulse to love his fellowmen and to work for their salvation. Let us thank St. Matthew for his Gospel, and study it diligently in order to learn to know Jesus better and to love Him all the more ardently.

What would have become of Matthew if he had not corresponded with God's grace? Can we afford to waste and reject such valuable sacred help?

Collect: Let the prayers of the blessed apostle and evangelist Matthew help us, Lord, obtaining for us by his intercession the boon which our own efforts cannot gain. Amen.

SEPTEMBER 24

Our Lady of Ransom

1. This feast of Mary had its origin in the founding of the Order of Mercedarians. Prompted by a vision of the Blessed Virgin, Peter Nolascus and Raymond of Pennafort founded the Order for the purpose of buying back Christian slaves from the Saracens. The Mercedarians were approved by Pope Gregory XI in 1225. They follow the Rule of St. Augustine, adding to the usual three vows a fourth binding them to labor for the freedom of Christian slaves, at the cost of their own freedom, if need be. The Order rendered many services to the Church both by this labor and by its extensive missionary la-

bors in Central and South America. Today's feast was extended to the entire Church by Pope Innocent XII in 1690. The Church looks upon the Mercedarians' activity as being in a special sense the work of the Mother of God, Help of Christians, and hence prays: "O God, who . . . wast pleased through the glorious mother of Thy Son to enrich the Church with a new family. . . ." We honor Mary as the foundress of this work as we ask her to free us, through her intercession, from our captivity to sin and Satan.

2. "*Ave Maria:* Hail Mary, full of grace . . . blessed art thou among women" (Offertory). In these words we greet her as "full of grace," in view of all the good she has done and still does as "foundress of this great work," this Order. Records show that up to the beginning of the eighteenth century the Mercedarians had, at the cost of innumerable sacrifices and heroic charity, liberated forty thousand captives from the hands of the Mohammedans in Spain and Africa. The Order also gave the Church about fifteen hundred martyrs. Owing to a change of circumstances the Order has turned to other tasks, particularly that of liberating Christian souls from sin. In this work also it experiences the evident help of Mary, and the Church praises her for that. We join the body of the faithful in the Eucharistic Sacrifice, returning thanks to the Father for giving Mary, Help of Christians, to His Church.

"My roots spread out among the people . . . my God has granted me a share in his domain" (Lesson). The existence of the Mercedarians is a definite expression of Mary's devoted love for the 'favored race' of Christians. Mary makes use of the influence she has over the heart of her divine Son to free us if we are languishing in the bonds of perdition. If she was so deeply concerned about those detained by material chains, how much deeper is her concern for us, chained by sin and inordinate attachment to mundane things, by error and illusion, and uncertainty, torturing doubts, undue self-seeking. She wants us to be free and unhampered in our striving for the

higher goal: God. In this holy freedom we are a "highly honored people," the patrimony of God, in whom Mary took root
and for whom she bears a motherly solicitude; for she wants us
to be free from every kind of slavery for all time, so we may
attain perfect inner liberty. That is the burden of our prayer to
Mary, Help of Christians, on this feast of hers.

3. Naturally, we are conscious of the captivity of many
Christians in the physical sense: those in concentration camps,
in prisoner-of-war camps behind barbed wire, in exile of all
kinds. We are thinking also of those spiritually enslaved, the
captives of sin, passion, selfishness, and error; we recommend
all of them to the intercession of the Mother of God for their
freedom.

We, too, were once slaves of the "old man"; but, thanks to
Mary, we now possess Christ and, in Christ, freedom in the
measure that we ourselves determine by reception of the life
and spirit of Christ in Holy Communion. "Where the Lord's
spirit is, there is freedom" (II Cor. 3:17).

"Blessed be the womb in which the blessed Mary bore the
eternal Father's Son" (Communion). These words of the
liturgy refer also to us as "blessed," for we attain to the liberty
of the children of God when we receive Christ in Holy Communion.

Collect: O God, who, for the deliverance of Christians from the
power of the heathen, wast pleased through the glorious mother of
Thy Son to enrich the Church with a new family, we pray Thee
grant that we, who devoutly venerate her as the foundress of this
great work, may likewise be delivered by her merits and intercession from all our sins and from bondage to the power of hell. Amen.

SEPTEMBER 27

Sts. Cosmas *and* Damian, *Martyrs*

1. Tradition tells us that Sts. Cosmas and Damian were
twin brothers of good Christian family, who worked as physicians in Sicily. It is said that they would accept no fees from
the poor and that they healed more often by means of the sign
of the Cross than by means of medicine. Furthermore, they
were interested in the spiritual well-being of their patients
and often used their medical skill to open the way for conversion of heathen patients. Their success in thus healing souls
soon brought down upon them the wrath of the pagans, whose
complaints to the governor resulted in their being condemned
and tortured. The Lord kept them miraculously from harm,
however, until at last they were beheaded. In the Eastern
Church, Sts. Cosmas and Damian were honored as early as the
beginning of the fifth century. In the following century many
churches bearing their names were to be found in Rome. The
Introit of today's Mass was composed in 530 for the dedication
of the Basilica of Sts. Cosmas and Damian near the Roman
Forum. The names of these saints occur in the canon of the
Mass.

2. "All the multitude was eager to touch him, because power
went out from him, and healed them all" (Gospel). Jesus had
often healed the sick by driving out the evil spirits that were
afflicting them; now He was sharing His power over sickness
with the holy physicians, and they gratefully used it in the
cause of Christlike charity. "When you did it to one of the least
of my brethren here, you did it to me" (Matt. 25:40). Cosmas
and Damian accounted themselves as poor by the fact that
they put their trust in Christ, who said: "Blessed are you who
are poor; the kingdom of God is yours." Those who are poor in
the sense that our Lord had in mind stand no longer in the do-

main of created things and earthly values; freed from the
dominion of these things, they are able to open their souls to
the light from above, to the graces God wants to pour on them.
"Blessed are you who are hungry now; you will have your fill."
These holy physicians understood our Lord's promise well; in
order to relieve the sick they sacrificed their time, and their
own health; they endured hunger in order to satisfy the hunger
of the needy. This is true Christianity, true charity; and God
blessed their sacrifices.

"Blessed are you, when men hate you, and cast you off and
revile you, when they reject your name as something evil, for
the Son of man's sake," that is, because you believe in Christ
and live for Him. True charity helps to destroy the kingdom of
Satan, and the evil one fights back. When the brothers were
subjected to torture they remembered that "it is the just that
will live forever," and that "a rich reward awaits you in
heaven." And, "How glorious is that kingdom, how beautiful
that crown, which the Lord will bestow on them!" (Lesson.)
"Roused by the cry of the innocent, the Lord sets them free
from all their afflictions. So near is the Lord to patient hearts,
so ready to defend the humbled spirit" (Gradual). Today we
think of Sts. Cosmas and Damian as being honored by God in
heaven: "When that day comes, rejoice and exult over it; for
behold, a rich reward awaits you in heaven" (Gospel). After
short-lived pain come an everlasting reward, an eternal plenitude of life with honor, every gladness, everything.

3. In the holy martyrs Cosmas and Damian we recognize
ourselves. Our Lord says to us: "Blessed are you who are poor;
the kingdom of God is yours. Blessed are you who are hungry
now; you will have your fill. Blessed are you who weep now;
you will laugh for joy" (Gospel).

As we unite ourselves with the priest and our brethren in
offering this Holy Sacrifice, we want Christ to make us sharers
in His sacrifice to the Father; we want to be sacrificed with
Christ, and we are prepared to be one with Him in His life of

poverty, humiliation, and self-denial. "Woe upon you who are rich; you have your comfort already. Woe upon you who are filled full; you shall be hungry. Woe upon you who laugh now; you shall mourn and weep. Woe upon you, when all men speak well of you" (Luke 6:24–26).

Collect: Grant, we pray Thee, almighty God, that we who are celebrating the birthday of Thy holy martyrs Cosmas and Damian, may by their intercession be preserved from all the ills that threaten us. Amen.

SEPTEMBER 29

The Dedication to St. Michael the Archangel

1. The Archangel St. Michael occupies a prominent place in the liturgy. In the struggle of God and the Church against Satan he plays an important role. The battle between God and his enemies, begun when Lucifer fell, still continues. The Son of God Himself came upon this earth as the armed warrior-hero, in order to strike down the enemies and to restore to the Father the honor that had been stolen from Him. In this warfare no creature can be neutral. Those sworn to Christ are St. Michael and his angels, the Church, and the saints; and St. Michael is their standard-bearer, sounding the battle cry, "Who is like to God?" On the side of God's enemies are Satan, his angels, and his companions among men. Today's feast was originally the anniversary of the dedication of the Church of St. Michael, on the Via Salaria, near Rome. The liturgy does not deal with St. Michael alone; rather it has in mind all the holy angels who have been assigned to protect us Christians and to assist us in the struggle toward what is good.

2. "Fierce war broke out in heaven, where Michael and his angels fought against the dragon. The dragon and his angels fought on their part, but could not win the day, or stand their

ground in heaven any longer; the great dragon, serpent of the primal age, was flung down to earth; he whom we call the devil, or Satan, the whole world's seducer" (Apoc. 12:7–9). The dragon had undertaken a direct assault upon heaven with all his forces, to thwart God's plan. A fateful decision hung in the balance: Would God's kingdom endure or not? Commander in chief of the faithful angels was Michael; his name was the watchword against the besiegers of heaven. There could never have been any doubt as to the outcome: the enemies of God were defeated and routed by Michael's victory with the host under his standard. Ever since, Michael has been looked upon as the protecting Patron of the Church, as he formerly was of the Chosen People. It is true that we children of the Church will always be molested by Satan, but the Church knows that St. Michael stands always at our side in the struggle. We joyfully repeat the battle cry, "Who is like to God?" We venerate the archangel Michael, leader of the angel army. Honoring him brings blessings to nations, and his intercession opens heaven (Fifth Response at Matins).

"They have angels of their own in heaven, that behold the face of my heavenly Father continually" (Gospel). And, "Woe to the world, for the hurt done to consciences." God takes care of the little ones, those who count for nothing in the eyes of the world. To each of them He assigns an angel to care for him, to guide and protect him, even as a man protects his own eye. God honors us to the extent of entrusting us to one of the princes of heaven, who will represent us before His throne. These princes stand at the throne of God and always behold His glory. They are the intimates and adorers of Him for whom they glow with love; in the hour of testing they kept faith and fought for His interests with sacrificial zeal. How encouraging it is to remember that God has given His Church this holy intercessor, this mighty conqueror of Satan, as her protector. She now has nothing to fear from the evil one's attacks, nor from his world, no matter how many despise her.

3. "An angel stood by the altar of the temple, holding a golden censer, and incense was given him in plenty; and the smoke of the perfume went up in God's presence" (Offertory). One of the "seven spirits who stand before God" took the censer and brought it to the altar before the throne of God, so that he might light it there. In fragrant clouds the incense rose to God, representing "the prayers of the saints," that is, of members of the Church Militant praying on earth. The cloud of incense created by the angel carries the Church's prayer aloft to the throne of God, where we hope to be heard. The feast of today brings us the consoling thought that God's holy angels unite their prayers and adoration with ours, and so with them we pronounce our "Sanctus, sanctus, sanctus!"

The Communion antiphon calls attention to the holy fellowship that we shall enjoy forever with the angels, as a fruit of Holy Mass and Communion: "Bless the Lord, all you the Lord's angels: praise him and extol his name forever!"

"Saint Michael the Archangel, defend us in battle, be our defense against the wickedness and snares of the devil. May God rebuke him, we humbly pray; and do thou, O Prince of the heavenly host, by the power of God, thrust into hell Satan and the other evil spirits who prowl about the world for the ruin of souls. Amen" (Prayer after Mass).

Collect: God, who ordainest the services of angels and men in a wonderful order, be pleased to grant that our life on earth may be guarded by those who stand always ready to serve Thee in heaven. Amen.

SEPTEMBER 30

St. Jerome, *Priest, Confessor, Doctor of the Church*

1. St. Jerome was a priest who was never distinguished by ecclesiastical or worldly honors, but who gained a name for himself by his greatness of spirit, exceptional learning, untiring labor, and holiness. Eusebius Jerome was born between the years 340 and 350; he studied in Rome and occasionally surrendered to the sensual charms of the world. It was in Rome that he received baptism and in Treves that he decided to become a monk. Returning to his home in Stridon, near Aquileia, Italy, he took leave of father and mother, in 372, and then made his way as a pilgrim through Asia Minor to Antioch, where he devoted two years to study. In 374 he retired to the desert of Chalcis to live a life of stern penance and hard work for four years. In Constantinople he attended the sermons of St. Gregory of Nazianz and perfected his knowledge of the Greek language. From 382 until 386, Jerome lived in Rome and served as secretary to Pope Damasus; then he went to Bethlehem for the remainder of his life, ruling a monastery for thirty-four years, devoting unspeakable pains to the translation of the Hebrew books of the Old Testament into Latin, and writing commentaries on many books of the Bible. He died on September 30, 420, in Bethlehem.

2. "God, who in Thy blessed confessor Jerome wast pleased to provide Thy Church with her greatest teacher in the interpretation of Holy Scripture . . ." (Collect.) St. Jerome's fame rests chiefly on his interpretation of the Scriptures. While in Rome he busied himself with a revision of the existing Old Testament text. In Bethlehem he continued this as a lifework, earnestly studying Greek and Hebrew and touring all Palestine in the company of learned Rabbis in order to gain a better

understanding of Scripture through acquaintance with its background, geography, and customs. For the purpose of refuting the "dogs that rave against Christ," he showed in his short biographies of famous men that the knowledge of Christians was in no way inferior to that of the most learned heathens. With burning zeal he defended the doctrine of Mary's perpetual virginity against Helvidius and Jovinian; he spoke out against Vigilantius in favor of veneration of saints, and against Pelagius in defense of the Church's doctrine of grace. Rightly then do we praise St. Jerome in the words of the Introit: "The Lord moved him to speak before the assembled people, filling him with the spirit of wisdom and discernment, clothing him in magnificent array."

"I buffet my own body, and make it my slave; or I, who have preached to others, may myself be rejected as worthless" (I Cor. 9:27). Jerome possessed a violent, passionate nature which sometimes caused him much trouble. As a young student he could very readily switch from the most distracting entertainment to the most profound and exacting studies. As a monk in the desert he lived on bread and water, slept on the bare ground, chastised his body severely, and, at the same time learned the rudiments of the Hebrew and Aramaic languages from a Jewish fellow-hermit.

Two enemies followed St. Jerome into his solitude. The one was the memory of enjoyments he had experienced in the world; and these were the cause of severe struggle in him because he so vividly recalled them. The other was his love for the works of Plato, Cicero, and Horace, amounting to an almost idolatrous worship. In spite of serious misgivings he would revel in these works as if in intoxication; but he finally gained a victory over himself and over them. Then he turned his undivided attention to the study of Holy Scripture. Having reached spiritual maturity, he could now win others for Christ. Under Pope Damasus he courageously denounced the avarice, luxury, and thirst for honors among the Romans, even the clergy. This made him the object of hatred and slander, so he went with some kindred souls back to Bethlehem. From there he wrote to St. Augustine, five years before his own death: "I have had my day, I have run as far as I could. Now I need rest." Surely he did need rest after his many labors, his trials of all kinds, his battles with his own nature, and his long years of stern penance and his hard fight for virtue.

3. To Heliodorus, who had left the monastery, Jerome wrote: "Dear brother, you are badly spoiled if you want to have pleasure on earth and yet reign with Christ hereafter. The happy day will certainly come when this mortal and corruptible flesh will put on immortality. 'Blessed whom the Lord will find watching.' Then, at the judgment, the world will lament and howl, and one generation after another will strike its breast. But the poor and the needy will rejoice and cry jubilantly: 'Behold, here is my Crucified, here is my God, here is my Judge, who once lay in a manger in swaddling clothes. He it was who was mocked in a purple garment and crowned with thorns.' "

St. Jerome has gained immortal renown in the Church; she numbers him among her most significant teachers; she gives him this honor even though she admits that he suffered from certain weaknesses and faults of character which somewhat mar his picture. His zeal for the right and the good sometimes carried him so far that he wounded and offended his best friends, among them St. John of Chrysostom and St. Augustine. Much light and strength of grace are required for combat against the enemies within oneself.

Collect: God, who in Thy blessed confessor Jerome wast pleased to provide Thy Church with her greatest teacher in the interpretation of Holy Scripture, we pray Thee let his merits plead with Thee to help us practice what he taught by word and deed. Amen.

�✲✲✲✲✲✲✲✲✲✲✲✲✲✲✲✲✲

OCTOBER

✲✲✲✲✲✲✲✲✲✲✲✲✲✲✲✲✲✲

OCTOBER 2

The Holy Guardian Angels

1. Revelation clearly teaches that a certain class of good angels fulfill the office of guardianship over men. Our Lord said of children: "They have angels of their own in heaven, that behold the face of my heavenly Father continually" (Matt. 18:10). Woe to him, then, who scandalizes a child, or anyone else who is a child of God through baptism, or who is even called to be such, as all men are; for God has assigned a Guardian Angel to every soul. All these angels are "spirits apt for service, whom he sends out when the destined heirs of eternal salvation have need of them" (Heb. 1:14). These comforting words of the Psalmist apply to all men: "He has given charge to his angels concerning thee, to watch over thee wheresoever thou goest" (Gradual). In the course of the year the Church celebrates the feast of individual angels, but on this day she honors all those spirits, to whom God has entrusted the protection of men, calling them Guardian Angels.

2. "God, who in thy transcendant providence deignest to send thy holy angels to watch over us . . ." (Collect). "Thus says the Lord God: now I am sending my angel to go before thee and guard thee on thy way, and lead thee to the place I have made ready for thee. Give him good heed, and listen to his bidding; think not to treat him with neglect . . . in him dwells the power of my name" (Lesson). God takes care of His children in a unique and kindly manner. "They will hold thee up with their hands lest thou shouldst chance to trip on a stone" (Gradual). St. Bernard amplifies this statement: "The Supreme Majesty commands his angels, those noble, blessed beings, His servants, and dwellers in His house, to protect you.

Who are you? What is man, that Thou shouldst be mindful of him, O Lord? What is he but misery? For thy protection, He has given His angels charge. What if you could see, hear, and touch this angel?" (Lesson for Matins.) Today we renew our faith in the holy Guardian Angel at our side. We believe in the providence of God over us and surrender ourselves to Him with complete, unshakable confidence. We are grateful to Him and to our Angel.

"He has given charge to his angels concerning thee." There is touching drama in some of the Scripture stories about the activities of angels on behalf of men. Any situation may have its angel. On all the paths traveled by nations and races from the beginning of history, angels have played a part as servants and messengers of the Most High, helping, enlightening, admonishing, warning, punishing. They have brought messages from God announcing His plans. They were especially active around His Incarnate Son. "You will see heaven opening, and the angels of God going up and coming down upon the Son of Man" (John 1:51). We can celebrate Christmas, Easter, and Ascension only in fellowship with angels. They stand at the crib and at the grave; they belong to the content of the great mysteries of Christ, the head of the Church. Therefore they belong to us, the members, too. With brotherly solicitude they watch over our physical welfare and protect us from misfortune and danger; they guard our spiritual life by enlightening and advising us; they remove this or that obstacle from our path; they stand by us in temptation; they comfort us; they prepare our heart for firm trust; they bring us joy and peace. They carry our prayers to God, support our efforts, and convey God's grace and blessing to us. In a word, "they will hold thee up with their hands."

3. "Lest thou shouldst chance to trip on a stone" (Gradual). They bear us up as a precious treasure entrusted to them by God. Just as older children carry and care for their younger sisters and brothers, so the angels wait on us until they have

conducted us happily to our home in our "Father's House." It is only after they have carried us past the abysses that yawn along our path in life and have rescued us from a multitude of dangers; it is not until we are safely home with our heavenly Father, that we shall fully realize what we owe them.

"They [the angels] . . . behold the face of my heavenly Father continually" (Gospel). They behold that face as the essence of their own bliss; but they behold it also as a means of serving us, for in their vision of God they see His plans for us. Out of this vision they gain the light, strength, and never-tiring love which enables them to serve us so carefully. They see how dear we are to the Father, and that makes us dear to them.

Every one of our fellow men, every brother and sister in Christ, even if he has failed or gone astray, has his angel who is concerned about him. In this the Guardian Angel gives us good example, for we should also be helping, loving guardians of our every brother in Christ.

Today we express gratitude to our Angel for his guidance, protection, and prayerful care of us. "Angel of God, my guardian, to whom the loving solicitude of God has entrusted me, enlighten, protect, lead and guide me."

Collect: God, who in Thy transcendent providence deignest to send Thy holy angels to watch over us, grant our humble petition that we may ever be safe under their protection, and may rejoice in their companionship through all eternity. Amen.

OCTOBER 3

St. Theresa of the Child Jesus, *Virgin*

1. The "Little Flower" first appeared in winter, having been born on January 2, 1873, in Alençon, Normandy. In baptism she received the name of Frances Theresa. At first stubborn and

proud, the lovely child soon recognized these faults and set out to overcome them. It was characteristic of her even then to abhor halfway measures: she would strive for holiness with all her might. When she became seriously ill in 1882, the Mother of God cured her. Overcoming many difficulties Theresa was permitted to enter the Carmel of Lisieux at the unprecedented age of fifteen years and three months, and pronounced her vows on September 8, 1890, taking the name of Theresa of the Child Jesus and the Holy Face. She lived a life of prayer, poverty, obedience, sacrifice and suffering, but above all, a life of love: love of God and love of the cross characterize the spirit of St. Theresa. Having consecrated herself to "the Father as a victim of merciful love," she realized that it was her mission "to teach others to love God as I love Him, and to show others the simple little way that I have walked. It is the way of spiritual childhood, the way of trust and complete surrender." Theresa went to her eternal nuptials on September 30, 1897. She was canonized by Pope Pius XI in 1925 and named the Patroness of the Missions.

2. "Unless you become like little children again, you shall not enter the kingdom of heaven" (Gospel). Theresa's love of God attained its perfection in a childlike attitude: "I am a helpless child, and yet it is precisely my weakness that gives me the boldness to offer myself as a victim of Thy love." This spirit urged her onward to boundless trust in the mercy of God. She makes no claim for any work of her own: "God has shown me that I am too small to pay even one of my spiritual debts, and that He wants me to remain in this poverty." That made perfection look easy to her: "It is sufficient if one acknowledges one's nothingness and places oneself like a child in the arms of God. . . . Holiness does not consist in this or that exercise: it is simply a readiness of heart that permits us to be little and humble in the arms of God; it gives us a consciousness of our own weakness and a bold trust in His fatherly goodness." Only

a few days before her death, Theresa confessed: "I am like a very small child; I have no thoughts. I simply suffer without being able to feel disturbed about what is to come." And what was the fruit of this childlike attitude toward God? "Oh, what joy floods my soul when it elevates itself above natural feelings! No, there is no joy that can compare with it. . . . As soon as the love that needed constant self-forgetfulness entered my heart, I was happy." That was Theresa's secret; we must try to learn from her what it means.

"He spread the eagle's wings to carry her, took her upon His shoulders. The Lord Himself would be her only guide" (Communion). "O Jesus, my adorable eagle. So long as you desire it, I shall keep my eyes fixed on You. I want to be the prey of Your love. Some day, You will pounce upon me, I hope, carry me off in the hand of Your love, and finally drop me into this burning abyss, so that I may forever be its happy victim. . . . Eternal Word, You are the eagle whom I love and who attracts me." So prays Theresa. He has "lowered Himself to me because I am little and weak." She can do nothing "but give herself up and abandon herself completely." She says: "A long time ago I gave myself entirely to Jesus. He is, therefore, free to do as He pleases with me." Nothing frightens, worries, or disturbs her any more; she knows only one fact, one joy: "Nothing makes me happy but to do the will of God." That is why the heavenly Father stooped down to her and lifted her up to the heights of love and holiness. God says, "My strength finds its full scope in thy weakness. More than ever, then, I delight to boast of the weaknesses that humiliate me, so that the strength of Christ may enshrine itself in me . . . when I am weakest, then I am strongest of all" (II Cor. 12:9–10).

3. "I want everything." That is the key to understanding Theresa's greatness. She wants a perfect work. God desires to be longed for, sought, and found with all of the soul's power. Only the whole-souled man can believe and love perfectly; it

is only such that God can help. He does not want mediocrity
in spiritual giving and striving. We have much to learn from
Theresa.

"We should like to be generous and to suffer nobly;
we don't ever want to fall. What self-deception! What does
it matter if we fall every moment? Thereby my weakness is
revealed; and that is to my great advantage. . . . Let us suffer if need be, in bitterness and without courage. Jesus also
suffered in sadness."

Theresa shows us the sure, simple way to holiness. We can,
we want to walk that way of love, of being little. "To remain
small means to acknowledge one's nothingness, to expect
everything from a loving God, not to be unduly troubled
about failings or to hoard up certain merits. Remaining little
means also not attributing one's virtues to oneself, as if one
were capable of any good, but, rather, acknowledging that they
are a treasure which a loving God places in the hands of a little child to be used by Him when He needs it."

Is it not strange, and also significant of the spirit of St.
Theresa, that Pope Pius XI chose the Carmelite nun, whose
proper vocation is contemplation, to be Patroness of the Missions? For Theresa religious life and contemplation were
above all else means of saving souls—prayer, sacrifices, self-
denial, suffering and intimate union with God. For her contemplation possesses a moving power and is the source of the
fruitfulness of activity. Theresa became a Carmelite in order
to pray for priests and to work for the spread of the kingdom
of God. She was right: Mary and Martha belong side by side,
and each makes the other fruitful.

Collect: Lord, who hast said: Unless you become like little children, you shall not enter the kingdom of heaven; grant, we pray
Thee, that by following the blessed maid Theresa in humility and
singleness of heart, we may win the prize of everlasting glory. Amen.

OCTOBER 4

St. Francis of Assisi, *Confessor*

1. In young Francis there lived the bold, ambitious spirit of his century, a time of knighthood, chivalry, aspiring citizenry, and of effervescent life in game and song. When the youth was twenty-four, he fell ill; that sickness brought him sense and he began to think about himself and his previous life. Having recovered he tried to escape God's hand, but God was stronger than Francis. On February 24, 1209, he heard the words of the gospel: "You are to have neither gold nor silver in your purse, nor a staff nor shoes" (cf. Luke 10:4). Francis took off his garments, shoes, and leather belt; he put on a gray smock, girded himself with a rope, and wore sandals on his feet. "That was what I had long sought; now my wish was fulfilled." He lived as an apostolic, itinerant preacher, in humility and utter poverty. Soon other men joined him, and he founded the Order of Friars Minor, the Order of Poor Clares, and the Third Order (1221). He died on the evening of October 5, 1226, at the age of forty-four. Two years later he was canonized by Pope Gregory IX.

2. "God forbid that I should make a display of anything, except the cross of our Lord Jesus Christ, through which the world stands crucified to me, and I to the world" (Introit and Epistle). Francis hung a large crucifix in the oratory of his monastery and led his brethren to it saying: "That is your meditation book." By gazing upon the cross Francis had come to understand the nothingness of all worldly things. Things he had formerly prized were now sources of temptation, objects of contempt and annoyance. Only the cross still had meaning for him; it was his only title to fame. In him the words of St. Paul were fulfilled: "Peace and pardon to all those who follow this rule, to God's true Israel" (Epistle). He took the

Cross of Christ as the standard by which all things are to be measured. So intimately was he united to the Crucified that he received the grace to "bear the scars of the Lord Jesus printed on [his] body." The stigmata marked him unmistakably as a disciple and "slave of Christ" (Gal. 1:10), who had become conformed to Him both internally and externally. In a certain sense Francis could say with Jesus: "If only I am lifted up from the earth, I will attract all men to myself" (John 12:32). He was not a priest but he founded an Order that circles the world; he effected so great a transformation in the religious and social realms of society that no one can fail to marvel at his success. He has attracted by the charm of his personality the noblest spirits of the centuries so that all do him honor, believers and nonbelievers alike, high and low. His great secret was devotion to the Crucified and a noble-minded rejection of all that the world had to offer; thus did he achieve interior liberty.

"Francis, poor and humble, enters heaven a rich man" (Alleluia verse). Because his profound understanding of the crucified Savior was so practical, he chose the way of poverty and humility. Poverty was the bride and queen of his heart and roused in him such a passion that he envied beggars in their rags. "Blessed are the poor in spirit" (Matt. 5:3). He founded a mendicant Order that was to live on small contributions, thus challenging an age that was in danger of being submerged in earthly dross because of its growing avarice and love of ease. His love of poverty was the more perfect because it was joined to simplicity and humility. His were not empty words when he said: "God has seen no more miserable man and sinner in the world than me." Admired and honored by everyone, Francis yet remained true to his standards: "I consider myself as nothing and give God credit for everything. I keep nothing for myself but the nothingness of my origin." What gives full brilliance to the picture of the Saint is his generous charity, the only thing that could make poverty and humility beget happiness. Francis loved God; he loved the Redeemer in His various mysteries, especially in His crucifixion; he loved the Church of Christ; he loved Christ's brothers and sisters; he loved the poor, the little, the children. He loved the sun, the flowers, the trees, and the birds. All were for him messengers of God. How rich the poor little man of Assisi was! And how greatly he enriched others!

3. "Blessed are the poor in spirit," those who are inwardly free from all earthly desires and possessions. "If thou hast a mind to be perfect, go home and sell all that belongs to thee . . . then come back and follow me" (Matt. 19:21). If only we realized what inexhaustible treasures we possess in Christ, we would empty ourselves and gladly sacrifice everything to gain Him. How imperfectly we understand the words of our Lord blessing the poor in spirit; yes, we who day after day offer ourselves as sacrifice in the celebration of the Eucharist. Our offertory is still too much a matter of formality, of words without deeds.

St. Francis can teach us much on this subject. Let us beg him to obtain for us the grace to love the cross and to despise earthly goods, according to his own example.

Collect: O, God, who through the merits of blessed Francis didst enrich Thy Church with a new offspring, grant that after his example we may despise earthly things and ever find joy in partaking of the gifts of heaven. Amen.

OCTOBER 5

St. Placid and his Companions, *Martyrs*

1. In his *Life of Holy Father Benedict,* Pope Gregory the Great states that "pious nobility used to come from Rome to St. Benedict at Subiaco and entrust their sons to him to be

educated for God. Among others Aequitius and the patrician
Tertullus, both prominent men, brought their promising sons,
Maur and Placid respectively, who were still children." Then
St. Gregory relates how St. Benedict took the boy Placid with
him one night up to the peak of the nearby mountain, and,
after praying for a long time, caused a spring to come forth from
the rocks to furnish water for the monastery there. Finally, St.
Gregory tells how Placid fell into the lake, from which he
was dipping water, and was rescued by St. Maur miraculously.
Beyond these incidents, nothing is known for certain about
St. Placid. Legend adds, however, that he was sent by St.
Benedict to found a monastery in Sicily and was martyred
there together with his monks.

2. "When affliction comes, the Lord is the refuge and defense of the innocent" (Introit: Mass of Martyrs: *Salus autem*).
This text reminds us of the boy incautiously stooping to fill his
jug from the lake, and falling in. As the waves were carrying
him farther from shore, St. Benedict in his cell became aware
of the danger and quickly commanded Maur to rescue him.
Having received St. Benedict's blessing, Maur hurried to his
companion and carried him to shore, without noting the fact
that he was walking on top of the water, until after he was on
land again. Who had accomplished this miracle? While St.
Benedict suggested that it was Maur's reward for his prompt
and unquestioning obedience, the latter attributed the marvel
to the blessing that his abbot had given him. Little Placid himself settled this contest of humility, for he said that while he
struggled in the water he had seen hovering over him as a sign
of protection the mantle of St. Benedict. In the wholly spiritual
atmosphere of Subiaco the supernatural was, as it were, the
very air that the first Benedictine family breathed freely, children as well as grown monks. This may account as well for St.
Benedict's taking the boy with him when he went to find a supply of water on the mountain. The child's prayer, united to that

of the mature man of prayer, would surely obtain from God the miraculous help of needed springs.

"A grain of wheat must fall into the ground and die, or else it remains nothing more than a grain of wheat; but if it dies, then it yields rich fruit" (Gospel; John 12:24). Even if Placid did not die for Christ by the martyrdom of blood, he certainly embraced the unbloody martyrdom of the perfect monk's life as St. Benedict taught it to him. The fact that the Abbot esteemed this young monk and offered him the distinction of sharing in the miracle on the mountain is proof that Placid had imbibed the spirit of his Father and was prepared to exemplify it. He would "truly seek God; he would be full of zeal for the praise of God and for prayer and obedience, ready for hardships, humiliations, and sacrifices inherent in the life of a monk in the company of his brethren" (cf. Holy Rule, chap. 58). St. Placid was a perfect disciple of his great and holy master in fidelity to the monastic vocation: a grain of wheat that had gone down into the earth and died by closely imitating Him who called Himself a grain of wheat, and who had humbled Himself even unto death, bringing forth superabundant salvation for men. "If any man has a mind to come my way [St. Placid did, as every monk does], let him renounce self, and take up his cross, and follow me" (Matt. 16:24).

3. Happy the disciple of St. Benedict who wholeheartedly accepts this teaching as St. Placid did. The Benedictine Order has chosen St. Placid as the model and heavenly patron of its novices. May he obtain for them the grace to grasp the true spirit of Benedictine monasticism and to exemplify it all their lives.

Prayer: O God, for those who renounce the world Thou dost prepare a dwelling in heaven. At the pleading of the merits of St. Placid, do Thou bless the earthly dwelling of this community with heavenly favors. Grant that its members may hold together in fraternal charity, observe Thy commandments con-

cerning moderation, lead a calm, simple, chaste life and acknowledge that Thy grace is a gift of pure love for them. May
their lives harmonize with their name of monk, and may their
faith manifest itself in good works. Amen.

Collect: Almighty, eternal God, who dost fill our hearts with
gladness on the feast of Thy saints, graciously grant that, while
rejoicing in their merits, we may be fired by their example. Amen.

OCTOBER 6

St. Bruno, *Confessor*

1. St. Bruno, the founder of the Carthusians, was a spiritual
son of the patriarch of Western monasticism, St. Benedict. His
Order represents a happy combination of the cenobitical and
eremitical ways of life. Born in Cologne in 1032, Bruno was
endowed by nature with great spiritual gifts. After early training in Cologne he went to the world-famous school of Rheims,
and was soon put in charge. Among his pupils was the future
Pope Urban II. On account of disorders that later developed in
the Church at Rheims, Bruno decided to withdraw from the
world. With a few like-minded companions, he went to the
bishop of Grenoble and asked for a secluded plot of land on
which to start a monastery. The bishop offered him a barren
tract in the Chartreuse mountains, and Bruno there laid the
foundation of the Carthusian Order in 1084. The monks lived
in separate cells or huts, pursuing prayer and work in perpetual
silence but coming together at stated times for common exercises. Pope Urban II called Bruno to Rome to serve as his
helper and adviser. After much petitioning Bruno obtained
permission to leave Rome and found another monastery, this
time at La Torre in Calabria. Bruno died there on October 6,
1101. Five hundred years later his body was found to be incor-
rupt, and Gregory XV extended his feast to the entire Church.

2. "Blessed is the man who lives unreproved, who has no greed for gold, puts no trust in his store of riches. Show us such a man, and we will be loud in his praise" (Lesson). Such a man was Bruno, light of the Church, teacher of teachers, ornament of the clerical state, boast of Germany and France. People came from all directions to be educated by him. Meanwhile, Bruno was devising plans for leaving the world and its promised greatness, nobility, and beauty; he wanted to devote himself exclusively to God. Above all earthly wisdom and scholarliness in his eyes stood the wisdom of the saints, as expressed in the Bible: "If any man has a mind to come my way, let him renounce self, and take up his cross, and follow me. The man who tries to save his life shall lose it; it is the man who loses his life for my sake that will secure it. How is a man the better for it, if he gains the whole world at the cost of losing his own soul? For a man's soul, what price can be high enough?" (Matt. 16:24–26.) St. Bruno accepted this doctrine. "Right reason is on the good man's lips, wellweighed are all his counsels: the law of God rules in his heart" (Introit). Do we act upon this wisdom?

"The innocent man will flourish as the palm-tree flourishes; in the house of the Lord he will grow to greatness as the cedars grow on Lebanon" (Gradual). In his solitude at Chartreuse and at La Torre, St. Bruno was a grain of wheat that died in order to produce much fruit. This fruit is, first of all, the Order of Carthusians, whose members live an austere life of poverty, self-denial, penance, prayer, contemplation, hard work, silence, and solitude in their cells. "These monks," says Cardinal Bona, "are a miracle to the world; they live in the flesh as though they had no flesh; they are angels on earth, a precious ornament for the Bride of Christ, the Church, comparable to eagles who fly up to heaven." They do great work for the Church and for the salvation of souls; they live not for themselves but for God. Just as the dove that Noah released from the ark returned to the ark because it "could find no resting place to perch on"

(Gen. 8:9), so these men leave the world and return to the ark of prayer, trying by the expiation and prayer of their holy lives to lead other souls to salvation. The Order has ever remained true to the spirit of its founder; it has never been found to need reform. What an inexhaustible source of blessing it has been for all of us in the Church!

3. "He who secures his own [temporal] life will lose it [for eternity]; it is the man who loses his life for my sake [by sharing My Cross] that will secure it" (Matt. 10:39).

"My faithfulness and mercy shall go with him; as my champion he shall rise to greatness" (Offertory).

Collect: May the prayers of Thy holy confessor Bruno come to our aid, we pray Thee, Lord; so that we who have grievously offended Thy majesty by our transgressions may obtain pardon through his merits and intercession. Amen.

OCTOBER 7

The Most Holy Rosary of Our Lady

1. "Let us celebrate the feast of the Rosary of the Virgin Mary: Come, let us adore Christ, her Son, our Lord" (Invitatory of Matins). With our words of praise, "Hail, thou art full of grace; the Lord is with thee; blessed art thou among women . . . and blessed is the fruit of thy womb" (Luke 1:28, 42), we plait a wreath of roses for our heavenly Mother. When we announce and meditate on the mysteries of the Annunciation, Visitation, and Nativity, we are ultimately thinking of Christ, who chose the Virgin for His Mother and gave her a place in His redemptive work; she is the one most intimately associated with Him in His saving sacrifice and His sanctification of us. The Rosary devotion offers praise to Mary and to her Son; it is a prayer of gratitude to God and to Christ, who did such great things for her; it is a petition for the grace to be able to imitate

Mary in her virtues and labor and suffering, all in union with Christ. The feast of the Rosary was instituted in 1573 and prescribed for the universal Church in 1716. It gratefully commemorates the victory of the Cross over the Crescent, an event which is rightly attributed to the power of this devotion in winning Mary's special help. In a sense, this is a feast of Mary the Conqueror (victories over the Turks occurred at Lepanto in 1571 and at Peterwardein in 1716).

2. "Take this staff in your hand; with it you will work wonders" (Responsory at Matins). Moses took the staff as the Lord commanded him, stood before the king of Egypt and wrought miracles, thus freeing the Church of the Old Testament from bondage. He led his people through the Red Sea, rescuing them from the pursuing Egyptians; he struck water from the rock to slake the thirst of Israelites in the desert; he conducted them to the gates of the promised land. "Take this staff" (cf. Exod. 4:1 ff.). The liturgy thus alludes to the Rosary. With this holy prayer we can do wonders; it is both a simple and an effective prayer obtaining wonderful favors from God. The Church highly recommends the daily use of the Rosary; it gives us joy to greet Mary over and over, while congratulating her on her part in the mysteries we are meditating on while we tell our beads.

"From me comes every grace of faithful observance, from me all promise of life and vigor. Mine to burgeon like a rose-bush that is planted by running water" (Offertory). This is a hymn of praise to divine wisdom that filled Mary with its power and fruitfulness in the Incarnation of the Son of God. "Blessed is the fruit of thy womb." Through her intimate association with Christ the Redeemer, Mary became for us the medium of salvation. By giving us Christ she gave us all grace, all truth, and all life, for time and eternity. We praise and approve this fruitful union of the Savior with her, the cause of our joy and our supernatural riches, whenever we pray the joyful, sorrowful, or glorious Rosary. We greet Mary in the Annunciation, the Visitation of Elizabeth, the Virgin-birth in Bethlehem, the Presentation in the Temple, and the happy moment of the finding in the Temple: "Hail Mary!" We share the pain of her maternal heart during the passion and death of her Son as she suffered with Him the Agony in the Garden, the Scourging, the Crowning with Thorns; as she accompanied Him on His Way of the Cross, and stood by Him on Calvary during the hours of Crucifixion. We felicitate Mary on her joy when her Son rose triumphantly and was exalted as King and Lord of all, in His Ascension; we congratulate her because He sent us the Holy Spirit; because He elevated her, His Mother, to the joys of heaven and crowned her Queen of angels and men.

3. "Yours to blossom like the lily and smell sweet . . . yours to sing songs of praise, and bless the Lord for all things He has made" (Communion). At this moment in the Holy Sacrifice we have become united with the same Christ with whom Mary was most intimately joined. By virtue of this union with Him, each of us ought to become, as it were, a sweet-smelling rose of Christian living, "Christ's incense offered to God" (II Cor. 2:15), a hymn of praise to God's great deeds which we have been honoring in the Rosary. This is a glorious program for the lover of the Rosary.

We believe in the power of the Rosary as a prayer, and we gladly respond to the call of the Holy Father when, year after year, he admonishes us to pray the Rosary regularly. May the oft-repeated "Hail Mary" enkindle and deepen our affection for our Mother and strengthen our confidence in her. If the Church attributes the victory over the Saracen army to Mary, should we not, in view of present danger from the East, have confident recourse to the Rosary, "the staff with which we shall work wonders"?

Collect: O God, whose only-begotten Son, by his life, death, and resurrection, has purchased for us the rewards of eternal life, we pray Thee grant that we who meditate upon the mysteries of the most holy Rosary of the blessed virgin Mary may imitate what they contain and obtain what they promise. Amen.

The Motherhood of Our Lady

1. Fifteen hundred years have passed since Nestorius, in Constantinople, dared to assert that the humanity of Christ is independent of His divinity, and to teach that there are two persons in Him. To teach, further, that Mary conceived only the human person, the man Christ, and was therefore not Mother of God, not God-bearer, but merely mother of a man in whom God dwelt as in a temple. In the year 431 the Council of Ephesus took a clear stand against Nestorius. It formulated the Catholic doctrine thus: In Christ there is only one person, and that a divine person. Therefore Mary gave birth to the Son of God, and she is God-bearer, *Theotokos.* We joyfully endorse this confession of faith. In memory of the Council of Ephesus Pope Pius XI introduced the feast of the Motherhood of Our Lady on the Council's fifteen hundredth anniversary, in 1931.

2. Mary is the Mother of Christ. We accept the prophecy of Isaias: "Behold, the virgin shall be with child and shall bear a son, and he shall be called Emmanuel" (Introit). The Gospel of the feast relates that, after Mary and Joseph had taken their Child on the annual pilgrimage to Jerusalem and "set about their return home, the boy Jesus, unknown to his parents, continued to stay in Jerusalem." Sorrowing, they sought the child, and after three days found Him in the Temple. "My son, why hast thou treated us so? Think, what anguish of mind thy father and I have endured, searching for thee." Mary is the mother of Him who had no earthly father; Joseph is his fosterfather. Jesus testified that His real Father is in heaven: "Could you not tell that I must needs be in the place which belongs to my Father?" The Child of Mary is conceived of the Holy Spirit. In the Communion antiphon we proclaim: "Blessed be the womb in which the virgin Mary bore the eternal Father's Son." Blessed art thou, holy Mother, for thou didst bear the Son

of God in the most intimate spiritual and bodily union: Thou
His Mother; He the fruit of thy womb. "The Lord is with thee!"

Mary is our Mother, "no vine ever yielded fruit so fragrant;
the enjoyment of honor and riches is the fruit I bear" (Lesson). Mary did not keep the Savior of mankind to herself, but
gave Him to us at Bethlehem, at the Presentation in the Temple, and on Golgotha. She accepted His testament from the
Cross: "Woman, this is thy son" (John 19:26). In John He intended all of us to be adopted. Amid the anguished sorrow
that she suffered at the feet of her dying Son she became our
Mother. From the Cross our Savior spoke to all of us in John:
"This is thy Mother." She gave us Christ, and, in Him, supernatural life. She is concerned about us and extends her love for
Jesus over to us. Happy we who have such a Mother—the best
and truest ever! The fact that Mary is truly the Mother of
Christ is the best pledge that she is truly our Mother and exercises a mother's care over us. We must thank her for that.

3. Full of faith, we repeat the invocations of the Litany of
Loreto: "Mother of divine grace, pray for us. Thou purest,
most chaste, immaculate, lovely, wonderful Mother, pray for
us." Mary is mother of mercy, all-powerful with her Son, full
of goodness and love toward us. All this because she is the
Mother of God.

"Hither turn your steps, all you that learned to long for me;
take your fill of the increase I yield" of Jesus Christ, my Son,
today, in the Holy Sacrifice, in Holy Communion. Just as God
the Father "gave him up for us all" so has Mary given us
everything with her Child. We believe this; we are grateful for
it; we consider ourselves fortunate indeed.

Collect: O God, who didst decree that, at the angel's message,
Thy Word should take flesh in the womb of the blessed virgin
Mary, grant to us, Thy suppliants, that we who believe her to be
indeed the mother of God may be helped by her intercession with
Thee. Amen.

OCTOBER 15

St. Teresa, *Virgin*

1. During the sixteenth century, a time of religious and political turmoil, God gave His Church a number of saints who effectively fostered the Catholic Counter-Reformation. Among these were St. John of God, St. Ignatius Loyola, St. Joseph Calasancti, St. Philip Neri, and St. Charles Borromeo. To this list we should add St. Teresa of Jesus, born on March 28, 1515, in Avila, Spain. A highly talented child, she took delight in reading the lives of the saints supplied by her mother, and was thus drawn powerfully toward God. But then she began reading novels of chivalry and weakened her desire for God. When she was twelve her mother died, and Teresa adopted such a worldly manner that her father felt obliged to place her in the Augustinian convent in Avila. In 1553 she joined the Carmelites and was happy to make her vows a year later. Still there continued in her a conflict between her inborn nobility of character and her natural love of pleasure until, one day in 1555, she chanced to be so deeply touched by a meditation on the suffering Savior that the conflict died, and from this time on she was filled with fiery love and burning zeal for souls. Under great difficulties she reformed the Carmelite Order. By her excellent writings she became for countless souls a great helper and guide to God. She died October 4, 1582, in her convent at Avila.

2. "One who has once begun the practice of prayer should never give it up, no matter how many faults he continues to find in himself; for this is the only means by which one can advance. On this point I speak from experience." Teresa prayed, and prayer saved her. Again and again she repeated in her writings the thought that one of the greatest graces God can grant a soul is the impulse toward prayer. She had, even

during those years when she was living only partly for God, devoted several hours every day to prayer. For her, the devil's worst temptation was that she give up contemplative prayer; the greatest catastrophe that could fall on anyone would be to give up prayer altogether. Such a soul would, as it were, be lamed by gout; a body without a soul; a pillar of salt, like Lot's wife, in the face of danger. Prayer, for Teresa, is the starting point for all good in man, the gateway to graces. "Prayer alone was the gate and road to all the graces that God gave me," she asserted, "and He never let me go away from Him without comfort." Her ascetical and even her historical writings are all in some degree an encouragement to prayer. She also remarks that it was not until she had overcome herself and renounced inordinate attachments that she began to make real progress in prayer.

"If I were to give one piece of advice, it would be this: Learn from my experience, never to listen to natural fears and never to repay God's goodness with mistrust, even if He were to give something great and sublime. If the sole purpose of such a gift is His glory, never doubt about success, for this great God is all-powerful." Teresa was noble enough to plan great projects and to face great difficulties and sufferings with fortitude. There was nothing in the world she feared except sin. She accomplished seemingly impossible things, and suffered beyond words, being able to do so because she was humble and sought only God's glory with boundless confidence and love. She overcame natural fear and vehemently loved suffering instead of fleeing it; only God is to be feared, as well as loved. Her advice is: "Be courageous, trustful, high-spirited! Your best asset is a love that despises creatures and knows nothing but God and everything else in God and for God."

3. Teresa wanted to "suffer and die." When both the papal nuncio and the king declared against her reform of monasteries and she was put in prison by the magistrate of Avila, she wrote: "Can there be a greater consolation than being allowed

to suffer for God: It is painful, but it is the surest way to heaven. Therefore, let the cross be our consolation, our joy. Let us seek it, desire it, embrace it!"

By her monastic reforms Teresa did more to preserve the Faith in Spain and spread it in the American colonies than all the fleets and regiments of the Spanish king. Except for this reformation, accepted in all Catholic countries and abroad by seventeen communities of nuns and fifteen of men, Spain would have fallen prey to Protestantism and would then have dragged the new world to destruction, humanly speaking. God had chosen a woman of courage to accomplish His designs, one courageous enough to rely wholly upon Him and on the invisible power of sacrifice and prayer. For us as for Teresa, prayer and self-conquest are the prerequisites for fruitful external activity.

"This is the wise virgin, the one of the number of the prudent, whom the Lord found waiting" (Vesper antiphon). Teresa's principle was: "All things are vain; God alone suffices."

Collect: Listen, to us, God our Savior, so that we who find joy in the festival of Thy blessed maiden Teresa may be nourished by her inspired teaching and learn from her the spirit of godly service. Amen.

OCTOBER 17

St. Hedwig, *Widow*

1. Hedwig was born in the castle of Andechs belonging to her father, Count Berthold IV of Merania, in 1174. Her mother began her Christian training and sent her at the age of seven to a Benedictine convent in France to be educated. In 1186 she was married to Henry I, Duke of Silesia and Poland, and in the ensuing years bore him six children. She was a virtuous wife and mother, not permitting the distractions of court life

to interfere with her prayers and severe penances. For forty years she abstained from meat, and took only water and bread on Wednesday and Friday. This austerity did not lessen her loving kindness toward others, however; she was a protecting mother to the poor and the sick. Since her heart was not attached to earthly things she was able to bear heroically the heavy trials God laid on her, the heaviest of which was the death of her husband and her sons. Hedwig founded the Cisterican convent at Trebnitz, near Breslau, and retired there after her husband died. She followed him on October 15, 1243, and was canonized by Pope Clement IV, in 1267.

2. "A man who has found a vigorous wife has found a rare treasure, brought from distant shores. Bound to her in loving confidence, such a man will have no need for spoil. . . . How briskly she girds herself to her task, how tireless are her arms! . . . Kindly is her welcome to the poor, her purse ever open to those in need. . . . Ripe wisdom governs her speech, but it is kindly instruction she gives. . . . Unrivalled art thou among all the women that have enriched their homes. Vain are the winning ways, beauty is a snare; it is the woman who fears the Lord that will achieve renown" (Lesson). This gives a good picture of St. Hedwig. At court she was the model of a Christian princess, a chaste wife, an unselfish, loving mother; and her good example exerted a powerful influence, particularly on her husband. Eventually he came to share her sentiments concerning religion and Christian conduct. At court and abroad in the Duchy of Poland, Christian discipline and fear of God prevailed. After they had been blessed with three boys and three girls, Hedwig and her husband decided to live in continence. During the thirty years which remained to them they avoided public festivities and external pomp, striving earnestly to advance in Christian perfection. Their people considered them saints. From the castle poured forth blessings on the land, the fruit of St. Hedwig's quiet activity, prayer, and sacrifices.

"The kingdom of heaven is like a treasure hidden in a field;

a man has found it and hidden it again, and now, for the joy it gives him, is going home to sell all that he has and buy that field" (Gospel). Hedwig had to contend with severe trials, among them the sudden death of her sister Agnes who had entered an invalid marriage with King Philip August of France, and the murder of her sister Gertrude, Queen of Hungary. Her two brothers wandered about, banished from the kingdom. Her own home, Castle Andechs, was completely destroyed; her niece, Elizabeth of Thuringia, was cast out of her Wartburg Castle and died in want and misery. Her husband fell into the hands of his enemy and died, excommunicated, after his release and before she could reach him. One of her sons died as a child, and the other two, between whom their father had partitioned Poland, were at war. Later Conrad rebelled against his parents and died of a broken neck while hunting; Henry led the Polish army against the Mongolian invaders and was killed. While everyone else bewailed these misfortunes, Hedwig, with only one daughter left of her six children, comforted the mourners with these words: "Whatever is the Lord's will, that must be best for His servants." Then she prayed: "Lord, I thank Thee for having given me such a son; he was the dearest treasure I had on earth. Now Thou hast taken him from me and for this, too, I thank Thee. He died in honorable warfare for the Faith and for the country whose protector Thou hast made him." Hedwig had found the precious treasure: a deep, lively faith which transfigured all suffering into confident love. "Let us have no other will but the will of God." This perfect conformity to His will made the Saint strong.

3. "Just are thy awards; I know it well, Lord, it was in faithfulness thou didst afflict me" (Introit). Thus St. Hedwig prayed in her trials, and the Church repeats her prayer today. This should be our prayer too: "God's will be done!" In this lies the secret of all abiding peace and true happiness, of all consolation and perfect security. May St. Hedwig be a powerful intercessor for our times!

Collect: O God, from whom blessed Hedwig learnt to renounce earthly splendors and to follow, humbly and wholeheartedly, Thy cross, let her merits and example teach us to spurn the transitory pleasures of this life, and, by embracing Thy cross, to overcome all adverse powers. Amen.

OCTOBER 17

St. Margaret Mary Alacoque, *Virgin*

1. Margaret Mary was born in France near Paray-le-Monial, on July 22, 1647, of highly respected parents. She possessed a cheerful disposition, a clear mind, a noble heart, and extraordinary power of will. On June 20, 1671 she entered the Visitation convent at Paray-le-Monial. Already in the novitiate, grace worked powerfully in her soul, and our Lord favored her with His constant, perceptible presence, filling her with such great reverence that she used to read and work on her knees whenever she was alone. Her life was a perpetual prayer; she had acquired such perfection of purity and unselfishness that she found bitter what was to other people pleasant. It soon became clear to her that she must walk the humiliating way of the Cross: she felt a passionate longing for suffering.

In this way God prepared Margaret Mary for a great mission. She was to be the instrument for the introduction of the liturgical cult of the Sacred Heart of Jesus. In the years 1673 to 1675 our Lord instructed her as to the nature of this devotion, and assigned her the task of preparing the way for a public feast of the Sacred Heart in the Church. From that time on her life had only this one purpose. Her first convert to the cause was her confessor, Blessed Claude de la Colombiére, and through him she gained the powerful support of the Society of Jesus, of which he was a member. Margaret Mary had the joy of seeing this devotion spread little by little throughout the Church. She died on October 17, 1690. In 1765 Pope Clement XIII approved a Mass and Office for the feast; in 1850 Pope Pius IX extended the feast to the entire Church, and in 1900 Pope Leo XIII ordered that the whole world be consecrated to the Sacred Heart of Jesus. Finally Pope Pius XI raised the feast to the highest rank, with an octave. Margaret Mary was declared blessed in 1864 and canonized by Pope Benedict XV in 1920.

2. "Brethren: On me, least as I am of all saints, God has bestowed this privilege, of making known to the Gentiles the unfathomable riches of Christ" (Epistle). Our Lord opened to a humble nun the inscrutable treasures of His Heart (cf. Collect). He showed her His Heart aflame with love and said: "Behold the heart that so loved men that it exhausted itself for them. And for this it receives only ingratitude and neglect." It was then that our Lord commissioned her to promote a feast in the Church to call forth a return of the Savior's love, and to offer satisfaction for the insults hurled against it. This was a difficult task. There had, indeed, been those who venerated and adored the Sacred Heart before this time, but there had never been an official apostle or representative of this form of piety. Very soon difficulties arose; many of the other nuns thought that Margaret Mary was the victim of a deception; outside the convent there were some, especially the Jansenists, who were suspicious of this new devotion and who opposed it with all their might. Margaret Mary bore all this with humility and patience, saying: "I can occupy my mind with nothing but the divine heart of Jesus. I shall die content, if only I can procure a little honor for Him." Still, the opposition to the Sacred Heart plunged her "into an ocean of bitterness." "By the grace of God, I have been totally annihilated in the esteem of men. That pleases me more than I can say."

"Shade cool to rest under, fruit sweet to taste, such is He my heart longs for continually" (Introit). Margaret Mary lived entirely for the love of the Sacred Heart, thinking of no other

vocation after she received her command. By word and pen she
tried to acquaint all with whom she came in contact, with the
love of the heart of Jesus. She offered all her prayers, sacrifices,
sufferings and humiliations for this intention. One could give
her no greater joy than to show oneself receptive to this devotion; on the other hand, nothing pained her more acutely than
to meet with difficulties in its promotion. "All my prayers and
actions have the sole purpose of establishing the reign of the
heart of Jesus." Our Lord declared that He had given her such
rich graces in order to make her a sanctuary "in which the
fire of love shall always burn. . . . I have established in your
heart the rule of pure love." Thus she was enabled more and
more "to measure, in all its breadth and length and height and
depth, the love of Christ, to know what passes knowledge"
(Epistle); to measure that love which reveals itself under the
symbol of the Sacred Heart. "Behold, the heart that has loved
you so much." In her love for the Savior she courageously accepted calumnies: "Love is a fire no waters avail to quench,
no floods to drown. This frame, this earthly being of mine must
come to an end; still God will comfort my heart, God will be,
eternally, my inheritance" (Gradual). "My beloved is all mine,
and I am his; see where he goes out to pasture among the lilies"
(Communion).

3. "God has chosen what the world holds base and contemptible . . . so as to bring to nothing what is now in being" (I
Cor. 1:28). This unpretentious nun received a magnificent mission for the benefit of the Church and carried it through.

In the concluding prayer of the Mass we ask Christ that we
"may have grace to strip ourselves of this world's overweening
vanities, and to put on the meekness and humility of [His]
own heart." May St. Margaret Mary obtain for us a profoundly
devout understanding of the divine gift that is ours and a
fervent love of this Sacred Heart.

With the Saint we pray: "I choose Thee, most Sacred Heart
of Jesus, to be my only love, the protector of my life, the pledge

of my salvation, the strength of my weakness and instability, as the atonement for all the sins of my entire life. O meek and kind Heart, be Thou my refuge in the hour of my death. Heart of love, in Thee I place all my trust. From my weakness and wickedness I fear everything, but from Thy goodness I hope for everything."

Collect: Lord Jesus Christ, who didst wondrously reveal the inscrutable treasures of Thy heart to the blessed maiden Margaret Mary, through her merits and example give us grace to love Thee above all and in all things, so that we may deserve to have in that same heart of Thine our everlasting abode. Amen.

OCTOBER 18

St. Luke, *Evangelist*

1. Luke the physician (cf. Col. 4:14) was a fellowworker of St. Paul. A convert from paganism he probably joined the Apostle about the year 50 or 51 when, on his second missionary journey, the latter first set foot on European soil (cf. Acts 16:10). Having gone to Philippi with Paul and remained there for some time, he went to Jerusalem about the year 58 and then to Rome, where he ministered to Paul in prison. During Paul's second captivity (about 65 to 67) Luke was again with him (cf. II Tim. 4:11). He is the author of the third Gospel and of the "Acts of the Apostles." Legend says that he later became a painter, the first to paint the Madonna, and that he died a martyr.

2. "We are sending with him [Titus] that brother of ours, who has won the praise of all the churches . . . [and] of whose eagerness we have had good proof, in many ways and upon many occasions" (Epistle). The liturgy understands St. Paul to be speaking of Luke here, for, by his authorship of the third Gospel the latter had become well-known in all the con-

gregations. The burden of his Gospel is the merciful love of God toward sinful mankind. He portrays Jesus as the Savior of the miserable and the neglected, the poor and the sinning, who announces the good tidings of God's goodness. For Luke Jesus is the kindly, pitying Redeemer who came to seek and save what was lost, who forgave the sinful woman (7:36–50), who entered the house of the Publican Zachaeus (19:1 ff.), who promised paradise to the penitent thief on the cross (23:42). Luke claimed to have "put the story [of Jesus] in writing . . . as it befell, having first traced it carefully from its beginnings" (1:3). We are grateful to him for this consoling picture of the Savior, and particularly for the lovely portrait of the Virgin-Mother that he alone of the Evangelists has given us (the Annunciation, Visitation, Magnificat, Shepherds at the Crib, Presentation in the Temple, Finding of the twelve-year-old Jesus in the Temple).

Luke "continually bore in his own body the sufferings of the cross" (Collect). We recall the occasion on which he traveled with St. Paul from Philippi over Miletus in Asia Minor to Jerusalem (Acts 20:5–15; 21:1–10), when Paul fell into the hands of the Jews. "The whole city was in a commotion, and the common folk ran up from all sides. They seized Paul and dragged him out of the Temple . . . and they were preparing to kill him" (Acts 21:30). The Roman officer rescued Paul from the rage of the Jews, had him bound with two chains, and eventually, took him to Caesarea, where the Apostle spent two years in mild captivity. Then followed the difficult journey to Roman captivity, with its many trials and dangers, all of which Luke described minutely as an eyewitness. He stayed courageously at Paul's side during both captivities (cf. II Tim. 4:11) and was probably a witness to his martyrdom. It is evident that Luke suffered much with his master. An ancient preface for the feast of this Evangelist speaks of the "cross of renunciation": "Thou, King of glory, hast granted invincible strength to those who fight against the snares of the ancient serpent and the weakness of their own body. One of them, Thy blessed Evangelist Luke, took up the shield of faith, the helmet of salvation, and the sword of the Holy Spirit; and thus, he fought bravely against vices, so that the stream of evangelical sweetness might flow to us."

3. "I am sending you out to be like lambs among wolves. You are not to carry purse, or wallet, or shoes; you are to give no one greeting on your way" (Gospel). The disciples were sent out to labor for the cause of the Master. A disciple of Jesus should be poor and uncomplaining; he should restrict his requirements to bare necessities and not allow himself to be hindered by useless talking in the fulfillment of his task. When he speaks it should not be in his own name, but as a messenger of God. Today's Gospel sketches the spirit and conduct of St. Luke.

We can honor the memory of this Evangelist in a special way by reading his book and contemplating the Savior whom he has depicted in such charming and encouraging style.

We are also indebted to St. Luke for the "Acts of the Apostles," in which he eloquently traces the victorious progress of Christianity from Jerusalem to the various parts of the Roman Empire. By means of this story, written for the converts of St. Paul, he hoped to strengthen the faith of Christians in the divine origin of their religion. With reason, the work has been called the "Gospel of the Holy Ghost," because Luke earmarks the great events he records as the work of the Holy Spirit.

Collect: Lord, we pray Thee let Thy holy evangelist Luke, who for the honor of Thy name continually bore in his own body the sufferings of the cross, make intercession for us. Amen.

OCTOBER 24

St. Raphael the Archangel

1. The name of this Archangel signifies, "God heals." Raphael accompanied Tobias on a trip, freed Raguel's daughter Sara from an evil spirit, and healed the blindness of the elder Tobias. Raphael is one of the seven spirits that stand before the throne of God (cf. Tob. 12:15; Apoc. 1:4–8:2). He is honored as the patron of travelers and of the sick.

2. "O God, who didst send the blessed archangel Raphael to accompany thy servant Tobias on his journey" (Collect). The story is contained in the book of Tobias. The father wanted to send his son to collect a debt in Medea. A young man offered to be the youth's guide on the long journey. They spent their first night on the bank of the Tigris and, when Tobias was washing his feet, a large fish swam up, frightening him. His companion called to him to pull it out on the land: "The fish . . . is worth the bowelling; heart and gall and liver of it thou must keep by thee, sovereign remedies all" (Tob. 6:4). The two young men traveled to the home of Raguel, a relative of Tobias, whose daughter, Sara, pleased Tobias, and, after Raphael had delivered her from an evil spirit, he married her. During the two-week celebration of the marriage, the angel went alone to Medea and collected the debt. Then the three returned to the home of the elder Tobias. The latter's blindness was cured by the medicine Raphael had prescribed, and joy then reigned in the home. Father and son offered their mysterious companion half of their new-found wealth; "but he, with a finger on his lip, bade them give their thanks to the God of heaven. . . . He it is that has shown mercy to you. . . . Come, let me tell you the whole truth of the matter. . . . When thou, Tobias, wert praying, and with tears, when thou wert burying the dead . . . I, all the while, was offering that

prayer of thine to the Lord . . . he has chosen me for his messenger. . . . I am the angel Raphael, and my place is among the seven who stand in the presence of the Lord." Thereupon, the angel disappeared, but the family lay prostrate for three hours, praising God (cf. Tob. 12:6–15). The ways of God are full of mystery. The elder Tobias had been subjected to many tribulations but had persevered in serving God faithfully. At length God had sent His messenger, Raphael, to change all his sorrows into joys. "How great a Lord is ours, how magnificent his strength!" (Gradual.)

"From time to time, an angel of the Lord came down upon the pool, and the water was stirred up" (Gospel). Here again the liturgy is thinking of Raphael, the angel who helps and heals. For us the waters of the pool are a symbol, the image of baptism and of the grace of the Holy Spirit who sanctifies the baptismal water; by His angel he stirs up the water, that is, He makes it capable of conferring life. "The first man who stepped into the pool after the stirring of the water, recovered from whatever infirmity it was that oppressed him" (Gospel). Gratefully we think of the moment when we were baptized. "Angels for my witness, I will sing of thy praise . . . giving thanks, Lord, to thy name" (Alleluia verse).

3. In the liturgy we are the ones led by the angel of God to a distant country, heaven. He leads wisely and safely; if there is danger he saves us from it, and then admonishes: "Bless the Lord of heaven and thank Him before all the living, because He has shown mercy to you," by calling you to Christ, so that one day you may be taken into the company of the angels and saints. We are the sick people of the Gospel story; we are the ones expecting a cure during the Holy Sacrifice. We beg St. Raphael to make his guidance and help effective in us.

Joyfully, in the celebration of the Eucharistic Sacrifice, we become conscious of our fellowship with the adoring angels. We call upon them to praise the Lord with us: "Bless the Lord, all you angels of his; angels of sovereign strength, that

carry out his commandment, attentive to the word he utters"
(Introit). "Thy majesty is praised by Angels, adored by Dom-
inations, feared by Powers; . . . the celestial virtues join with
the blessed Seraphim in one glad hymn of praise. We pray thee
let our voices blend with theirs as we humbly praise thee,
singing: Holy, Holy, Holy Lord God of hosts. Thy glory fills
all heaven and earth. Hosanna in high heaven!" (Preface.)
Holy Communion enables us to behold and desire the eternal,
blessed com-union with the praising angels.

Collect: O God, who didst send the blessed archangel Raphael
to accompany Thy servant Tobias on his journey, grant that we Thy
servants may ever be guarded by his care and strengthened by his
aid. Amen.

OCTOBER 28

Sts. Simon *and* Jude, *Apostles*

1. Simon, called "The Zealot," probably because he had
formerly clung passionately to the observance of the Mosaic
law, was chosen by our Lord to be an Apostle of the New Law
(Matt. 10:4; Mark 3:18). There is reason to believe that he
succeeded St. James as bishop of Jerusalem and prudently
directed his people during the turmoil of the Jewish war. Tradition says he gained a martyr's crown by crucifixion under
Emperor Trajan, about the year 107.

Jude was a brother of the Apostle James the Younger, son
of Alpheus and Mary, the "sister" of the Blessed Virgin. Known
as a "brother of the Lord" (cf. Matt. 13:55), he was also called
Thaddeus. He is said to have announced the gospel in Syria
and to have become a martyr in Beirut. Another account assigns his preaching to Mesopotamia and Persia. He is the
author of the so-called "catholic Epistle" in which he urgently

warns the Christian communities of Palestine to beware of heretical teachers.

2. "Great reverence have I for thy friends, O God; sovereign power is theirs in abundance" (Introit). The Apostles were the friends of Christ: "I do not speak of you any more as my servants; a servant is one who does not understand what his master is about, whereas I have made known to you all that my Father has told me; and so I have called you my friends" (John 15:15). Because they are intimate friends of our Lord, with whom He lived for three years, whose meals He shared, in whom He confided, and whom He made the pillars of His Church, the Church honors them, and reveres them as Apostles. We recognize their dignity, their oneness with Christ, the rich graces and the privileged position of honor He gave them in His kingdom. We joyfully recognize their authority in the kingdom of the Church. We honor the faithfulness with which they followed our Lord, carried out His command to teach all nations, and sealed their testimony with their blood. "Great reverence have I for thy friends, O God."

"If you belonged to the world, the world would know you for its own and love you; it is because you do not belong to the world, because I have singled you out from the midst of the world, that the world hates you. . . . They will persecute you just as they have persecuted me; they will pay the same attention to your words as to mine" (Gospel). Christ honored his Apostles by asserting that they were not of the world. They judged, thought, and lived differently from earthly-minded people, who were "children of disobedience," giving themselves up to the impulses of their lower natures (cf. Col. 3:5), "whose lives make them the enemies of Christ's cross" (Phil. 3:18). That was why the Apostles were rejected and persecuted by the world. Woe to the apostle of Christ, woe to the Church, woe to the priest, woe to the Christian who is considered as one of its own by the world, by the enemies of the

Crucified. In the offering of the Holy Sacrifice as in the rough reality of life we unite ourselves with Him who chose the Cross and who segregated us from the world so that we might become one victim with Himself, offered and dedicated to God with Himself. "No servant can be greater than his master. They will persecute you just as they have persecuted me." It was in baptism that we entered into this fellowship with the cross and Christ: in the Eucharistic celebration we renew it. The Apostles lead the way; we follow them.

3. Are we truly not of the world? We can give a positive answer to this question if we are doing as our Lord did, returning love for hatred—a love that barters life itself to redeem anyone who has done evil to us. "Love your enemies, do good to those who hate you, pray for those who persecute and insult you" (Matt. 5:44), for the sake of Christ. Such was the conduct of Sts. Simon and Jude.

"It is for you, beloved, to make your holy faith the foundation of your lives, and to go on praying in the power of the Holy Spirit; to maintain yourselves in the love of God, and wait for the mercy of our Lord Jesus Christ, with eternal life for your goal. . . . There is but one who can keep you clear of fault, and enable you to stand in the presence of his glory, triumphant and unreproved, when our Lord Jesus Christ comes; to him, who alone is God, to him, who gives us salvation through Jesus Christ our Lord, glory and majesty and power and domination are due, before time was, and now, and for all ages" (Jude 20–25).

Collect: O God, who through Thy blessed apostles Simon and Jude hast brought us to a knowledge of Thy name, grant that by advancing in holiness we may celebrate their lasting glory, and by celebrating it become holier still. Amen.

Feast of the Dedication of a Church

With gratitude and joy we commemorate the day on which the bishop solemnly blessed our church. First, he prayed the seven penitential psalms; then he blessed water and sprinkled the walls of the church from the outside. Entering in to take possession of it for God, he walked around the interior three times, sprinkling the walls. He then called down the grace of consecration upon the building and carried relics in solemn procession to place them in the "tomb" of the altar stone. Then the church was a holy place, a dwelling of God among men.

2. "This is a fearsome place: it is the house of God, the gate of heaven: it shall be named the palace of God. Lord of hosts, how I love thy dwelling-place! For the courts of the Lord's house, my soul faints with longing" (Introit). God is present everywhere, in the house in which we live as well as in every stone or grass blade we tread on. He also lives in our souls and draws them lovingly to Himself, filling them with His light and strength, speaking to them, admonishing them, enlightening them, inspiring them to good deeds and preserving them from sin and misfortune. But in the church God dwells and acts in an entirely unique manner. Here alone does the Son-of-God-made-man dwell in the tabernacle, with His divinity and humanity, flesh and blood, body and soul, sympathizing with us and remaining near us. Here on our altar He continues the Sacrifice of adoration, thanksgiving, praise, atonement, satisfaction, and petition for us. Here in our church He lives and prays to the Father unceasingly in our stead.

In this "House of God" we may come to Him, holding loving conversation with Him, open our hearts, and tell Him that we want to love Him; that we are sorry for weakness and shortcomings that prevent us from giving Him joy. Here we may present all the needs and cares of our own or of loved ones, of the entire Church, of the well and the sick, and of those in danger of losing faith or innocence. Here He exercises His office of Savior through the sacraments. Here, in Holy Communion, He daily becomes the sweet nourishment of our souls. His mysterious union with the divine nature of God the Father and God the Holy Spirit is closer here than elsewhere: "Here is God's tabernacle pitched among men; he will dwell with them, and they will be his own people, and he will be among them, their own God" (Lesson).

"O God, fill this house with the magnificence of thy powerful presence, and grant that all who assemble here for prayer may obtain the grace of Thy consolation, no matter what tribulation it was that made them cry out to Thee." Thus the bishop and the Church prayed on that day of dedication. As she prayed, so the Church believes that her prayers will not go unanswered in this holy place. Here, "Everyone that asks, will receive; that seeks, will find; that knocks, will have the door opened" (Matt. 7:8). "Open my eyes shall be, my ears attentive to every man's prayer that here prays to me; I have set this place apart and hallowed it, to be the shrine of my name for all time; never a day but my eyes shall be watching, my heart be attentive here" (II Par. 7:15 ff.). (These words God addressed to Solomon at the dedication of the Temple in Jerusalem.) The dedicated church is called a sacramental, a holy place, in which, by virtue of the prayer that the Church recited, we may expect to have our petitions granted.

3. "On this day, salvation has come to this house," that is, on the day when, for the first time, the Lord entered into it at the celebration of the Holy Sacrifice. Today, every day, salvation comes when Christ appears on the altar at the Consecration. Then the church becomes the house of Zacchaeus, where He is "received with joy." We are the Church; the Lord comes to us; we receive Him joyfully on the altar and in our mouths.

How we should miss our parish church if we had none! We should miss the baptismal font, the pulpit, the altar, the tabernacle. God has been good to us in giving and preserving our church. On the anniversary of its dedication we look back and consider the many graces we have received in the House of God since our childhood. This is an occasion that calls for humble gratitude.

Our church, in which God so graciously dwells among us, is a reminder of the goal of all of us—heaven and God. There "he will dwell with them, and they will be his own people, and he will be among them, their own God. He will wipe away every tear from their eyes, and there will be no more death, or mourning, or cries of distress, or more sorrow; those old things have passed away" (Lesson).

Collect: O God, who year by year renewest for us the dedication-day of this holy temple of Thine, and still bringest us safe and sound to take part in its sacred rites, heed the prayers of Thy people, and grant that whosoever enters this church to seek Thy favors may receive with joy all that he asks. Amen.

Last Sunday of October

The Kingship of Our Lord Jesus Christ

1. "The Lord is King." This is a day of thanksgiving to the Father, who has conferred universal kingship on His divine Son, the glorious hero of untold sufferings and humiliations. It is a day of homage to the man Christ, to whom "all power was given in heaven and on earth." "His dominion will reach from sea to sea, from the great river [Euphrates] to the ends of the earth. All the kings of the earth shall bring their homage, all the nations serve him" (Gradual). We, too, do homage and serve Him.

2. The Gospel of today's Mass concerns itself with that important moment in the history of mankind when Jesus was brought by the Jews to the judgment seat of Pilate, representa-

tive of pagan Roman world-power. "Art thou the king of the
Jews? . . . Thou art a king, then? Pilate asked. Jesus answered: It is thy own lips that have called me a king. What I
was born for, what I came into the world for, is to bear witness
to the truth. . . . My kingdom . . . does not belong to this
world." It is, rather, the kingdom of God, which is the Church,
full of grace and truth. It is God's realm, in which we are safe
from the dominion of Satan and sin, and become sharers in the
divine freedom. It is God's rule that rejoices our hearts with
its divine activity in us. It postulates that our thinking and
striving be rooted in God by virtue of our living union with
Christ, the Head. Jesus brought this kingdom to earth, establishing it by His teaching and example, but especially by His
death on the Cross. He gives laws and commands; all judgment
is His (cf. John 5:22). "Everything in heaven and on earth
and under the earth must bend the knee before the name of
Jesus, and every tongue must confess Jesus Christ as the Lord,
dwelling in the glory of God the Father" (Phil. 2:10, 11). We
render joyful homage: "Power and Godhead, wisdom and
strength, and glory are his by right, the Lamb that was slain.
Glory and power be his through endless ages" (Introit). "The
Lord sits enthroned as King forever; the Lord will give his
people his own blessing of peace" (Communion).

God has transferred us "to the kingdom of his beloved Son"
and made us partakers of this kingdom. "In the Son of God, in
his blood, we find the redemption that sets us free from our
sins." Emancipated from the power of sin, we obtain the life of
grace, sonship of God, power over the world, over the flesh,
over the urge of evil passions; we receive God's gift of interior
freedom of heart and spirit in the possession of His life. In
addition there is the expectation we have of being taken up
into the future kingdom of endless glory. "We return thanks
to God our Father for making us fit to share the light which
saints inherit, for rescuing us from the power of darkness, and
transferring us to the kingdom of his beloved Son" (Epistle).

3. He is the true likeness of the God we cannot see; His is that first birth which precedes every act of creation"; He is the eternal Son of God, God from God, light from light, begotten, not made. It was through Him that all things came into being; everything was made by Him and for Him. All the marvelous and beautiful things that the universe contains are His property. He is the rightful master of the spirit, will, heart and body of man. To Him belong heaven and earth; He has the might and the right to make use of all earthly things. In every way the primacy was to become His. It was God's pleasure to let all completeness dwell in Him, the man Jesus Christ. He must be King also over me, my very being and existence. I must live for whatever He wishes of me.

We rejoice with Holy Church that the Father made Him Lord and King of the universe, saying: "Ask thy will of me, and thou shalt have the nations for thy patrimony; the very ends of the world for thy domain" (Offertory). "Christ conquers; Christ rules; Christ is King" (Inscription on the obelisk in St. Peter's square, Rome).

The Lord is a king; He directs with strong hand His kingdom, His Church, our souls. Powerful enemies will besiege His kingdom in vain. "Do not be afraid, you, my little flock. Your Father has determined to give you his kingdom" (Luke 12:32).

We dedicate ourselves and all we have to Christ the King. We pray that all men, all races and nations of the earth may bow to His dominion.

Collect: Almighty, everliving God, who hast willed that in Thy beloved Son, the universal king, all things should be made new, grant in Thy loving-kindness that all peoples of the earth, now torn asunder by the wound of sin, may be subdued to the gentle sway of Him who is God. Amen.

NOVEMBER

NOVEMBER 1

All Saints

1. *"Gaudeamus!* Rejoice we all in the Lord, as we keep holiday in honor of all the saints; whose feast makes angels joyful and sets them praising the Son of God" (Introit). We join the angels in singing the praises of the "King of all the saints," of Christ, our Lord and Redeemer. We are conscious of our fellowship with our happy brethren in heaven in the oneness of the body of Christ.

2. "Then I saw a great multitude, past all counting, taken from all nations and tribes and peoples and languages. These stood before the throne in the Lamb's presence, clothed in white robes, with palm-branches in their hands, and cried with a loud voice, To our God, who sits on the throne, and to the Lamb, all saving power belongs. And all the angels that were standing round the throne, round the elders and the living figures, fell prostrate before the throne and paid God worship; Amen, they cried, blessing and glory and wisdom and thanksgiving and honour and power and strength belong to our God through endless ages, Amen" (Lesson). These are blessed, happy ones who are saved and are praising God for His goodness to them. It is these whom the Gradual addresses: "Those who fear him never go wanting. Those who search for the Lord are denied none of his blessings." They possess Him and in Him the fullness of good things. They are perfectly satisfied, eternally content. "Come to me, all you who labor and are burdened; I will give you rest [in heaven]" (Alleluia verse). We rejoice with our redeemed brethren in their happy attainment of their goal. We, too, have been created for heaven.

The road on which they have sought and found their goal is the one pointed out unmistakably by Christ: "Ever since John the Baptist's time, the kingdom of heaven has opened to force: and the forceful are even now making it their prize" (Matt. 11:12). Anyone who thinks he can gain heaven without doing violence to himself, without conquering, without daily dying to his own will—such a one is deceiving himself. Those who enter heaven are the "poor in spirit," who have freed themselves from everything that is not God: the meek, who bear insult and injustice calmly, without returning evil; those who have renounced the world's enjoyments to find their joy in God; those who hunger for justice and earnestly work to sanctify themselves; the merciful, who sincerely sympathize with their brethren in bodily or spiritual distress; the clean of heart who fly from every willful imperfection; the peace-lovers, who cling to God's good pleasure and thus preserve peace of soul; those who for Christ's sake bear rash judgment and slanderous abuse in patience. To all these our Lord's promise applies: "Be glad and light-hearted, for a rich reward awaits you in heaven" (Gospel).

3. "These . . . have come out of the great affliction; they have washed their robes white in the blood of the Lamb. And now they stand before God's throne. . . . They will not be hungry or thirsty any more. . . . The Lamb, who dwells where the throne is, will be their shepherd, leading them out to the springs whose water is life; and God will wipe away every tear from their eyes" (Apoc. 7:14–17). "God's throne (which is the Lamb's throne) will be there, with his servants to worship him, and to see his face, his name written on their foreheads . . . the Lord God will shed his light on them, and they will reign for ever and ever" (Apoc. 22:3–5). Truly, "the souls of the just are in God's hands, beyond the reach of their tormentors' malice. Fools account them dead, but all is well with them" (Offertory).

All Saints is the day of the triumph of grace over fallen human nature; the triumph of the Church; the triumph of her doctrine, her preaching, her sacraments and her priesthood. By the power of the Holy Eucharist, especially, the Church has turned sinners into saints. In the strength of this Sacrament our brothers and sisters in Christ have, in spite of human weakness, walked the way of the beatitudes and become holy. We therefore remain true to the Church and her Sacrifice; we too are on the sure way to heaven.

The saints of heaven whom we contemplate admiringly today are the fruit of the Incarnation of the Son of God, of His "emptying Himself and becoming obedient unto death." In the saints we see ultimately Christ Himself, the working of His grace, of His spirit, of His power. He continues to live His life on earth in them, just as the vine lives on in the branches. It is a life of voluntary self-denial, obedience, virginity, adoration, surrender to God, penance, and atonement. The saints are what they are entirely through Christ; they are reflections of the power of the King of apostles, martyrs, confessors, and virgins. We recognize in them the power of the Redemption. The same power of Christ that was operative in the saints and led them to the heights of holiness is at work in us too, who are called to the heights of Christian virtue and sanctity; and it will accomplish that end in us.

Collect: Almighty, everlasting God, by whose leave we pay homage to the merits of all Thy saints in one great festival, we pray Thee bestow upon us, at their manifold intercession, the fullness of that mercy of Thine, for which we long. Amen.

NOVEMBER 2

All Souls' Day

1. In the Martyrology the following announcement appears: "Today, the commemoration of all the faithful departed is observed. Mother Church, through her powerful intercession with their Lord and Spouse, is at pains to help all those who are

detained in purgatory, so that they may soon attain to the fellowship of the saints in heaven." The Church exercises a loving solicitude for the departed on this day, in a special observance; her love is one not only of sympathy but also of action.

2. The Mother of all the faithful sympathizes with those who are in need, that is, those who are temporarily excluded from the possession and enjoyment of God. These souls are indeed at rest in Christ by a living union with Him; they are in the state of grace; they are saved and know for certain that they will one day come to the eternal vision of God. But they are still deprived of the enjoyment of "eternal light"; they are still held by the "bonds of sin" until they will have suffered the punishment deserved by their sins. There clings to them still the "stain of their earthly guilt." They long for God, for their eternal home, for the place of "refreshment, light, and peace," for the "bliss of rest," for "everlasting joy in the Land of the living." This separation from God is most painful to them: they love Him alone, and yet they may not possess or see Him, nor rest on His heart. They are still not worthy of this, and they are aware that their sins and infidelities and their insufficient sorrow are causing this painful delay. Though they deeply regret their earthly negligences, such compunction is no longer worthy of merit; their time of earning ended with death. For them night has fallen, "when there is no working any more" (John 9:4). Now they can only suffer until they have canceled their debt to divine justice. The Church realizes their helpless need; that is why she has set aside this day of co-suffering, on which she wants us to assume a share of their atonement through sympathetic prayer and penance.

The Church's love for the faithful departed, however, does not stop at sympathy. She knows she can assist them by her prayer, especially by the Sacrifice of the Mass; so she prays earnestly and lets every priest offer the Holy Sacrifice three times on this day, so that a veritable flood of grace may inundate the place of purgation and carry many souls away to heaven.

On this day the faithful on earth may gain any number of plenary indulgences for the Poor Souls. In a spirit of charity we should second the efforts of the Church by making November in a special sense a month of active solicitude for the Poor Souls. In addition to private prayer and the offering of Masses, we should exert ourselves to gain many indulgences for those bound in purgatory.

3. When we offer the Holy Sacrifice we take the heart of Jesus with its redemptive blood into our hands, as it were, and offer it to the Father in satisfaction for the debt of atonement owed Him by the souls in purgatory. In that way we blot out their sentence with the Precious Blood, praying meanwhile: "Remember . . . Lord, Thy servants who have gone before us with the sign of faith and sleep the sleep of peace. To them, Lord, and to all who rest in Christ, grant, we entreat Thee, a place of cool repose, of light and peace" (Memento in Mass).

"Lord, in praise of Thee we offer sacrifice and prayer; accept them for the good of those souls whom we call to mind this day. Lord, make them pass from death [purgatory and exclusion from God] to life, which Thou of old didst promise to Abraham and his posterity" (Offertory).

Collect: O God, creator and redeemer of all the faithful, grant to the souls of Thy departed servants forgiveness of all their sins. Let our loving entreaties obtain for them the pardon they have always desired. Amen.

NOVEMBER

The Month of All Souls—I

1. In the liturgy we repeat over and over again the petition that God may grant the "remission of all sins" to the souls in purgatory; that they may, by the power of the Holy Sacrifice, be "cleansed of all sin, freed from every bond of guilt"; that they may receive pardon, "being purified by this Sacrifice and freed from sin." "If any stain of earthly filth still clings to them, may it be washed away by this merciful forgiveness of thine."

2. "Grant to the souls of thy servants the remission of all sins." Do the Poor Souls still have venial sins to atone for? According to a well-founded opinion of theologians, the Christian receives, whether at the moment of death or immediately after, the grace to make an act of perfect contrition. This would, of course, wipe out the guilt of venial sins, without, however, removing the necessity of atonement for them. With this in mind, then, we pray with the Church: "Grant, O Lord, to thy servants and handmaids the remission of all sins," that is, of the temporal punishment which would have to be undergone after death. Nothing unclean can enter heaven. The prayers of the Church, no matter how long after a person's death they are applied to him, are accepted by God as having been offered in the moment of his death and are thus fitted into God's eternal plans for his soul. In this way, the prayers which the Church offers today benefit the soul at the hour of death. As we participate in the Church's suffrages each year, then, we confidently expect to be heard and never weary of repeating our "*Requiem aeternam;* Lord, grant them eternal rest, and let everlasting light shine upon them." Surely we are partly to blame for the stay of many souls in purgatory, and this realization should spur us on to greater efforts to obtain their release.

"Grant the souls of all the departed liberation from every bond of sin." What debt is it then, that still burdens the souls in purgatory? Not the guilt of venial sins, nor of possible perverse attachments. These souls have their wills intimately united with the will of God; they love Him with all their being; their wills are so completely one with His that they desire nothing but what He desires. Therefore they submit to the sufferings of purgatory willingly, gladly, because they know their beloved God wills it. They want to suffer all that He imposes as long as He chooses. No, the souls in purgatory have no sinful attachments or inclinations any more. The "bonds of guilt" that hold them are solely the so-called temporal punishments. God is holy and just: every sin, even the smallest, against His majesty calls for atonement, if it was a conscious offense. Unless the punishment has been undergone on earth, it will be imposed in purgatory. Death puts a stop to all growth in grace or virtue or merit; however, no contrition in purgatory can alter the soul's status or hasten the union with God, or bring greater bliss in heaven. Whatever happens in purgatory, up to the moment when all temporal punishment has been remitted, is only satisfaction due for the past. Only at that last moment is the soul pure enough to appear before God to be assigned to the place won by the merits it possessed at the hour of death.

3. The Poor Souls are subjected to a twofold penalty: the first is temporary exclusion from the vision and full possession of God while they satisfy justice for all their infidelities; this is the essential punishment of purgatory, and its severity surpasses all power of the imagination. In addition there are specific punishments to match the particular created things which each soul clung to sinfully. These are severe pains, because the soul freed from the body has acquired such tenderness and sensitivity that it suffers intensely. Small wonder that our brethren in purgatory long for the day of liberation. Their desire for God and for release from torment makes

minutes and hours seem like years and centuries. We can help
to lift their burden; we can free them from temporal punishment. Does this not become a sacred duty of charity for us?

God is holy; nothing defiled can come in contact with Him.
God is just; no one shall leave the prison until he has paid the
last farthing (cf. Matt. 5:26). But God is also merciful; He is
pleased when we assume the debt which the Poor Souls themselves cannot pay. He loves them and wants to shorten the
time of their exclusion from heaven. As fellow members of the
body of Christ, we can do that. No doubt we could do more
than we have been doing; we could participate in the Holy
Sacrifice with keener consciousness of our power to satisfy the
heavenly Father for our brothers in purgatory. We could pray
more assiduously and offer up more work, more self-denial. We
could carry our crosses more patiently, offer our satisfactions
more consistently and more earnestly for them. Is not the so-
called "heroic act" something greatly pleasing to God, a magnificent "good work"?

Collect: O God, creator and redeemer of all the faithful, grant to
the souls of Thy departed servants forgiveness of all their sins. Let
our loving entreaties obtain for them the pardon they have always
desired. Amen.

NOVEMBER

The Month of All Souls—II

1. In offering Mass for the deceased the Church places herself, as it were, beside the deathbed of the one for whom the
Holy Sacrifice is being offered. Her thought is that the deceased will, through this holy Mass, come to enjoy the longed-
for glorification in heaven. To the Church the Mass is not only
a sacrifice of praise and thanksgiving, but it is also one of
propitiation. Here our Lord offers, together with His Church,

all His infinite satisfaction to the Father, for the benefit of the living and the dead. "Lord, grant them eternal rest and let perpetual light shine upon them."

2. "O God, thou shalt have praise in Sion; to thee let the vow be paid in Jerusalem" (Introit psalm). This is a song of thanksgiving taken from the harvest psalm of the Church of the Old Testament. When one of her children dies, the Church celebrates a harvest feast. In the departed for whom she offers the Mass she reaps the fruit of God's merciful grace sown by the labors of her own motherhood. With grateful and hopeful heart, she offers the fruit of the Holy Sacrifice as golden wheat on the paten. At the consecration this gift is united with the Sacrifice of our Lord and carried by Him, the High Priest, into the realm of Light. There it becomes a never-ending hymn of praise to God and His mercy, of thanks that will forever recall His graces. Thus does the Church believe and act regarding her departed children. Her Requiem Mass is not so much a lament as it is a rejoicing that God has once again perfected and received one of her children into His glory. It was for this reason that the liturgy of ancient times added to our present Introit the psalm verse: "Blessed is he whom thou dost select and take up in grace: he is privileged to dwell in thy courts." This was believed to be the fruit of the Holy Sacrifice in which the departed had participated during life and which now is being offered as if at the moment of his death. By virtue of this Sacrifice, then, he receives for his soul the "eternal light" of glory; for his body, the right of eventual resurrection from the grave (cf. Gospel).

"Lord, in praise of Thee we offer sacrifice and prayer; accept them for the good of those souls whom we call to mind this day." At the Offertory, the Church offers gifts of bread and wine as tokens of her prayers and petitions to Christ, the "King of Glory." The liturgy looks upon this act as taking place at the moment of death when the departed soul appeared before its Lord to receive sentence regarding admission to or exclusion from the kingdom of eternal glory. Meanwhile, the Church prays fervently: "Lord Jesus Christ, king of glory . . . save [this soul] from the lion's jaws . . . let [it] not be engulfed in hell nor swallowed up in darkness. Let St. Michael the standard-bearer bring [it] into that holy light which thou of old didst promise to Abraham and his posterity" (Offertory). In this attitude of prayer and sacrifice the Church awaits the coming of the Lord; and He comes at the moment of consecration. He comes laden with graces; He comes to take home the soul that the Church and St. Michael have presented and recommended. He unites it with His own offering and pays the price of its redemption with His own blood. This gives full satisfaction for the temporal punishment still due. The Church has offered to the heavenly Father Christ's prayers and atonement, His suffering and death, His precious blood, as a fully effective expiatory sacrifice for all that this child still owes its Father. "Look kindly upon our offerings and graciously accept them." We receive Holy Communion, and, by virtue of the fellowship that unites our departed brother with us and with Christ, the deceased is invisibly joined to God in the Communion of eternal life. That is the hopeful expectation of the Communion song: "Eternal light shine upon them, Lord: with thy saints . . . thou art merciful."

3. The Church is fully convinced of the effectiveness of the Holy Sacrifice in regard to life, death, and purgatory. She counts on the satisfactions of Christ and His saints which ascend to God during Holy Mass. With the same faith we join in the Sacrifice.

Fortunate is he who is a member of the Church, who lives in and with her. If we are true to our incorporation in the Church we become, in life, the mature fruit that will be appropriated at the hour of our death by the Church as a gift of gratitude and praise to God and Christ, our Lord. Happy we, if we live fully with the Church. She is our most reliable helper in life, in death, and in purgatory.

Collect: Lord, we pray Thee release the souls of Thy servants and handmaids from every bond of sin, so that in the glory of the resurrection they may rise again to life among Thy saints and Thy elect. Amen.

NOVEMBER

The Month of All Souls—III

1. In the liturgy of the Requiem Mass two thoughts predominate: deep sympathy with the need of souls detained in purgatory; the joyful certainty of their ultimate admission to heaven, and the resurrection of their bodies.

2. "Lord, grant them eternal rest." We think of those who died in Christ but are still, unfortunately, separated from God. They love Him devotedly and have broken with all else, clearly perceiving the emptiness of life without Him. They understand how foolishly they acted in not giving up sin and inordinate attachments to friends and honors, while on earth. They realize that they lightly shirked the mortifications which would have controlled certain secret desires. All these "trifles" have become chains that still hold them away from the Object of their longing. This is the keenest suffering of the Poor Souls, that through their own fault they must be separated from God. They long for nothing any more, only for God, their All. Their hunger becomes more violent and consuming the more they are purified, just as a stone falling from a height increases in velocity the nearer it approaches to earth. Every moment of delay increases their tormenting hunger; hence the liturgy begs: "Lord, give them eternal rest by admitting them to the blessed face of God. Let perpetual light shine upon them."

"It is the will of him who sent me, not my own will, that I have come down from heaven to do; and he who sent me would have me keep without loss, and raise up at the last day, all he has entrusted to me. Yes, this is the will of him who sent me, that all those who believe in the Son when they see him should enjoy eternal life; I am to raise them up at the last day" (Gospel of second Mass). The unalterable sentence of death depresses us, but the promise of future immortality encourages us. In Christ "there has dawned for us the hope of a blessed resurrection. . . . The life of those who are faithful to thee, Lord, is but changed, not ended; and when their earthly dwelling-place decays, an everlasting mansion stands prepared for them in heaven" (Preface). In the heart of the Church there dwells the hope of an early entrance into everlasting life, the confidence in a blissful resurrection for her children who have been taken out of this life. Her sadness at their distress is lessened and transformed to such an extent that she considers the Requiem Mass a thanksgiving (Eucharistic) service as well. "Right indeed it is and just, proper and for our welfare, that we should always and everywhere give thanks to thee, holy Lord, almighty Father, eternal God, through Christ our Lord. In him there has dawned for us the hope of a blessed resurrection. . . . Therefore . . . we chant an endless hymn in praise of thee, singing: Holy, holy, holy" (Preface). The Church knows that her children in purgatory are saved. God has already assigned them places in heaven; after a short time they will be permitted to rest on the Heart of God in eternal bliss.

3. "Eternal rest grant unto them, O Lord, and let perpetual light shine upon them. . . . Lord, release the souls of all the faithful departed from every bond of sin. By the help of thy grace enable them to escape avenging judgment. And to enjoy bliss in everlasting light" (Tract).

We share in the sufferings of the souls in purgatory, but, like the Church, we do so in the confident belief that they died in Christ and are saved. "In him there has dawned for us the hope of a blessed resurrection, heartening us with a promise of immortality."

Even if we make earnest efforts to help the Poor Souls, we are still not sure just how much profit this or that soul will derive from our prayers. St. Augustine holds the opinion that our prayers will help not only those for whom we offer them, but other souls also, if they disposed themselves during life by works of charity to receive our help. Did not our Lord say: "Forgive, and you will be forgiven. Give, and gifts will be yours" (Luke 6:38).

Collect: O God, creator and redeemer of all the faithful, grant to the souls of Thy departed servants forgiveness of all their sins. Let our loving entreaties obtain for them the pardon they have always desired. Amen.

NOVEMBER

The Communion of Saints

1. "Lord, grant them eternal rest, and let perpetual light shine upon them" (Introit). "Lord, release the souls of all the faithful departed from every bond of sin. By the help of thy grace enable them to escape avenging judgment" (Tract). "Grant, we pray thee, almighty God, that the souls of thy servants who have today departed from this world, may be cleansed by this sacrifice, and being thus rid of their sins, may find both forgiveness and everlasting rest" (Postcommunion). These and similar sentiments are the burden of our petitions to God in favor of the Poor Souls. We are convinced that prayers can still profit our dear departed after their remains have been consigned to the grave. The sacred bonds that united us with them during their earthly life have not been suddenly severed. We are still members of the same family; and spiritual intercourse is possible by virtue of the Communion of Saints.

2. "And you are Christ's body, organs of it depending upon each other" (I Cor. 12:27). "It was his [God's] loving design,

centered in Christ, to give history its fulfillment by resuming everything in him. . . . He has made him the head to which the whole Church is joined, so that the Church is his body" (Eph. 1:10, 22). All who are incorporated in this body of Christ belong to the Communion of Saints, that supernatural sharing of life by which all who are redeemed and sanctified in Christ are joined with Him and with one another. The saints of heaven, the suffering souls of purgatory, and we members of the Church Militant on earth are united to form the one body of Christ; and we are destined to reach the goal of eternal life, working together and helping each other in charity. For we stand in the same living relationship with one another as do the members of a body. "If one part is suffering, all the rest suffer with it; if one part is treated with honor, all the rest find pleasure in it" (I Cor. 12:26). In virtue of the vital bond uniting all Christians in this body, we are expected to help the souls in purgatory attain to perfection in Christ and the enjoyment of the life of the blessed. This we can do by offering prayers and sacrifices for them. "Thus God has established a harmony in the body. . . . There was to be no want of unity in the body; all the different parts of it were to make each other's welfare their common care" (I Cor. 12:25). In God's plan, we are responsible for helping the Poor Souls.

"Bear the burden of one another's failings; then you will be fulfilling the law of Christ" (Gal. 6:2). The souls of our brethren in purgatory are bearing the burden of temporal punishment which they incurred during life by their sins, failings, and infidelities, and have not yet satisfied for. To us in the Communion of Saints is given the power to lighten their burden in a greater or less degree; for we can take their place and do what they are no longer able to do: We can offer to God, in their stead, the atonement which He must demand and which they are unable to render. Whenever we offer to God the merits of Christ at Holy Mass for them, we are bearing the burdens of the Poor Souls. In this august Sacrifice, we possess the most excellent and most effective means of helping the dear departed (Council of Trent, Session 25). Whenever we gain indulgences and apply them to the Poor Souls, we are bearing their burdens. Likewise, all our prayers, sacrifices, efforts, labors, self-denials, and sufferings have value in satisfying for sin, provided we perform them or accept them for love of God. They are so many means of bearing the burdens of the Poor Souls, of lightening or even reducing their debt. And they will be effective in the measure that we exert ourselves to grow in intimacy of fellowship with Christ and His Church through growth in love, in purity, and in other virtues. Is this not a noble undertaking, to bear the burdens of the Poor Souls and thus cooperate in their Redemption? How grateful they will be for our help!

3. It is by virtue of our incorporation in Christ and His Church that we are able to be of assistance to the souls of our brethren in Christ; and our ability to benefit the deceased will be in proportion to our love.

"I may speak with every tongue that men and angels use. . . . I may have powers of prophecy, no secret hidden from me, no knowledge too deep for me; I may have utter faith, so that I can move mountains; yet if I lack charity, I count for nothing" (I Cor. 13:1 ff.). "Make charity your aim" (I Cor. 14:1) in the Communion of Saints, in the Church at large, as well as in the sanctuary of your home, in your family, your parish, your cloister!

Prayer (Tract of the Requiem Mass): Lord, release the souls of all the faithful departed from every bond of sin. By the help of thy grace enable them to escape avenging judgement and to enjoy bliss in everlasting light. Amen.

NOVEMBER 4

St. Charles Borromeo, *Bishop and Confessor*

1. In the bull of canonization, Pope Pius V called St. Charles "a martyr of charity, a shining example for shepherd and flock, an angel in human form." Born in 1538, son of Count Gilbert Borromeo of Arona, Charles was created cardinal archbishop of Milan at the age of twenty-two by his uncle, Pope Pius IV. Many criticized the Pope for showing this preference for his nephew, but the youthful prelate at once set about acquiring the virtues expected of a prince of the Church. It was not until 1566, as a matter of fact, that the pope permitted him to reside in his See. Charles devoted himself wholeheartedly to his clergy and people. He energetically upheld the reforms of the Council of Trent. His Christlike charity shone during the famine of 1570 and the plague of 1576. The Cardinal personally visited the stricken in their homes to hear their confessions and administer the last sacraments. In order to be able to help the sick materially, he gave them everything he had in his palace, even his bed. St. Charles died on November 4, 1584, when he was only forty-six years old.

2. "Here was a great priest, whose life was acceptable to God" (Lesson). In his time, the so-called age of the Renaissance, many of the clergy, even some at the papal court in Rome, had become very worldly-minded. St. Charles was not of their number. While studying law at Pavia, among students who wasted a great deal of their time in theaters and dance-halls, or endangered their health by duelling and drinking, Charles had pursued his studies diligently in a secluded life of prayer and self-discipline. His life at the papal court afterwards followed the same pattern; his uncle showed his approval by making him papal prothonotary, president of the Council of State, and later, archbishop and cardinal. But the

splendor of wealth and dignity could not blind Charles; the acclaim of men never robbed him of his Christian humility; the multiplicity of weighty duties could not disturb his interior union with God; thus, "he proved faithful and acceptable to God." The untimely death of his brother, Count Frederic, proved to be a great trial for Charles; many insisted that instead of becoming a priest he should marry in order to save his family from extinction, since his brother had died without heirs. Charles' answer was to have himself secretly ordained to the priesthood in Rome. "Here was a priest whose life was acceptable to God."

"So it was the Lord took an oath that he should be the father of his chosen people. The Lord gave him the blessing which should extend to all nations" (Lesson). Charles employed all his adroitness and energy to bring to a conclusion, after its two lengthy interruptions, the Council of Trent, whose decisions have proved a great blessing to the Church, even in our own day. He led in carrying them out by his own example, in his own house. He renounced all the benefices that his uncle had assigned to him, maintained an unpretentious household and insisted on orderly Christian living and justice among his appointees. Soon he directed his attention to a reform of the divine services in his churches; he abolished noisy entertainments, such as dances. One man was so violently incensed by this that he fired a shot at the Cardinal, who escaped death only by a miracle. St. Charles also brought great blessings to his diocese by his charity. During the famine and plague years, Milan and its vicinity suffered the loss of some 520,000 people, among them 120 priests. The truly good Shepherd of the flock was spared and he became a leader in prayer, service, and penitential works. When civil officials fled the city he remained at his post, prepared to die for his people and with them. Milan justly praised him as a savior and liberator.

3. "He was a great priest." At the time of the pestilence, Charles carried the cross in processions of atonement and, in

every regard conducted himself as if the entire guilt lay upon him. He made his will, solemnly dedicating his body and his life for the salvation of his people, "such grace he found in the eyes of the Lord."

Here was a truly great saint. All the good things of earthly life were at his disposal: wealth, property, high offices, honors, esteem, and influence. St. Charles rose above all these things; he sacrificed them to become poor, to the extent of looting his own palace of useful and valuable treasures, such as precious tapestries, fabrics, and carpets, whatever could be used to clothe the poor or procure food for them. "Blessed are the poor in spirit," those who have detached themselves from earthly goods so that nothing stands in the way of their living entirely for the love they bear Christ in His brethren.

Collect: Lord, keep Thy Church under the continual protection of Thy holy bishop and confessor Charles; and let the intercession of one so renowned for watchful care of his flock kindle in us an everburning love of Thee. Amen.

NOVEMBER 9

Dedication of the Archbasilica of Our *Holy Savior*

1. The Church of the Lateran holds the unique distinction of being the mother of all the churches in the world; it is the first Roman Church dedicated to the Savior and was built by Emperor Constantine. Since all the popes resided in the Lateran palace for almost ten centuries, this basilica was considered to be the cathedral of the pope and thus stood as a symbol of papal authority in the eyes of the Catholic world. Pope Sylvester consecrated the Lateran Basilica on November 9, 324. In the year 896 it collapsed as the result of an earth-

quake, but was rebuilt under Pope Sergius III, receiving the name St. John the Baptist. Fire destroyed successive buildings in 1308 and 1361. Finally, in the seventeenth century the church lost much of its ancient and medieval character when the baroque style was introduced into the interior. On a feast of dedication the liturgy is not thinking merely of the house of stone, but takes the material structure as a symbol of the living Church here on earth, and in heaven as well. This symbolism applies to the mother Church, the papal basilica, in a very special way.

2. "At this time: Jesus had entered Jericho, and was passing through it; and here a rich man named Zacchaeus, the chief publican, was trying to distinguish which was Jesus, but could not do so because of the multitude, being a man of small stature. So he ran on in front, and climbed up into a sycamore tree, to catch sight of him, since he must needs pass that way. Jesus, when he reached the place, looked up and saw him; Zacchaeus, he said, make haste and come down; I am to lodge today at thy house. And he came down with all haste, and gladly made him welcome" (Gospel). In Zacchaeus, the heathen publican, we recognize the Church that has come to Christ from among the pagans. An unimpressive minority despised by the chosen people of Israel, heathenism longed for the Savior whom Jewry in its blindness had rejected. In the form of Zacchaeus it hurried ahead of the people of Israel and was the first to receive salvation; our Lord went to dwell in the Church of the converted pagans and blessed it. That Church welcomed Him. "I am to lodge today at thy house," in your church, for the church of the pagans had become "God's tabernacle pitched among men." In the Church "he will dwell with them and they will be his own people" (Lesson). The Church knows that she is the house of God, filled with His presence, treasury of grace and truth, the "gate of heaven." That is why she is praising God unceasingly. She receives the Lord with joy in every Holy Sacrifice, in every word of His, in

every grace He gives her children. "Salvation has been brought to this house."

"Zacchaeus stood upright and said to the Lord, Here and now, Lord, I give half of what I have to the poor, and if I have wronged anyone in any way, I make restitution of it fourfold" (Gospel). No sooner had our Lord entered the house of Zacchaeus than He wrought a complete change in the heart of the Publican. What were we, what had we before we came to the Church, to Christ? "He found you dead men; such were your transgressions, such were the sinful ways you lived in. . . . We did what corrupt nature or our own calculation would have us do, with God's displeasure for our birthright, like other men. How rich God is in mercy, . . . in giving life to Christ [He] gave life to us too" (Eph. 2:1 ff.). Our Lord went to stay with Zacchaeus; He lifted heathenism out of its confusion and ruin, filled men with His light, His life, and His spirit of holiness. Heathenism abandoned its former perversion and became the "holy" Church, the Bride of Christ, "no stain, no wrinkle" (Eph. 5:27). As our Lord said: "I make all things new" (Lesson). This is the reason for the Church's joy, and ours, today.

3. On the day when Pope Sylvester consecrated the Lateran Basilica, Christ entered it in the Blessed Sacrament and took up His abode there, and from this mother church He has saved and sanctified innumerable souls. In today's feast we thank Him for the continued action of His grace.

In this mother church of the world we recognize the exalted model of the Church founded by Christ. He lives on in His Church through all ages; He supports and guides by penetrating her with His spirit and power, with His truth and grace, so that ultimately, "it is He who baptizes and teaches, binds and looses, offers sacrifices through the Church." If the people of Israel found in the city of Jerusalem "the fountainhead of its greatest joy" (cf. Ps. 136:5–6), "how much greater then should be the joy and exultation that should fill our hearts 'who dwell in a City built on the holy mountain of living and chosen stones, Jesus Christ himself being the chief cornerstone' (Eph.

2:20; I Pet. 2:4–5). For nothing more glorious, nothing nobler, nothing more honorable can be imagined than to belong to the holy, catholic, apostolic, and Roman Church, in which we become members of one body as venerable as it is unique; are guided by one supreme head; are filled with one divine Spirit; are nourished during our earthly exile by one doctrine and one heavenly Bread, until at last we enter into the one, unending blessedness of heaven" (Pius XII on The Mystical Body; N.C.W.C. translation, par. 91).

Collect: O God, who year by year renewest for us the dedication-day of this holy temple of Thine, and still bringest us safe and sound to take part in its sacred rites, heed the prayers of Thy people, and grant that whosoever enters this church to seek Thy favors may receive with joy all that he asks. Amen.

NOVEMBER 11

St. Martin, *Bishop and Confessor*

1. St. Martin was the first great father of monks in the West, and the successful apostle of Gaul. He was born about 316 in what is now Hungary, of heathen parents. Growing up in Pavia, he enrolled among the catechumens at the age of ten, because he was attracted to Christ. At fifteen he had to enter service in the royal army, and he proved himself a good soldier. Proven as a Christian, he was baptized at eighteen, and upon being released from the army he went into solitude, where he could live undisturbed for Christ. In 355 he visited St. Hilary, bishop of Poitiers, and received the order of exorcist from him. His zeal for the cause of Christ impelled him to return to Hungary to try to win his parents for Christ. His father refused but his mother gladly received the good tidings he brought. Martin had to suffer much at the hands of the Arians. In 360 he went again to visit St. Hilary, just returned from exile.

Near Poitiers Martin founded, at Ligugé, the first large

monastery for cenobites in the West. Here he lived an austere
life with his brethren. Meanwhile, news of his sanctity and
miracles reached Tours, and the people there elected him by
unanimous vote to be their bishop, in 372. Even as bishop,
Martin lived in monastic poverty and simplicity, and before
long he built, near Tours, the monastery of Marmoutiers, as-
sembling eighty monks for it. He often went out to work for
the conversion of the pagans in the vicinity, and the fearless
power of his preaching gained results. Wherever a heathen
temple fell a Christian sanctuary was established. In this way
he quickly overcame the opposition and won the confidence
of the people; he also won them by charitableness and by defending their rights against certain governors. While on an
apostolic journey St. Martin died at Candes on November 8,
397. He was buried at Tours. In Martin, monk and apostle
were happily united, so that he became a trail-blazer for all
Western monasticism.

2. "Nobody lights a lamp, and then puts it away in a cellar
or under a bushel measure; it is put on the lamp-stand, so that
its light may be seen by all who come in" (Gospel). St. Martin
was a lighted lamp placed on the lampstand by God so we all
may see it and be illumined and warmed by it. "You are the
light of the world" (Matt. 5:14). He sought seclusion from the
world; he wanted to be unknown. It was only by a trick that
the people of Tours were able to secure him as their bishop;
but he immediately began to let his light shine for all to see.
In the silence of the cloister, in the school of poverty, self-
abnegation, and prayer, Martin learned to cooperate with grace
and thus became the great Apostle of Gaul. He carried his light
into the darkness of paganism and drew many to Christ by his
prayers, example, and miracles. St. Martin is a light for our
age to look at, too.

"Thy body has the eye for its lamp; and if thy eye is clear,
the whole of thy body will be lit up. . . . Take good care,
then, that this principle of light which is in thee is light, not

darkness" (Gospel). The liturgy presents St. Martin, monk
and bishop, as a man of faith. Faith—profound, living faith—is
the bright light in him that makes him a light for the world. It
was toward this faith that the boy of ten was reaching as a
catechumen, and which he received eight years later in baptism. By its light he was able to see Christ in the poor man to
whom he gave half his mantle. Filled with its light, he opposed
Arianism even in the person of Emperor Maximus, and won
out. This faith gave him strength to bear insults both from
opponents and from those who should have been true to him.
He never became excited, but proved himself one of those men
who are called to establish the reign of charity in the world by
kindness and mildness. It was his living faith that gave him the
strength to continue tireless efforts on behalf of the kingdom
of God and to say on his deathbed: "Lord, if I am still necessary to thy people, I shall not shirk labor; thy will be done."

3. "Martin is taken to Abraham's bosom, rejoicing. Martin,
needy and poor on earth, enters heaven rich and is celebrated
with heavenly song. O fortunate man, whose soul dwells in
paradise. Therefore, the angels rejoice, the archangels are
happy, the choir of saints exult, the throng of virgins sing their
invitation: 'Stay with us forever!'" (Respon. of III Noct.)

His disciples said to St. Martin: "Why are you leaving us,
Father, and to whom do you entrust your orphans? Behold,
ravening wolves will fall upon your flock." And he: "Lord . . .
thy will be done!" Hail, "O incomparable man, whom neither
labor subdued nor death conquered; who neither feared to die
nor hesitated to continue living" (Antiphon at Vespers).

Collect: O God, who seest that we put no reliance in our strength,
grant us this boon, that by the intercession of Thy blessed confessor
bishop Martin we may be fortified against all harm. Amen.

NOVEMBER 13

All Saints of the Benedictine Order

1. After the feast of All Saints on November 1, the liturgy provides celebrations for the saints of the various religious families. On this day, then, the children of St. Benedict look up to the many saints who on earth lived according to the spirit and Rule of St. Benedict, the patriarch of Western monasticism, and thereby sanctified themselves. "Rejoice we all in the Lord, as we keep holiday in honor of all holy monks. On their feast day the angels rejoice, praising the Son of God in chorus" (Introit). They belong to us and we to them. What we are, they have been; they followed the Holy Rule as we now do; where they are now, thither leads the path we are treading.

2. "And what of us who have forsaken all?" (Gospel.) How happy and grateful they now are that they were called by God to forsake all things by pronouncing the vows: "I promise stability, conversion of my morals, and obedience according to the Rule of our Holy Father Benedict." They are happy because they received from God the grace to live in voluntary poverty, to renounce earthly love, and, for the sake of God, to subject themselves to a man. It was a life of self-denial and sacrifice that they chose by their vows. They understood the advice of their Founder: "To deny oneself in order to follow Christ". (Holy Rule: chap. 4). They took seriously his enthusiastic challenge to die to their own wills through perfect, all-embracing obedience. They chose the way of self-humiliation, of being little, as St. Benedict so masterfully outlines it: "To hold fast to patience amidst hard and repulsive things, and even to be calm and composed under injustices of every sort; to bear all disagreeable things for the love of God." And, "Struck on one cheek, they offer the other; robbed of coat, they

give away their mantle too; forced to walk one mile, they go two; with Paul, they bear with false brethren, and bless those who curse them". (Chap. 7, *ibid.*). "See, we have left all things." They thank God today, and forever, for their religious vocation. They are grateful to St. Benedict, to their abbot, to their confreres all of whom helped them to become what they now are.

"And followed thee" Christ, their Master. To do that, they renounced the world and their own will so as to be free to walk the way of love and to cling to God without hindrance. Certainly, they found from experience that the way to the heights is steep and difficult at first; but they also experienced the truth of St. Benedict's prediction: "Progress in monastic living and in faith expands our heart, and we run the way of God's commandments with unspeakable sweetness of love, so that we shall never withdraw from His guidance, but shall persevere in His teaching until death in the monastery, sharing in patience the sufferings of Christ and thus deserving to be companions in His kingdom", (*ibid.*, Prologue). They loved Christ above all things. With ardent love they exercised "the good zeal that separates from evil and leads to God"; they bore patiently with the physical and spiritual weaknesses of others; they obeyed one another eagerly; they did not seek what was to their own advantage, but rather what would profit another; they exercised fraternal kindness with chaste minds; they feared God; they loved their abbot with humble and honest devotion. But Christ meant more than all else to them.(cf. chap. 72, *ibid.*). Here was Christ's word, Christ's example, Christ's honor, Christ's cause. The monks happily arrived at "that perfect love of God which casts out all fear and enables them to do now without any difficulty, naturally and out of good habit, no longer for fear of hell but out of love for Christ, all those things that they formerly could do only with trepidation" (*ibid.*, chap. 7).

3. Therefore, "we rejoice in the Lord as we keep holiday in

honor of all monks." This is a day of honor for Holy Father St. Benedict and all his sons and daughters: for the entire Benedictine family in heaven and on earth.

The spirit of St. Benedict, incarnate and visibly evident in the saints of his Order, is a spirit of breadth and of interior freedom, as the Lesson magnificently describes it: "Truly to seek God," "to serve God in honor and in disgrace, in bad as in good repute, regarded as deceivers and yet true, as unknown and yet well-known, as dying and, behold, we live, as chastised and yet not killed, as sorrowing and yet always joyful, as poor and yet enriching many, as having nothing and yet possessing all things" (II Cor. 6:4–10). Inwardly free, the monks live entirely for the service of God in the common celebration of prayer in choir, in the firm discipline of a life devoted to work and prayer in obedience to the Rule and the abbot, and in self-less devotedness to the fellowship of the brethren: "So that in all things, God may be glorified" (Holy Rule: chap. 57).

"Come to me, all who are tired and burdened: I will give you rest" (Alleluia verse). Our saints became what they are now through Christ.

Collect: Almighty God, we pray Thee: grant that the example of the holy monks may spur us on to a better life; then we shall imitate the virtues of those whose feast we are celebrating. Amen.

NOVEMBER 15

St. Albert the Great, *Bishop, Confessor,* *Doctor of the Church*

1. Albert was born of noble parents in Germany, in 1193. Having completed his studies in Padua, he became a Dominican in 1221. Following his novitiate, he won brilliant success in philosophical and theological studies, and soon became the

most celebrated teacher of his time. His assignments were to the schools of his Order in Hildesheim, Freiburg i. Br., Regensburg, and Cologne. From 1245 until 1248 he also studied and taught with outstanding success in Paris, where he was called "the Wonder and Oracle" of the century. After that he taught in the school he had founded in Cologne. Here he had as one of his pupils St. Thomas Aquinas and was the first to recognize the significance of that young Dominican's gifts. From 1254 to 1257 Albert was provincial of the German Dominicans. He was then called by the Holy Father to Italy, and was made Bishop of Regensburg, in 1260. Two years later he resigned this office, and in 1264 he again submitted to the jurisdiction of his Order, living in Cologne after 1269. In 1277 he was called to defend the teachings of St. Thomas, who had died several years before. St. Albert himself died on November 15, 1280. On December 16, 1931, Pope Pius XI canonized him and declared him a Doctor of the Church. His was the most universal spirit in the field of Scholasticism; he was a pioneer in the introduction of Aristotelianism into Western philosophy and the natural sciences, as well as exercising a significant influence on medieval mysticism and piety.

2. "You are the salt of the earth . . . the light of the world" (Gospel). Albert received the title, "The Great," during his lifetime. His chief claim to greatness lies in the sphere of ecclesiastical science: he dared to substitute for the hitherto accepted Platonism the philosophy of Aristotle as being closer to reality. As a result, Aristotle received the title of "The Philosopher." Of him Albert says: "Nature has placed him as the rule of truth, as the highest perfection of human thought." Previously, study of the pagan Aristotle had actually been forbidden in Church circles. St. Albert's authority, Christian and human, in the difficult philosophical and theological shift of the thirteenth century was a guarantee that Aristotle could be assimilated into Christian thought without harm. Albert proved, in fact, that the philosophy of Aristotle could, when

rightly viewed and employed, raise sacred sciences to new heights; and time has shown him to have been correct. He did this at a time when the pagan Emperor Frederick II posed a great danger to the faith and culture of the Christian West. Albert truly became the "salt of the earth" and "light of the world." We gratefully acknowledge the grace that God gave him for the advantage of His Church.

"A lamp is not lighted to be put under a bushel-measure; it is put on the lamp-stand to give light to all the people of the house." St. Albert was such a light; all Europe looked up to him; adherents of the natural sciences, philosophy, and theology cried out to him in their troubles; cities and nations appealed to him to settle their feuds; as arbitrator he analyzed differences and pronounced judgments with such clear-cut finality that everybody came to trust him. He would say: "I, Brother Albert, take it upon my conscience." During the Council of Lyons, 1274, when the fearful period without an emperor came to an end, King Rudolph of Hapsburg, who had been elected several years earlier, came to enlist the aged Albert's support. Albert pleaded his cause before pope and Council, opening his speech with the words: 'Behold, I send the savior and champion who shall liberate them.' They were won over, and history has vindicated the wisdom of Albert's advice.

3. With St. Albert we pray to the Eucharistic Lord: "Permeate our souls with Thy holy body as with leaven; satisfy our longings with good gifts, and grant that the wonderful Sacrament of Thy flesh and blood may communicate to us its treasures: truth and virtue, unity and love, purity and piety, resignation and sanctity. Cause us to be incorporated in Thee through Thy holy body, so that union with Thee may bring us salvation and we may rejoice over this partaking of Thee. May the spirit that lives in Thee also enliven us and bring light to our thoughts and renew in our souls the holy life that we have lost. Create in us faith and love, give us a spiritual outlook, anoint and strengthen us so that we shall dedicate

ourselves entirely to Thee. Give us solicitous charity, a tireless zeal, and an attentive readiness to serve Thy brethren. Give us true faith, firm hope, and perfect charity."

Collect: God, who didst make Thy blessed bishop and doctor Albert truly great in setting divine faith above his own human wisdom, we pray Thee grant that by closely following the path of his teaching we may come to enjoy perfect enlightenment in heaven. Amen.

NOVEMBER 17

St. Gertrude the Great, *Virgin*

1. St. Gertrude of Helfta (frequently mistaken for the abbess of Helfta who died in 1292) was born in Thuringia in 1256. At the age of five she was sent to the convent school at Helfta, where she received an excellent spiritual and religious training. Entering this convent she began, at the age of twenty-six, to live a life that was intimately affected by the liturgy of the Church and was mystically blessed by a mysterious, tender familiarity with Christ. Her two writings, "Ambassador of Divine Love" and "Spiritual Exercises" give an impressive view of her pure, childlike, amiably simple yet noble and powerful soul, with its glowing love. (Book 2 of the "Ambassador" is Gertrude's own work; books 3, 4, and 5 were written under her direction; book 1 was composed by the nuns of Helfta shortly after her death.) Gertrude's writings exercised great influence on the development of the Sacred Heart devotion. The probable date of her death is 1302.

2. "I know no other content but clinging to God, putting my trust in the Lord, my Master; within the gates of royal Sion I will be the herald of thy praise" (Introit; Ps. 72:28). As a young nun Gertrude took delight in study. At first she cultivated the so-called liberal arts, but later took up the study of

Holy Scripture and the Church Fathers, particularly St. Augustine and St. Gregory the Great. On January 27, 1281, she enjoyed her first vision of our Lord. From this moment on she knew nothing but Christ, the Beloved of her heart. There was a tender exchange of love between them. Our Lord imprinted the marks of His wounds upon her heart and mysteriously exchanged hearts with her as a symbol of His indissoluble mystical marriage with her. When she was thus one spirit with Him, our Lord revealed to her the secret treasures of His love. Repeatedly He opened His heart, the instrument of merciful redemption and the mysterious furnace of ineffable human-divine love, to the ecstatic gaze of His spouse. She is thus rightly counted among the first founders of the modern devotion to the Sacred Heart.

On one occasion, when St. Mechtild saw Gertrude walking up and down and always looking up at the image of His face, our Lord assured her: "Such is the life of my chosen one; she always walks before me, ceaselessly desiring to recognize the good pleasure of my heart. When she has seen something as My will, she hastens to carry it out at once. That is why she keeps turning to Me, seeking to know My will, and thus her entire life gives Me honor and glory." Gertrude was a wonderful bride for Christ, being so intimately bound to Him that our Lord assured her sisters: "Nowhere can you find Me more truly than in the Sacrament of the altar, and then, in the heart of My lover, upon whom I have poured all the joy of My divine heart" (cf. "Ambassador" I, chap. 3).

"Within the gates of Sion [the Church] I will be the herald of thy praise." Gertrude became a holy praise of God in the midst of her sisters. They testified that she was a "strong pillar of religious life," and they listed these points as proof: holy recollectedness that could not be disturbed by any external activity; heavenly unction and dedication that breathed from all her works; meek lovability which won all hearts; profound humility which made her consider it a miracle of God that the earth should bear such an unworthy sinner as herself; admirable patience throughout her protracted illnesses; abundant love of God that burst into mighty flame on any occasion, to give light and warmth to all around her; unsullied innocence that transfigured her whole being. All this splendor of virtue drew Gertrude's companions to imitate her. Nor was the zeal of her charity bounded by convent walls; it reached to all who were in any need. Her great heart's words and prayers brought many sinners to repentance, and her tender sympathy brought comfort to the sick and troubled, who were also effectively helped by her gift of miracles. She was a source of many great blessings for her time and she continues to benefit the Church through the centuries by her admirable life and writings, her spirit, and her powerful intercession with her Lord and heavenly Bridegroom.

3. "O thou worthy spouse of Christ, splendid in the light of prophetic gift, inflamed with the zeal of the apostles, crowned with the diadem of the virgins, consumed by the fire of divine love" (Antiphon at Benedictus). Do thou obtain for us the grace to love our Lord truly, above all else!

St. Gertrude was a true daughter of St. Benedict, governed by the spirit of a free heart which, liberated from all that is not God, "runs its course rejoicing, like a giant" (Ps. 18:6), in the impetuous force of love of God, full of enthusiasm and joyful desire for suffering. "The lover flieth, runneth, and rejoiceth; he is free and cannot be restrained. He giveth all for all, and hath all in all; because he resteth in one sovereign Good above all, from whom all good floweth and proceedeth. . . . Love feeleth no burden, thinketh nothing of labors . . . conceiveth that it may and can do all things" (*Following of Christ*: 3, 5).

Collect: O God, who didst prepare for Thyself a pleasant abode in the heart of Thy holy virgin Gertrude, let her merits and pleadings move Thee to wash away the sins by which our hearts are stained, and grant us fellowship with her in bliss. Amen.

NOVEMBER 18

Dedication of the Basilicas of

Sts. Peter and Paul

1. Both of these basilicas were built in the time of Constantine the Great, at the beginning of the fourth century. In place of an earlier monument marking the grave of St. Peter, prince of the Apostles, the Emperor erected a church with five aisles and a length of over a hundred feet. In the course of centuries this structure fell into decay, and in the sixteenth century the present St. Peter's was erected. It was dedicated by Pope Urban VIII on November 18, 1626. Likewise, Constantine replaced a monument to St. Paul on the Via Ostia with a new church having five aisles, a transept, and a hundred magnificent pillars. Owing to the carelessness of a roofer, this venerable basilica was destroyed by fire in 1823. Restored by Pope Pius IX, it was solemnly dedicated on December 10, 1854, two days after the declaration of the dogma of the Immaculate Conception. The feast of the dedication of these two basilicas reminds us of the day on which we ourselves were consecrated as temples of God by baptism. "You are the temple of the living God" (II Cor. 6:16). "It is a holy thing, this temple of God which is nothing other than yourselves" (I Cor. 3:17). In baptism we received sanctifying grace and the promise of our Lord was fulfilled in us: "If a man has any love for me . . . he will win my Father's love, and we will both come to him, and make our continual abode with him" (John 14:23). The texts of the Mass may be understood as referring to both the church building and to the spiritual edifice in the soul.

2. "Today, salvation has been brought to this house" (Gospel). The publican Zacchaeus, the sinner, as the Jews called him, represents each of us. "He has gone in to lodge . . . with

one who is a sinner." At the moment of baptism God entered our soul, and its previous inhabitant, Satan, had to leave. Grace came with God Himself: the Father, Son, and Holy Spirit. From a child of wrath and of eternal rejection, each of us was changed to a child of election, "a child of Abraham." For, "that is what the Son of Man is come for, to search out and to save what was lost" (Gospel). "You are the temple of the living God," a holy place. God entered lovingly to give Himself to us for our happiness, and to make us His own property in much the same way that He made the church of brick and stone His House. "I will live and move among them, and be their God, and they shall be my people" (II Cor. 6:16). We are a sanctuary in which God Himself lives and acts—the holy God who loves good and hates evil; the Almighty who protects us; the infinitely wise God whose hand guides us over life's dangerous paths. God's generous, strong love lives in us, to forgive our sins, to bring strength for good works, and to make sacrifices sweet and burdens light. What have we to fear if we believe in the indwelling of God? "Salvation has been brought to this house" at the moment of baptism, in every participation in the Holy Sacrifice and reception of Holy Communion.

"I give half of what I have to the poor; and if I have wronged anyone in any way, I make restitution of it fourfold" (Gospel). Our Lord's visit made Zacchaeus so happy that earthly goods and treasures meant nothing to him any more. "I know no other content but clinging to God," who dwells in my soul. "My trust is in the Lord" (Ps. 72:28). In our consciousness of God's dwelling in us, we withdraw more and more from external things and fix our gaze on Him who is living and working in us. We speak to Him in intimate prayer and exchanges of love, listening for His voice and acting gladly on His suggestions. In the light of God we see everything in every day as arranged, given, willed, or permitted for our salvation. He opens His heart to us, for it is His delight to be among us men (cf. Wisd. 8:31). He gives us an appreciation of the mysteries of His

presence, especially that "peace of God, which surpasses all
our thinking" (Phil. 4:7). Truly, "salvation has been brought
to this house." How insignificant are all other goods and values
compared to the wealth of our possession of God, as His abode!

3. "Today, at thy house . . . salvation has been brought."
It has come today in Holy Communion. When He enters, He
makes us new. "I give half of what I have to the poor." Filled
with the spirit of Christ we share our goods with the poor, His
brothers. That must be the fruit of Holy Communion.

"You are the temple of the living God." How well-guarded,
well-arranged, and well-cared-for must the tabernacle of the
Most High be! "Holy is thy house, and must needs be holy until
the end of time" (Ps. 92:5). Our thoughts, our emotions, our
inclinations, our wishes, our words, our works, our movements,
our whole deportment must be holy. "It is a holy thing, this
temple of God, which is nothing other than yourselves" (I Cor.
3:17).

Every one of our fellow men, whoever he may be, is also a
temple of God; every child, every poor, dispossessed, despised
person; each one must be holy to me, must be treated with holy
reverence.

Collect: O God, who year by year renewest for us the dedication-
day of this holy temple of Thine, and still bringest us safe and
sound to take part in its sacred rites, heed the prayers of Thy
people, and grant that whosoever enters this church to seek Thy
favors may receive with joy all that he asks. Amen.

NOVEMBER 19

St. Elizabeth of Hungary, *Widow*

1. Elizabeth was born in 1207, daughter of King Andrew of
Hungary. At the age of four she was placed in the Wartburg
castle of Landgrave Hermann of Thuringia, where at eleven

years she was betrothed to Prince Louis of that realm. The pleasures of court life did not harm her innocence nor lessen her frequent visits to our Lord in the tabernacle. Courtiers despised the girl's humility, simplicity, and mortifications, and accused her of wanting to make herself a ruling princess. Some tried to dissuade Louis from marrying her, but he had the marriage solemnized with great pomp in 1220. During the famine of 1226 Elizabeth aided the poor so generously that officials bewailed her "extravagance" to her absent husband; but Louis was convinced that the charity of the Princess would bring blessings upon his house.

Unfortunately, Louis died as a Crusader in 1227, and Elizabeth's brother-in-law, Henry Raspe, robbed her of all her property and rights. In the depth of winter she was forced to leave the palace with her children. Begging from door to door in Eisenach, she met with rough treatment and had to spend the first night in a barn. At midnight she went to the church of the Franciscans and asked the friars to chant the "Te Deum" in thanksgiving for the misfortune that God had permitted to befall her. The Abbess of Kitzingen, her aunt, took pity on the poor family and helped them find a refuge in Bamberg. After a time Raspe yielded to the protests of her relatives and permitted Elizebeth to return to the Wartburg as its rightful princess. In due time she renounced the government in favor of her son, but retained her right to Marburg and went there to live. Here, in 1228, she founded a hospital, where she and two companions served the sick brothers and sisters of Christ with generous kindness until her death on November 19, 1231, at the age of twenty-five. She is considered the first member of the Third Order of St. Francis in Germany. Only four years after her death, Pope Gregory IX canonized her.

2. "The kingdom of heaven is like a treasure hidden in a field; a man has found it and hidden it again, and now, for the joy it gives him, is going home to sell all that he has and buy that field" (Gospel). From the very beginning of her stay at

court, Elizabeth realized that a life of enjoyment and pleasure
was not her ideal. Rejecting the luxury to which she was en-
titled, she devoted almost all her income to the poor, and much
of her time to prayer and recollection. The sudden death of
Louis affected her deeply: "Thou knowest, Almighty God, that
I loved no one on earth more than my husband. Since he had
to depart this life in obedience to Thy will, I do not complain.
In fact, I am so thoroughly resigned to Thy providence that I
would not wish to call him back to life by my prayers if I
could. I ask only that Thou grant him eternal rest and give me
the grace to remain true to Thee and Thy commandments until
death." She was prepared to give up not only her husband, but
also her station, her possessions, and her home. In the words of
the Gospel, she had discovered the true treasure: God. "Just
are thy awards; I know it well, Lord, it was in faithfulness thou
didst afflict me" (Introit).

"A man who has won a vigorous wife has found a rare treasure. . . . Kindly is her welcome to the poor, her purse ever
open to those in need" (Lesson). To lighten the burden of
taxes and compulsory service, Elizabeth had induced Louis to
abolish the foolish expenditures for tourneys and feasts. The
lot of their subjects improved visibly, even before the royal
marriage. She became the mother of the poor and needy. Her
husband fully approved of her caring for lepers and orphans,
of her helping everywhere with her generous charity. In the
hospital her marvelous compassion found countless devices for
comforting and encouraging the sick. Now her stern spiritual
director took her children from her in order, he said, to give
them an education befitting their rank; next, he deprived her
of the two companions with whom she had been living a religious life next door to the hospital; there was nothing left to
her but God. In prayer she gained the strength for these sacrifices, always borne up by the thought of future union with God
in heaven. Truly, a strong woman!

3. The bull of canonization calls Elizabeth "a new master-

piece." She was a product of the Holy Spirit, incomparably beautiful; she is still a vessel of the Holy Spirit, from which the blessings of her life and work are dispensed throughout the Church and the world.

Elizabeth modeled her life on norms given by Konrad of Marburg, her spiritual director: "Be patient in voluntary poverty. Renounce human comfort and the desires of the body. Keep God always in your heart and thoughts. Thank God for having saved you from hell by Christ's death on the Cross. Since He suffered so much for you, carry your cross patiently. Consecrate yourself, body and soul, entirely to God. Remember that you are the work of His hands, and strive for eternal union with Him. Treat people as you wish them to treat you. Ponder the shortness of life; young and old must die, but you must strive for everlasting life. Constantly bewail your sins and plead with God for forgiveness."

Collect: God of mercy, enlighten the hearts of Thy faithful, and at the prayer of blessed Elizabeth, now in glory, give grace to scorn worldly prosperity and to look to heaven for our joy and comfort. Amen.

NOVEMBER 20

St. Mechtild, *Virgin*

1. In 1241 Mechtild was born to a noble family in Hackeborn, Saxony. At the age of seven she was entrusted to the nuns of the nearby convent of Rodersdorf, but later followed her sister, Gertrude of Hackeborn (not "the Great") to Helfta, of which Gertrude later become abbess. Mechtild was highly educated, having special talent for art among her rich gifts of heart and mind; but, although she headed the convent school, hers remained a contemplative nature, and, through a life which was one long series of trials and illnesses, she at-

tained to a high degree of contemplation. After the death of Abbess Gertrude, Mechtild revealed some of her sublime graces to several sisters, among whom was Gertrude the Great, who recorded them in her "Book of Special Grace." Many passages of these sketches refer to the love and grace of the Sacred Heart, which Mechtild often beheld in sublime transfiguration. By her numerous prayers to the Sacred Heart, in use since the fourteenth century, she contributed substantially to the spread and deepening of devotion to the heart of Jesus. Mechtild died on November 19, 1299.

2. "God, thou didst make the heart of Thy holy virgin Mechtild, glowing with love, into a pleasant abode for Thyself . . ." (Collect). Being a frail infant, Mechtild was baptized immediately after birth; later, our Lord told her He had arranged matters thus so that she would become a temple of God without delay. From the day the seven-year-old girl was taken to the convent, she was so firm in her determination to remain that neither begging nor threatening could induce her to return to the parental castle. Love for her heavenly Bridegroom bound her to the cloister; to Him she consecrated her love and virginity. The genuineness of her vocation was proved by her life: it was one of most ardent love for God, for her Lord and Savior and His Sacred Heart; it was a life of poverty and simplicity; it was a life of obedience and the complete renunciation of self; it was a life of uninterrupted prayer so profound and fervent that she scarcely noticed what was going on around her; it was a life of love for neighbor which impelled her to help with advice and comfort, to suffer penance and pray in order to obtain God's grace and to serve wherever she could.

Our Lord was well pleased with St. Mechtild. On one occasion when she heard in the Gospel of Easter Monday the words, "Lord, remain with us," she begged of Him: "Stay with me, for it is towards evening in my life." Jesus answered: "I will remain with you like a father with his son; I will share with you

the heavenly inheritance that I purchased with My blood, and
I will give you, as your own, all My good deeds on earth. I will
stay with you as a friend with his friend, as a bridegroom with
his bride; there will be no separation any more. When you
are sick, I will attend you like an experienced physician, and
cure you; I will faithfully help you carry every burden, so that
you will be able to bear and suffer everything easily." In effect,
He says the same to all of us: "If a man has any love for me,
he will be true to my word; and then he will win my Father's
love, and we will both come to him, and make our continual
abode with him" (John 14:23).

One day God made her understand how our Lord comes to
us in Holy Mass for our salvation: "He comes in such profound
humility that He stoops to unite Himself with anyone who
desires such a union, no matter how lowly he may be. He comes
with such great patience that He bears with the sinner and, in
answer to his earnest petition, gives him the grace of repentance and of conversion. He comes with such love that He is
able to soften and influence the heart of even the coldest and
most obdurate sinner. He comes with such goodness and gen-
osity that He can enrich even the poorest. He gives Himself
to all in Holy Mass as the sweetest, most pleasing, and most refreshing food; there is no needy, no hungry man who cannot
be satisfied and strengthened by Him. He comes with such
glory that His presence can enlighten and purify every heart,
no matter how blinded and darkened it may be. Finally, He
comes with such an abundance of holiness and graces that He
can awaken anyone from spiritual sleep, no matter how lazy
or undevout he may be." Then God added that if she, Mechtild,
wanted to make good all her evil deeds and neglect, she should
go to the Most Blessed Sacrament of the altar, for it is the
source of all goodness, a mine of all graces. Consoling thoughts
for us!

3. In the spiritual life the interior comes first, and then the
exterior, but in such a way that the spirit itself forms our life

from within, without ever losing the inner freedom that our
Lord's redemption merited for us. This law was fulfilled in
Mechtild's life; she knew only God. She was not a creature of
habit, but was prepared at any moment to sacrifice her rightful
preference, or to give up her favorite work, or her opinion.
She possessed complete freedom of spirit and heart in her love
for Christ.

We ask St. Mechtild to obtain for us from God the grace to
love Him with undivided affection and to live for Him alone.

Collect: God, Thou didst make the heart of Thy holy virgin
Mechtild, glowing with love, into a pleasant abode for Thyself. We
beg Thee, through the intercession of this virgin, that as long as
we live we may ever rise more and more from earthly things and
thus come to triumph with her on the day when the just shall rise.
Amen.

NOVEMBER 21

The Presentation of Our Lady

1. Mary was brought by her parents to the Temple. In one
of the Lessons at Matins St. John of Damascus says: "Planted
in the House of God and nourished by the Holy Spirit, she became like a fruitful olive tree, a dwelling-place of all the virtues. She turned away from all earthly desires of life and of the
flesh, preserving virginity of spirit and body. This was fitting
for one who had been called to conceive God in her body."

2. "Mine to minister before him in his holy dwelling . . . I
made Sion my stronghold, the holy city my resting-place, Jerusalem my throne. My roots spread out among the people that
enjoys his favor; my God has granted me a share in his own
domain; where his faithful servants are gathered I love to
linger" (Lesson). Mary was consecrated to God in the Temple,
a more pure and precious offering than the priests had ever

offered there, and one with which the Holy Trinity was well pleased. She was an offering surpassed in worth only by the Victim on the Cross and on our altars. When the child Mary was enrolled among the virgins of the Temple she gave herself without reserve, with all the ardor of her great soul, to her Lord and God. For this reason, she ever after chose a life of seclusion, prayer, obedience to superiors, and charitable service to her companions. She was a perpetual, holy sacrifice before God. "Joyful are the thoughts that well up from my heart, a King's honor for my theme" (Introit Psalm). On this day of her consecration to God, her "profession," the liturgy admiringly greets her: "*Ave Maria*—Hail Mary, full of grace! The Lord is with thee; blessed art thou among women and blessed is the fruit of they womb" (Offertory).

"A King's honor for my theme." The liturgy looks upon Mary in her Presentation as a type of the Church. Like Mary, the Church has from her very infancy deliberately turned her back on worldliness and dedicated her life to God alone. When our Lord had ascended into heaven, the young Church, the apostles, "went back full of joy to Jerusalem, where they spent their time continually in the temple, praising and blessing God" (Luke 24:53). The first Christians in Jerusalem "occupied themselves continually with the apostles' teaching, their fellowship in the breaking of bread, and the fixed times of prayer. . . . They persevered with one accord, day by day, in the temple worship . . . and winning favor with all the people" (Acts 2:42 ff.). Many of the Church's noblest and bravest children of all ages and nations, representing their Mother, have cheerfully withdrawn from the world's affairs into the silent solitude of religious life, even into perpetual enclosure: Mary in the Temple! "(Listen, my daughter, and consider my words attentively; thou art to forget, henceforward, thy own nation, and the house of thy father; thy beauty, now, is all for the King's delight; he is thy Lord and worship belongs to him). . . . All her splendor is the splendor of a princess through and through; so bedecked is she with embroidery and tassels of gold. Maidens will follow in her retinue into the King's presence, all rejoicing, all triumphant, those companions of hers, as they enter the King's palace!" (cf. Ps. 44:11–16.) Happy those who, with Mary and Holy Church have left all and gone to dwell in the house of the Lord! "I promise to live for my God and Savior, and for Him alone, in poverty, chastity, and obedience": My whole life is for my Bridegroom.

3. Mary's life in the Temple was a life of holy silence. When God wishes to do great things in a soul, He leads it away from the noisy unrest of life in the world, into solitude; in the restful silence of a life of prayer, God speaks to it, purifying and sanctifying it as a preparation for its future apostolic activity of saving souls with Him. Mary was soon to be given back to the world by the Temple in order to save the world.

The liturgy of today's Mass sees in the child offered in the Temple the future Mother of God: "Blessed art thou, and worshipful, Mary, virgin; who without loss of maidenhood wast found to be the mother of our Savior. Virgin Mother of God, He whom the entire world cannot hold enclosed Himself within thy womb and was made man" (Gradual).

Collect: O God, by whose will the blessed, ever-virgin Mary, dwelling-place of the Holy Spirit, was on this day presented in the temple, we pray Thee grant that through her pleading we may be found worthy to be presented in the temple of Thy glory. Amen.

NOVEMBER 22

St. Cecilia, *Virgin and Martyr*

1. Cecilia is one of the most highly venerated virgin-martyrs of the Church; her name occurs in the Canon of the Mass. There are no reliable records regarding either her person or her martyrdom. She may have gained her crown in the perse-

cution of Alexander Severus (222–235), or in that of Valerian
(258) or in that of Diocletian (304). One fact stands, however: that there was in the fourth century a church in Rome
founded by a Cecilia. Tradition affirms that she was of noble
stock and that she was married to a certain Valerian, against
her will. On the first evening they were together she persuaded
him not to touch her, by promising that he would be able to see
the Guardian Angel at her side if he would go to Pope Urban
and receive baptism. Thus did she preserve her virginity and
gain a convert to Christ; in fact, both Valerian and his brother
Tiburtius suffered martyrdom for the Faith. Then Almachius,
the Prefect of Rome, arrested Cecilia, who had already given
all Valerian's possessions to the poor. An attempt to murder
her in her home by means of steam met with failure; an execu-
tioner then vainly attempted to cut off her head, and left her
dying after three strokes of his axe. Her house was converted
into a church, to which her body was transferred by order of
Pope Paschal I (817–824), after resting for a time in the Cata-
combs of St. Callistus.

2. "I will reveal a secret to you, Valerian: the angel of God
is my protector and he jealously guards my body." Although
Cecilia submitted to marriage with the pagan Valerian, she was
determined to preserve her virginity and to lead her husband
to Christ. While the noisy merriment of the wedding celebration was in progress she spoke to our Lord: "Keep my heart
unspotted and let me not be confounded" (Vesper antiphon).
She had promised Him to remain a virgin and she trusted in
His help, in spite of the marriage forced upon her by her parents. Valerian was impressed by her sincere promise that he
should see her angel, and he respected her convictions. After
receiving baptism and seeing the angel, he went at once to
lead his brother to the font. By a miracle God had rewarded
Cecilia's filial obedience and trust; she remained a virgin after
marriage.

"Be bold, you soldiers of Christ; throw away the weapons

of darkness and take up those of light." These were Cecilia's last words to her husband and his brother as they were led away to death. She was seized and locked in her bathroom, which was then heated until it seemed certain she must suffocate. She prayed, however, and remained unharmed. She joyfully exposed her neck for the stroke of the axe, but had to linger three days in her blood before she secured the crown of life. "Behold, the bridegroom is on his way; go out to meet him" (Gospel). "Come, spouse of Christ, receive the crown that the Lord has prepared for thee from eternity. For love of Him, thou hast shed thy blood" (Responsory at Matins).

3. "God dwells within her, and she stands unmoved" (Ps. 45:6). With what great zeal did Cecilia set about winning souls for Christ! This prompts the liturgy to sing: "Cecilia, Thy handmaid, O Lord, serves Thee like a busy bee." "The virgin, crowned with glory, constantly carried the gospel of Christ in her heart and never ceased either by day or night, to carry on holy conversations and to pray" (Antiphon at the Magnificat).

What a magnificent spirit it was that motivated Cecilia! It was the valiant spirit of the Church of martyrs; and it still lives.

Collect: O God, who year by year dost gladden us with the feast of Thy blessed virgin-martyr Cecilia, grant that we who venerate her with sacred rites may also follow her example in holy living. Amen.

NOVEMBER 24

St. John of the Cross, *Confessor and Doctor*

1. John de Yepes, son of a poor weaver, was born in Fontiberas in Old Castile, in 1542. Poverty compelled his mother to move into Medina del Campo after her husband's death, and there the founder of a hospital hired the boy to tend the sick,

allowing him time for his studies in the hope that he would eventually become the hospital chaplain. In 1563, however, John entered the Carmelite Order and lived from the beginning a life of self-denial and prayer. In fact, the manner of life at Medina del Campo did not seem severe enough for him, and he was about to transfer to the Carthusians, when St. Teresa visited his monastery. She directed him to remain and to join her in an effort to restore the Carmelites to their original austerity. They were successful, but at the cost of great sacrifices. In 1580 Pope Gregory XIII approved the founding of a new province of so-called "Discalced (shoeless) Carmelites." John was appointed superior of various monasteries but, in 1580, the general chapter relieved him of all offices and sent him to a secluded house at Ubeda, for he was a sick man. He died there after many sufferings, on December 14, 1591. Canonized in 1675, he was declared a Doctor of the Church by Pope Pius XI in 1926. St. John wrote a number of mystical works which constitute the most significant system of Christian mystical theology ever compiled.

2. "God, who didst endow Thy confessor and doctor St. John with a spirit of utter self-denial" (Collect). Becoming a Carmelite at twenty-one, St. John at once cultivated familiarity with God and practiced severe mortification. His bed was a hollow log, his clothing a rough, penitential garb; he frequently scourged himself and constantly fasted and kept night-vigils. He lived what he taught and taught what he lived. His principle was: "All the natural desires of the heart must be mortified and suppressed; otherwise, the soul cannot attain to union with God. In this life it is impossible to escape involuntary and spontaneous impulses altogether; however, even while they exist in the lower part of man, the higher part may be freed of them. But, if the soul is to attain to perfect union with God, it must free itself of all voluntary desires, even the least, whether they tend to mortal or venial sin, or even only to imperfections" (*Ascent to Carmel:* I, 11). Indeed, he who "wishes

to attain to perfect union with God may not depend on understanding; he may not rely on what he has enjoyed or experienced or seen in his imagination; he must believe in the perfec-
tions of the divine Being." The soul must "overstep its natural
limitations"; it must rise above the natural; it must, "above all,
go out of itself," out of lower things "to the Most High" (*ibid.,*
II, 4). To accomplish this God himself interferes to purify the
soul and place it in complete dryness and interior darkness,
that is, in the "dark night." Here the soul will gain strength
and firmness in the virtues and, little by little, attain to the de-
lights of divine love. St. John had experienced all these stages
in himself. He longed incessantly for participation in the Cross
of Christ. After his life had been consumed by labors and sufferings, our Lord asked him what reward he desired. He replied: "Lord, to suffer and be despised for Thy sake." By self-
denial and patient suffering the soul lifts itself to the heights of
love.

"Why are there so few who arrive at the state of perfect
union with God? It is not because God has called only a few
spiritual persons to it—He would like to see everybody perfect
—but He finds comparatively few who will submit to this
stern but sublime treatment (the dark night of the spirit). If
He tries them even slightly, most people will show their weakness and soon run away from the required effort; then, God
does not lead them any farther. O you souls who wish to enjoy
a spiritual life of security and consolations, if you only knew
how necessary suffering is for acquiring this comfort!" (*Living
Flame of Love:* II, 5.) "The soul will be greatly retarded in its
progress toward the sublime state of union if it relies on its
own understanding, feeling, judgment or will; if it trusts
its own way or anything else of its own; if it fails to understand
the necessity of tearing itself away from all these things" (*Ascent to Carmel:* II, 3). John was a thoroughgoing saint; he was
looked upon as being radical. Happy are those who imitate his
virtue!

3. "The Lord moved him to speak before the assembled people, filling him with the spirit of wisdom and discernment" (Introit). We ought to listen to the wisdom of this remarkable teacher and follow his instructions, for they would guide us on the sure, straight way to the goal of holy love, of union with God.

"O you souls who are created for and called to such glory, what are you doing? Miserable blindness! How can you close your eyes to such a brilliant light?" (*Spiritual Song:* IV, 39, 1.)

The ways of God are wonderful. At one time St. John was so thoroughly despised and mistrusted that he was locked up in a small dark cell with little more than water and bread for sustenance; every Friday during those nine months he was made to kneel in the refectory while being whipped and otherwise mistreated. Finally, although extremely weak from sickness and starvation, he succeeded in letting himself down through a window, on a rope made of cloth strips. After hiding in a friendly home to regain his strength, he left the city to escape from his brethren. God miraculously rescued him and later vindicated and exalted him.

Collect: God, who didst endow Thy confessor and doctor St. John with a spirit of utter self-denial and a pre-eminent love of the cross, grant that by constant following of his example we may win eternal glory. Amen.

NOVEMBER 25

St. Catherine, *Virgin and Martyr*

1. Tradition makes this St. Catherine the daughter of a distinguished family in Alexandria. She received a thorough education in science and religion. At eighteen she defended the Christian religion before Emperor Maxentius (305–312) and his fifty philosophers, and she convinced the latter so com-

pletely of the truth of it that they were converted and died for the Faith. Catherine was also condemned to death, and after the most frightful tortures was beheaded. God glorified her by having angels carry her body to the top of Mount Sinai to bury it. Honoring this legend Emperor Justinian founded a famous monastery, named after her, on Mount Sinai. St. Catherine enjoyed great veneration in the Middle Ages and her cult continues to the present time. She is numbered among the "Fourteen Helpers in Need."

2. "Fearlessly will I talk of thy decrees in the presence of kings, and never be abashed" (Introit). In the year 306 Emperor Maxentius had come to Alexandria and proclaimed a great feast in honor of his pagan gods. There were animal sacrifices; clouds of incense hung over the altars, while pagan priests chanted. In the midst of the celebration Catherine appeared with her servants and asked to be admitted to the Emperor's presence. She then addressed him: "Emperor, you surely must realize that your gods and your sacrifices are all illusion and folly. It is evident that there can be only one supreme being." The Emperor took her to his palace and called together a great number of learned men—orators, rhetoricians, and scientists—to dispute with her. She refuted the reasonings of all of them, and then convincingly proved the inanity of heathen beliefs. It is to this incident in the legend that the Introit alludes, for Catherine came forth victorious from the disputation: "I give thee thanks, O God. . . . I extol thy name, for all the succor and protection thou hast given me" (Lesson). Our Lord had said: "I will give you such eloquence and such wisdom as all your adversaries shall not be able to withstand" (Luke 21:15).

"The kingdom of heaven will be like ten virgins, who went to bring the bridegroom and his bride home, taking their lamps with them. Five of these were foolish and five were wise . . . those who were wise took oil in the vessels they carried" (Gospel). Catherine was a wise virgin; she had her lamp filled with

the oil of charity, the love of a bride of Christ, as she went to
meet her bridegroom, and, though the way led through painful
martyrdom, she preserved her invincible love. When a wheel
set with sharp blades was readied to torture her, it miraculously broke: "Thou in that great mercy, that renowned mercy
of thine, didst deliver me" (Lesson). At this everybody cried:
"Great is the God of the Christians!" Only the Emperor remained unmoved; he was devising new tortures. When Catherine had withstood all his cruelties he ordered her beheaded.
"Behold, the bridegroom is on his way; go out to meet him."
Catherine entered into the wedding feast with her Bridegroom.
She had not trusted in vain.

3. "Thou hast been a friend to right, an enemy to wrong.
And God, thy own God, has given thee an unction to bring thee
pride" (Gradual). "Come, Christ's betrothed, and take the
everlasting crown the Lord has prepared for thee, that Lord
for love of whom thou didst shed thy blood" (Tract).

Words of St. Catherine: "Pain is brief, glory is eternal. It is
not so hard to bear torments: Christ stands at the side of anyone who suffers for Him."

Collect: God, who gavest the law to Moses on the summit of
Mount Sinai, and didst miraculously place the body of thy blessed
virgin-martyr Catherine in the selfsame spot by the ministry of thy
holy angels, we pray Thee grant that her merits and pleading may
enable us to reach the mountain which is Christ. Amen.

NOVEMBER 26

St. Conrad, *Bishop*

1. As soon as Conrad, the son of the Duke of Altdorf in
Germany, had acquired sufficient education, he was sent to the
cathedral school at Constance. He soon gained the esteem of
Bishop Noting, who adopted him, gave him sacred orders, and

shortly thereafter entrusted to him almost all of his own episcopal duties. At the funeral of Bishop Noting, Bishop Ulrich of
Augsburg recommended Conrad as the successor, and the
clergy elected him. As bishop, Conrad directed his priests by
doctrine and example, shepherding them with tender care. He
built a special lodging for the poor and pilgrims, founded a
number of parish churches in Constance, and in many other
ways labored tirelessly for the honor of God and the salvation
of souls. He made three pilgrimages to the Holy Land. Once,
at the Communion of his Mass, he noticed a poisonous spider
in his chalice. He consumed the precious blood, trusting in the
word of the Lord: "They will drink poisonous draughts without
harm" (Mark 16:18). He died on November 26, 976, and was
canonized by Pope Callistus II, in 1123.

2. "Let thy priests go clad in the vesture of innocence, thy
faithful ones cry aloud with rejoicing" (Introit of Mass: *Sacer-
dotes tui*). In the priest ascending the altar today the liturgy
sees the great Bishop Conrad. Justice and holiness were his
vestments, for his priesthood was a reflection of the priesthood
of Christ, "who continues forever, and his priestly office is
unchanging; that is why he can give eternal salvation to those
who through him make their way to God; he lives on still to
make intercession on our behalf. Such was the high priest that
studied our need, holy and guileless and undefiled, not reck-
oned among us sinners" (Epistle). St. Conrad had a share in
this eternally holy priesthood of Christ, which effects grace
and salvation. He possessed not only the inviolable power
and honor of Christ's priesthood—every Catholic priest has
these—but he also had personal holiness, derived from the
prayerful renunciation, work, and suffering of his long and virtuous life. The entire Church thanks God today for this great
and holy bishop. The good priest or bishop is the protector,
the treasure, the intercessor, the mediator, the comfort and
joy of his people. He draws down on them the merciful forgiveness and grace of God. "He can give eternal salvation to

those who through him make their way to God" (Epistle). Our Saint saves his people even now by his prayer and merits in heaven and by the memory of his holy example on earth. St. Conrad stands before us in today's feast as "holy, guileless, and undefiled among us sinners," and entirely dedicated to God.

"Think of thy servant David, and do not refuse audience to him thou hast anointed" (Introit Ps.). The "servant David" of today's celebration is Conrad; the "anointed" are we, the faithful, who have been touched with holy oil in baptism and confirmation and thus made members of Christ, "the Anointed One." We cry out to God, begging Him to grant us grace and pardon of sin, for the sake of this holy Bishop who loved the poor so much that he lived in voluntary poverty; who never counted the money he gave to a fellow man in need; who with his own hands helped carry stones to build a home for the poor; who never allowed a petitioner to depart without consolation and help. All this gives us confidence in our prayer to God: "For the sake of Thy servant Conrad, do not despise our petitions." By virtue of his priestly holiness St. Conrad has influence over the heart of Jesus for our welfare. By virtue of the communion of saints, we have a right to consider his merits as belonging to us as well, and to offer them to God for ourselves.

3. "Which of you, then, is a faithful and wise servant, one whom his master will entrust with the care of the household, to give them their food at the appointed time?" (Gospel.) Conrad was such a servant: he gave his people the nourishment of God's Word in exhortations, of God's body in the Holy Eucharist, of God's love in material aid. We thank him for his fidelity to God and to us.

"I promise you, he will give him charge of all his goods" (Gospel). In heaven he sees us all in God; he knows our needs, and will obtain the strong help we need. He knows we are praying to him.

Collect: Humbly we pray to Thee, O Lord on this feast of Thy holy bishop and confessor Conrad; grant in Thy goodness, that we may have him as our advocate whom Thou hast appointed as a mediator of our salvation. Amen.

NOVEMBER 30

St. Andrew, *Apostle*

1. Andrew, the first Apostle called by our Lord, was born in Bethsaida of Galilee. He was a disciple of St. John the Baptist, but when Jesus came to Jordan and the Baptist announced: "Look, this is the lamb of God; look, this is he who takes away the sin of the world" (John 1:29), Andrew went to Jesus. Satisfied with the new Teacher, he found his brother Simon Peter and said: "We have discovered the Messias." Both then went back to their occupation as fishermen until our Lord called them formally, as recorded in the Gospel of this feast: "Come and follow me; I will make you into fishers of men." Tradition says that after Pentecost Andrew labored for Christ in Scythia, Asia Minor, and Greece, until his death.

2. "Brethren: The heart has only to believe, if we are to be justified; the lips have only to make confession, if we are to be saved" (Epistle). Andrew proved himself a man of faith by promptly accepting the new Teacher on the recommendation of his previous master. Again, when our Lord said, "Follow me," he immediately left all he had and obeyed. It was such men that Christ needed for His mission, and He named Andrew not only among His seventy-two disciples, but also among the chosen twelve. As a zealous and faithful preacher of the word of God, Andrew encountered contradiction and failure. The Roman proconsul of Achaia imprisoned him and condemned him to death by crucifixion. The Apostle was happy to die for Christ; for two days he made his cross his

pulpit. On the third day it became the altar on which he completed his sacrifice. "Any one who believes in him [the Lord] will not be disappointed" (Gospel).

"Do not hinder my death as a martyr." Later tradition reports that when the proconsul imprisoned Andrew, the people rose up threatening to release "the just, holy man beloved of God." But the prisoner himself calmed them saying: "Do not hinder my martyrdom; rather, prepare yourselves for a courageous fight." When the proconsul threatened crucifixion, Andrew responded: "That will only make me more pleasing to the Lord. I am, after all, a servant of the Cross and must desire rather than fear it." As soon as he saw the cross prepared for him he exclaimed: "O excellent cross that I have so long desired, so earnestly loved; that I have sought without ceasing! Finally I find you ready for me. Take me up, away from men, and give me back to my Master, so that He who redeemed me through thee may receive me back through thee." Then the Saint was fastened with ropes and lifted up on the cross. He lived thus for two days, preaching and praying. Then he cried out: "Lord Jesus, take up my spirit in peace; it is time for me to come to thee" (cf. Breviary). St. Andrew was a lover of the Crucified and of His Cross.

3. "They [Peter and Andrew] dropped their nets immediately and followed him [Jesus]." St. Gregory the Great comments as follows: "They had not yet seen Him perform any miracles. And yet, at the single call of the Master they parted with all they had. How many miracles we have seen the Lord work! With how many rods He has chastised us! And still we do not follow Him. He is sitting on His throne in heaven; He is waiting for our conversion. But, day after day, our proud spirit will not voluntarily give up even what we inevitably lose against our will. He abandons much, who fully abandons the little that he does abandon; who also abandons the desire to possess" (St. Gregory the Great). What a splendid example St. Andrew is for us!

Andrew considered it a great glory and honor to share with Christ the ignominy of the Cross. Such was the conviction and conduct of our Lord's first pupil. Similarly, St. Paul declared: "God forbid that I should make a display of anything, except the cross of our Lord Jesus Christ, through which the world stands crucified to me, and I to the world" (Gal. 6:14).

We pray to St. Andrew, that lover of the Cross, to obtain for us from the Lord a profound understanding of the Cross, so that, by sharing in the Cross of Christ, we may obtain the grace to learn to treasure and to love it. In the Cross is salvation.

Collect: We humbly entreat Thy majesty, Lord, that the blessed apostle Andrew may be as constant an advocate for us in Thy court as he was eminent in preaching and ruling over Thy Church. Amen.

DECEMBER

DECEMBER 3

St. Francis Xavier, *Confessor*

1. Francis was born of noble parents in their castle Xavier, in the kingdom of Navarre, in 1506. His exceptional brilliance marked him for advanced studies; and at the age of eighteen he entered the University of Paris, where he merited the title of Master. He began to teach fine arts there; being clever, noble, and handsome, and having connections with the court of Paris, he was in danger of sacrificing all his knowledge and ability on the altar of pleasure. At this critical stage he met St. Ignatius of Loyola. Little by little he fell in with Loyola's plans, and on August 15, 1534, joined him and his five companions in making a vow to devote their lives to the conversion of infidels and saving souls. Francis took up the study of theology; later, he also devoted some time to caring for the sick in Venice. In 1537 he became a priest; the next year he went to Rome, whither St. Ignatius had summoned the entire group.

King John III of Portugal had begged Ignatius for missionaries to India, and Francis was assigned to that mission. His trip from Lisbon along the West coast of Africa to Goa, India, required thirteen months. At Goa he began missionary work immediately, moving through southern India, Indo-China, and the Moluccas south of the Philippines. God blessed his efforts with remarkable success. When several helpers arrived from Europe he introduced these to the work in India and betook himself to Japan, where he gained many thousands to Christianity at the cost of superhuman effort and suffering. Convinced that Japan would follow China to Christianity, he first returned to India in 1552, to assure himself that the Faith was growing stronger there, and then set out to China. He landed after a perilous voyage, on the island of Sancion, opposite Canton, and died there on December 2, 1552, in the forty-sixth year of his life, a victim of his own restless activity. He never really trod Chinese soil. His last words were: "In thee, O God, I put my trust; may I never be disappointed!" (Ps. 70:1.)

2. "Fearlessly did I talk of thy decrees in the presence of kings, and was never abashed. Full of love for thy commandments, I made them my study" (Introit). The priest at the altar represents for us the noble apostle and missionary, St. Francis Xavier. Filled with love for God and souls, he carried the gospel fearlessly into the distant lands of India and Japan, and far out to the Islands of the Pacific. On the long voyage from Lisbon to Goa, and for some time while at Goa, St. Francis had devoted his attention to the Portuguese who, by their un-Christian behavior, especially by their injustice and cruelty toward the natives, were endangering the conversion of India.

Then he turned to the pagans. With the help of some native Indians he translated the Apostle's Creed, the Commandments, the Our Father, Hail Mary, and the entire catechism into the Malabar language. Next he memorized the most necessary portions verbatim and set out, ringing his little bell in one village after another. He proceeded similarly in Indo-China and Japan, without means, without help, without protection, with nothing in fact but unbounded trust in Him whose work he was doing. "You are not to carry a purse, or wallet" (Luke 10:4). That was the way he entered Japan in 1549. With unbelievable effort and the help of a Japanese friend, he learned the difficult Japanese language and at once proceeded to publish an explanation of the Creed, a catechism, and a life of Christ in that tongue; then he also composed Japanese hymns and prayers. He set up crosses in many places, gained the good will of the governor of the province of Sakuma, and, little, by little, won many Japanese for Christ. He was counselor, physician, nurse, father, and brother; he was "all things to all men." The Buddhist priests compelled him to leave his congregation after a year, and then he went from island to island establishing Christian communities. Thirty years later there were about 400,000 Christians in Japan, so well had Francis laid the foundations. Nobody could resist his sincere love, his zeal, his holy enthusiasm, and the Christlike nobility that lifted him above sensuality and earthly pleasure to selfless optimism.

"O Lord, still more!" St. Francis had to win success not only through strenuous effort, prayer, and miraculous powers, but also, and chiefly, through suffering. Laboriously he climbed steep cliffs; barefooted he traveled the hot, stony roads of India; on tree-trunks he crossed rapid streams, ever praying: "Lord, yet more!" He felt the derision of the Brahmans, the fanaticism of the bonzes and the mistreatment of the rabble. Hunger, thirst, exposure, pain, and need were his companions; a handful of rice for food, a cotton smock for clothing, three hours for a night's rest. When his feet were bleeding from thorns and he had emerged dreadfully tired and weak from a night in a filthy cave or in a tree, out of reach of his persecutors; when battle-axes hovered and poisoned arrows whirred about him, he always repeated the same prayer: "Still more, still more!" Only when thousands stood on the shore praising him and watering his hands with tears of joy while they kissed the hem of his garment and called him father; when they carried him into the church in their arms, thanking him prayerfully for having brought them to Christ—only then did he pray: "Enough, Lord, enough!"

3. In the case of St. Francis our Lord's words found fulfillment in a very special sense: "They will cast out devils in my name, they will speak in tongues that are strange to them: they will take up serpents in their hands . . . they will lay their hands upon the sick and make them recover" (Gospel).

To what did St. Francis attribute the wonderful blessings that resulted from his prayerful exertions and sufferings? Simply to his faith-inspired obedience to St. Ignatius, to whom he always wrote on his knees. An obedience with such a supernatural foundation was bound to bring down God's gifts. Whatever Francis undertook he did as an agent of another; the foundation for his success lay in his intimate union with Christ, his life of faith and charity, the selfless, self-sacrificing resignation of his will to the will of God. May this remarkable man obtain for us the grace to believe, to love, and to sacrifice as he did!

Collect: O God, who by the preaching and miracles of blessed Francis wast pleased to bring into the Church's fold the peoples of the Indies, grant us this favor, that we who revere his shining merits may also imitate the pattern of his virtues. Amen.

DECEMBER 4

St. Peter Chrysologus, *Bishop, Confessor,*
Doctor of the Church

1. Peter was born at Imola, about the year 400. Pope Sixtus III appointed him bishop of Ravenna in 433. A trusted friend of Pope Leo the Great, Peter was so highly esteemed that even the heretic Eutyches sought his opinion. Because of his brilliant pulpit oratory Peter was given the name Chrysologus, or "man of golden words." A good many of his sermons are extant. He died in the city of his birth about 450.

2. "I adjure thee in the sight of God, and of Jesus Christ, . . . preach the word, dwelling upon it continually, welcome or unwelcome; bring home wrongdoing, comfort the waverer, rebuke the sinner, with all the patience of a teacher. The time will surely come when men will grow tired of sound doctrine, always itching to hear something fresh" (Epistle). Peter understood the seriousness of St. Paul's words; he knew that the

bishop or priest will have to give a strict account of all the souls entrusted to him; that he must conscientiously perform the first and essential duty to "preach the word." "When I preach the gospel, I take no credit for that; I act under constraint; it would go hard with me indeed if I did not preach the gospel" (I Cor. 9:16). "A lamp is not lighted to be put under a bushel measure; it is put on the lamp-stand to give light to all the people in the house" (Gospel). The bishop, the priest has a mission to mankind, and may not remain hidden; like the Church, he must be the "light of the world . . . a city built on a mountain-top," visible to everybody in order to lead all to Christ and salvation by word, prayer, sacrifice, and holy example. St. Peter was such a bishop and priest, and we praise him today for his fidelity to Christ's Church and to his vocation.

"He who wishes to have a good time with the devil will not be able to rejoice with Christ." That is what Peter once told the frivolous people of Ravenna. No one can serve two masters, God and the devil, though life places us in a world between their respective kingdoms. Our choice must be Christ; we have to be detached from the enjoyments and possessions of this world and cling to Christ alone. The kingdom of heaven is a treasure hidden in a field, but we must have a trained eye to recognize its surpassing value. We have to sacrifice earthly values and believe that God speaks to us through His Son. "For the man who believes in him, there is no rejection; the man who does not believe is already rejected" (John 3:18). If one wishes to serve the kingdom of God he must do so with his whole being. "No one who looks behind him, when he has once put his hand to the plough, is fitted for the kingdom of God" (Luke 9:62). It was this deep comprehension of Christianity that motivated St. Peter.

3. "Lord, . . . it was five talents thou gavest me, see how I have made a profit of five talents besides. . . . Well done, my good and faithful servant; since thou hast been faithful over little things, I have great things to commit to thy charge; come

and share the joy of thy Lord" (Matt. 25:20). The talents were the word of God entrusted to St. Peter. He traded with his talents and won rich profit in the conversion and spiritual progress of his people; therefore, the Lord took him into His joys. In the Secret of the Mass we say: "Let not the godly prayer of thy holy bishop and doctor Peter fail us, Lord: may it make these gifts of ours acceptable, and win us thy continuing forgiveness." It is a great comfort to know that the saints, filled with the fire of the love of God, lend power and fervor to our prayers and present them to God. I believe in the communion of saints!

Collect: God, who didst miraculously point out the admirable doctor Peter Chrysologus, and ordain that he should be chosen to rule and instruct Thy Church, grant, we pray Thee, that we may be worthy to have as advocate in heaven him who on earth taught us the way of life. Amen.

DECEMBER 6

St. Nicholas, *Bishop and Confessor*

1. History offers no facts concerning St. Nicholas. According to legend he lived in Asia Minor in the third century. Educated as a Christian and left wealthy by the early death of his parents, he devoted himself and his means to helping the poor. A certain noble family had fallen into poverty and the father was thinking of selling his three daughters. When Nicholas learned of this, he went to the home and threw a small sack of gold through an open window. In this way he provided a dowry for each of the daughters and they were happily married. All Christendom knows about the three golden apples on St. Nicholas' tree of neighborly charity. Once, on a pilgrimage to Jerusalem, Nicholas' power saved himself and all aboard the ship in a terrific storm. About 270 or 280, he went to Myra

and was chosen bishop of that city. Imprisoned under Diocletian in 305, he was released by Constantine and returned to his See. Legend says that he took part in the Council of Nice, in 325. His feast is celebrated in both East and West.

2. "You must remember to do good to others and to give alms; God takes pleasure in such sacrifice as this" (Epistle). What, above all, made this legendary hero famous was his great generosity and the profound wisdom with which he grasped the word of God and translated it into act. "Make use of your base wealth to win yourselves friends, who, when you leave it behind, will welcome you into eternal habitations" (Luke 16:9). He must have pondered also: "Warn those who are rich in this present world not to think highly of themselves, not to repose their hopes in the riches that may fail us, but in the living God, who bestows on us so richly all that we enjoy. Let them do good, enrich their lives with charitable deeds, always ready to give, and to share the common burden, laying down a sure foundation for themselves in time to come, so as to have life which is true life within their grasp" (I Tim. 6:17–19). And again: "Blessed is the man who lives, for all his wealth, unreproved, who has no greed for gold. . . . Show us such a man, and we will be loud in his praise; here is a life to wonder at. A man so tested and found perfect wins eternal honor" (Ecclus. 31:8 ff.). Nicholas possessed his wealth in such a way that it did not possess him. He did not lose sight of the true treasures with which he could enrich himself for eternity, that is, good deeds.

"God takes pleasure in such a sacrifice as this" (Gospel). "Give, and gifts will be yours; good measure, pressed down and shaken up and running over, will be poured into your lap" (Luke 6:38). When Nicholas arrived at Myra the election of a new bishop was in progress. The oldest bishop proposed a plan: Let the man entering the church first on the following morning be made bishop. All agreed. Very early next morning, entirely unaware of this agreement, Nicholas hastened to church. At once he was hailed as bishop of Myra, for he had abundantly demonstrated his love of Christ in his brethren. "Dost thou care for me more than these others? Yes, Lord . . . thou knowest well that I love thee." To Nicholas, as once to Peter, the commission was given: "Feed my lambs. . . . Feed my sheep" (John 21:15 ff.). Thenceforth, he devoted all his love and care to the flock entrusted to him; he became a true father to all, a refuge for the oppressed, a high priest who prayed and sacrificed and consumed himself in the service of souls. But he, too, was to experience treatment similar to that promised to Peter: "As a young man, thou wouldst gird thyself and walk where thou hadst the will to go, but when thou hast grown old, another shall gird thee, and carry thee where thou goest, not of thy own will" (John 21:18). Emperor Diocletian issued an edict: Bishops and presbyters of churches were to be taken into custody and subjected to torture. Nicholas was put in chains and banished, but he was a brave soldier of Christ and confessor of the Faith. Love proves itself in suffering.

3. "Suppose that a man has the worldly goods he needs, and sees his brother go in want; if he steels his heart against his brother, how can we say that the love of God dwells in him?" (I John 3:17.) Nicholas knew that earthly wealth may easily become a danger. He knew the truth of St. Leo's words: "Whatever good one has, death robs him of it; whatever good one does, heaven returns it to him. He who gives perishable things falls heir to eternal goods."

"Well done, my good and faithful servant; since thou hast been faithful over little things, I have great things to commit to thy charge; come and share the joy of thy Lord" (Gospel).

Collect: O God, who didst glorify the blessed bishop Nicholas by countless miracles, grant, we pray Thee, that by his merits and prayers we may be delivered from the fires of hell. Amen.

DECEMBER 7

St. Ambrose, *Bishop, Confessor,*
Doctor of the Church

1. Ambrose was born of a noble family about the year 240, probably in Treves. After having studied law in Rome and begun a very successful practice there, he received from Emperor Valentinian the appointment as governor of Liguria and Aemilia, with headquarters in Milan. When this city's Arian bishop had died and the people were gathered in the cathedral to elect a successor, Ambrose was assigned to keep peace between the contending factions. As he entered the church a child cried out, "Ambrose, bishop." He was promptly chosen, though he had not yet received baptism. After he had been persuaded to accept the nomination, he was baptized and successively elevated through the various clerical orders, becoming bishop of Milan on December 7, 374. From that time forward he led an austere life, diligently studied the Scriptures, preached every Sunday and holy day, listened to the spiritual problems of the faithful, personally directed the care of the poor, wrote numerous letters, and, in all, exercised heroic charity; he was a bishop after God's own heart. He nevertheless had to put up with much vexation at the hands of the Arian Empress Justina, who resided in Milan. Ambrose excommunicated Emperor Theodosius and exacted public penance of him for his terrible massacre in Thessalonica in 390, answering the Emperor's plea of immunity with the famous sentence: "If you have imitated David in sinning, you must also imitate him in doing penance." In the spring of 397 Ambrose fell ill. He died on the vigil of Easter, April 4. Since feasts are not celebrated during this season, the anniversary of his consecration, December 7, was chosen as the date for his festival.

2. "The Lord moved him to speak before the assembled peo-

ple, filling him with the spirit of wisdom and discernment"
(Introit). With these words we greet the priest approaching
the altar, for we see in him the holy bishop Ambrose, a priest
and teacher of noble stature preaching the word of God,
"dwelling upon it, welcome or unwelcome," even opposing the
Empress and Emperor, whom he otherwise esteemed. He was
watchful lest the false Arian doctrine poison his flock, and was
prepared "to accept every hardship, to employ [himself] in
preaching the gospel, and perform every duty of [his] office"
(cf. Epistle). He was the "salt of the earth," full of supernatural wisdom and possessing such powerfully attractive eloquence that even worldly-minded people were captivated by
the magic of his words and won for Christ. Even the rhetori-
cian Augustine was so deeply impressed by the force of Ambrose's personality and preaching that he asked for baptism at
Easter, 387.

Mindful of the Apostle's admonition that a bishop ought not
to seek gold and possessions but should be satisfied with little,
Ambrose distributed his property among the poor and lived
entirely for the care of souls. The work of grace in him is especially apparent in his inspired writings, but he was also an outstanding speaker, a master of graceful language and of noble
poetry. Firmly rooted in faith, he possessed a strong but tender
love of Christ. Ambrose preached on Christian virginity with
such sincerity and fervor that the mothers of Milan would not
let their daughters hear him lest they lose interest in marriage.
The empress Justina, mother of the young Valentinian II and a
rabid Arian, tried in every way to deprive Ambrose of his
See. She assembled bishops agreeable to her for the purpose of
deposing him. Ambrose appeared at the gathering surrounded
by an excited crowd of his faithful. The Arian bishops found
themselves completely overpowered and Ambrose calmed the
people. Emperor Valentinian then demanded that one church
be given up to the Arians, but Bishop Ambrose declared with
finality: "The secular buildings belong to the emperor, the

churches to the bishop. If you forget that you are a Catholic prince, I shall not forget that I am a Catholic bishop. I will not surrender the temple of God to those who falsify the Faith." Fearless preaching, and effective, too.

"Every soul is in the hands of God, and Christ must be all to all. Perhaps you need a healing balm for your burning wounds: He is a physician. Or, you are being consumed by the fever of temptation: He is a cooling fountain. Or, the burden of sin on your conscience is oppressing you: He is holiness and justice. Are you seeking a remedy for your weakness? He will be strength and power to you. Are you afraid of death? He is life. You long for the bliss of heaven: He is the way. You wish to escape the darkness of error: He is the light. Is your soul hungry? He is bread. Come and see how loving the Lord is. Blessed the man who places his hope in Him." For "the worst kind of ignorance is to be ignorant of Christ. Anyone who does not grow great on Christ remains small. He walks in deepest darkness who lives without Christ. Ignorance of Christ is death to the soul. Knowledge of Christ brings everlasting life, now, in a dark manner, hereafter in lightsome vision, face to face." These sentiments reveal the faith and the life of St. Ambrose.

3. The last words of the great Bishop were: "I have so lived that I need not be ashamed; I am not afraid to die. We have a good Master." His fearlessness in the face of death was due to his conviction that he had exercised the spiritual and corporal works of mercy to the best of his ability. He had always been ready to help; the door of his room had always been open and everyone had found free access to the bishop without appointment. He had settled every type of case brought before him: helping the oppressed, widows and orphans; deciding questions of conscience for his people; reconciling enemies. When the Goths overran Thrace in 377 and set up slave-markets everywhere, Ambrose sold even the precious vessels of the altar in order to redeem captives. One whose charity is so sincere and self-sacrificing surely heard at death the words

of our Lord: "I was hungry, . . . a stranger, . . . a prisoner, and you came to me. . . . Take possession of the kingdom which has been prepared for you" (cf. Matt. 25:34).

"Here was a great priest whose life was acceptable to God. . . . Where shall we find another to keep the law of the Most High as he kept it?" (Gradual.)

Collect: O God, who didst give blessed Ambrose to Thy people as a minister of eternal salvation, grant, we pray Thee, that we may be worthy to have as our advocate in heaven him who on earth taught us the way of life. Amen.

DECEMBER 11

St. Damasus, *Pope and Confessor*

1. Damasus was born in Rome about the year 304, of Spanish parents. He entered the service of the Church at an early age but was not ordained deacon until 355, under Pope Liberius. While that pope was in exile by order of the Arian Emperor Constantius, Damasus, as archdeacon of the Roman Church, strongly defended papal interests. After the death of Liberius in 366, a small party elected the deacon Ursinus as bishop of Rome and had him consecrated at once. The majority of the clergy and people, however, chose Damasus. A bloody feud ensued, lasting until Emperor Valentinian I recognized Damasus as pope and sent Ursinus into exile. In Rome Damasus vigorously opposed the Donatists; in the Roman synods of 368 and 369, he condemned Arianism. He sent his legate to the general council of 381 in Constantinople; he called St. Jerome to the Eternal City to revise the Latin text of the Bible; he took an enthusiastic interest in the tombs of the martyrs, beautifying them and even composing exquisite epitaphs for them. Damasus died on December 11, 384.

2. "Thou art Peter, and it is upon this rock that I will build my Church" (Gospel). The pontificate of Damasus saw the rise of great difficulties. The horrors of the bloody persecution of Christians by the Emperors Diocletian and Maxentius began in his reign. Then, hardly had Constantine granted the Church its right to exist in the Roman state, when, in 320, the heresy of Arianism reared its ugly head. Though condemned by the Council of Nice in 325, it continued to be a serious threat to the integrity of Catholic doctrine, during that century, because many bishops, as well as the emperor, favored it. Pope Damasus exercised moderation in the struggle; but he demanded that every bishop subscribe to certain doctrinal norms, and inflicted punishment when necessary. As champion of the true Faith against all heresy he proved himself a providential pope, a veritable rock of truth in the midst of storms. "Thou art Peter!"

"Simon Peter, if thou dost love me, feed my lambs, feed my sheep" (Introit). Peter had to give assurance of his love before he could undertake the leadership of the Church. It is not natural human prerogatives that qualify a man for the tiara; the decisive and essential requirement is love of God. "Simon, lovest thou Me?" The more perfect Peter's love, the more perfect will be his union with Christ and the more successfully will he feed the Lord's sheep. "Be shepherds to the flock God has given you. Carry out your charge as God would have it done, cordially, not like drudges, generously, not in the hope of sordid gain" (Epistle). In spite of the bitter opposition and foul slanders of his Arian enemies, Damasus labored zealously to overcome the heresy and to show the erring their way back to truth and to the Church. His charitable mildness toward the heretics brought criticism from one of his own bishops; but Damasus was motivated solely by love for souls, love like that of the Good Shepherd, who will not rest until the last sheep has been saved. Such was his love of Christ that he could forget the injustice done him and say with his Master: "Father,

forgive them; they do not know what it is that they are doing"
(Luke 23:34). In this way he proved himself worthy to stand
beside St. Peter and say: "Thou knowest that I love Thee."

3. St. Damasus is considered the most significant pope of
the fourth century. Fearless in the fight against heresies, he
was a priest full of goodness, courage, and energy; he was filled
with zeal for the word of God as revealed in the Scriptures. We
thank God today for having given His Church this saint as its
pope in the critical times of the fourth century.

"See, I have inspired thy lips with utterance: I give thee
authority over the nations; with a word thou shalt root them
up and pull them down, with a word thou shalt build them up
and plant them anew" (Offertory). This is the program of
every bishop, priest, and superior of the Church of Christ!

Collect: Be pleased to watch over Thy flock, eternal Shepherd,
and keep it under Thy continual protection, through Thy supreme
pontiff, blessed Damasus, whom Thou didst establish as chief
shepherd of the whole Church. Amen.

DECEMBER 13

St. Lucy, *Virgin and Martyr*

1. St. Lucy probably suffered martyrdom about the year 304,
during the persecution of Emperor Diocletian. She belonged
to a prominent family in Syracuse, Sicily, and was brought up
as a Christian by her mother Eutychia. On the occasion of the
latter's miraculous restoration to health at the tomb of St.
Agatha in Catania, Lucy obtained her permission to remain a
virgin and to distribute her property among the poor. This
fired the wrath of her intended husband, and he denounced
her as a Christian. The judge ordered her to be taken to a
brothel; but she became miraculously fixed to the spot, and no

one could move her. Nor did fire harm her. Finally, the thrust
of a sword ended her life. This is the legendary account of
Lucy's death. History attests only to her existence and her martyrdom.

2. "Thou hast been a friend to right, an enemy to wrong"
(Introit). This does not imply that Lucy would have done
wrong by accepting matrimony. But God gave her the grace
to see that "he who is unmarried is concerned with God's claim,
asking how he is to please God. . . . So a woman who is free
of wedlock, or a virgin, is concerned with the Lord's claim, intent on holiness, bodily and spiritual; whereas the married
woman is concerned with the world's claim, asking how she is
to please her husband" (I Cor. 7:32, 34). For this reason, Lucy
chose to remain unmarried. She distributed her wealth among
the poor, thereby removing the greatest hindrances to her
total dedication of herself to the Lord. At St. Agatha's tomb
she had found the "treasure hidden in a field" and the "pearl
of great cost" (Gospel); she had come to recognize the nobility of a life for and with Christ. Therefore, she sold all her possessions and purchased the field, the pearl (cf. Gospel).

"Maidens shall follow in her retinue into the king's presence;
all rejoicing, all triumph, those companions of hers, as they
enter the palace of their Lord and King" (Offertory). In Lucy,
the "lucent" saint of the Advent season, we recognize ourselves;
we long for the coming of Christmas, the coming of Christ.
Our gaze rises above earthly things to the heavenly realm of
grace and supernatural life; we look up to the heaven which is
Christ, whose coming we are now anticipating. St. Lucy leads
the way as we hasten to meet Him when He comes to us in the
Holy Sacrifice, in Holy Communion, in order to fill us with the
holiness of His own divine life. We look forward to the time
when He will take us to His home for the blessed nuptials.
But we cannot claim to be good imitators of St. Lucy unless
we free ourselves from inordinate attachment to creatures in

daily life, for the sake of the "treasure" that we hope to acquire; unless we walk the way of martyrdom, of sacrifice, and suffering out of love for Christ.

3. During the Advent of earthly life, let us walk in the footsteps of St. Lucy, virgin and martyr, on our way to meet the coming Redeemer; and let us persevere in this holy practice until, at the hour of death, we shall be admitted to the celebration of an everlasting Christmas in heaven.

"Vexed by the causeless malice of princes, my heart still dreads thy warnings. Victors rejoice not more over rich spoils than I over thy promises" (Communion). Amid the afflictions of life, we will place our confidence in the promise given in the Holy Eucharist: "The man who eats my flesh and drinks my blood enjoys eternal life, and I will raise him up at the last day" (John 6:55). This promise of our Lord gives us strength and courage.

Collect: Listen to us, God our Savior, so that we who find joy in the festival of Thy blessed virgin and martyr Lucy may learn from her the spirit of godly service. Amen.

DECEMBER 21

St. Thomas, *Apostle*

1. When Jesus was preparing to go to Judea (and to His death) in answer to the call of Mary and Martha for His help in the serious illness of their brother Lazarus, Thomas said to the other apostles: "Let us go too, and be killed along with him" (John 11:16). During our Savior's farewell discourse to His apostles, Thomas interrupted with the question: "Lord, we do not know where thou art going: how are we to know the way there?" Our Lord answered him: "I am the way; I am truth and life" (John 14:6). The Gospel selection for today's

feast records the reaction of St. Thomas to the testimony of the other apostles in regard to the Resurrection. "Until I have seen the mark of the nails on his hands, until I have put my finger into the mark of the nails, and put my hand into his side, you will never make me believe." When our Lord again appeared, a week later, Thomas fell on his knees before Him declaring: "Thou art my Lord and my God." His preaching later on gave evidence of his firm conviction, of his faith in the divinity of Christ. He carried the good tidings of redemption to the Parthians, Armenians, Persians, and above all, to India, where he is said to have gained King Gundaphar for Christ. In this land he died a martyr.

2. "Great reverence have I for thy friends, O God; sovereign power is theirs in abundance" (Introit). Our Lord Himself applied this psalm verse to His apostles when He said: "I do not speak of you any more as my servants; a servant is one who does not understand what his master is about, whereas I have made known to you all that my Father has told me; and so I have called you my friends" (John 15:15). He had chosen them from among His disciples to be apostles, that is, messengers; now He sent them forth to preach to all men, as eyewitnesses to His public ministry and His resurrection. They were "Christ's servants, and stewards of God's mysteries" (I Cor. 4:1), ministers of Christ commissioned to establish "in our hearts his message of reconciliation. We are Christ's ambassadors, then, and God appeals to you through us; we entreat you in Christ's name, make your peace with God" (II Cor. 5:20). Their faithful execution of the mission entrusted to them, gained for them the right to be laborers with Christ in the work of building up the kingdom of God among men. They were the foundation wall, the fundament upon which we have been placed as living stones of God's holy house. "The chief cornerstone of it is Jesus Christ himself. In him the whole fabric is bound together, as it grows into a temple dedicated to the Lord; in him you too are being built in with the rest, so

that God may find in you a dwelling-place for his Spirit" (Epistle). Christ transferred His own mission to His apostles: "I came upon an errand from my Father, and now I am sending you out in my turn" (John 20:21). He gave them His power and authority to teach: "To me is given all power, in heaven and upon earth. Go, therefore, and teach all nations." The apostles were the princes of the people, the judges of the world: they were to give testimony of Christ. Among them we greet St. Thomas this day.

"If the world hates you, be sure that it hated me before it learned to hate you" (John 15:18). An apostle is to the world, "ipso facto," an object of hatred and persecution; he shares the lot of Christ, to whom he is bound and belongs. "They will persecute you just as they have persecuted me; they will pay the same attention to your words as to mine" (John 15:20). Thomas perceived clearly and was determined: "Let us go too, and be killed along with him." No doubt he was deeply disturbed after His Lord and Master had died on the Cross. Like the other apostles, he was so utterly crushed by the apparent failure of Christ that he could not at first believe in the Resurrection; but once he had been convinced, he declared firmly: "My Lord and my God!" In his missionary preaching he boldly proclaimed: "The Lord has indeed risen," and "I put my finger into the mark of the nails, and put my hand into his side," quite near to His heart. After gaining many souls for Christ by his zealous preaching, Thomas received the grace to die a martyr.

3. "You are no longer exiles, then, or aliens; the saints are your fellow-citizens, you belong to God's household" (Epistle); you are full-fledged members of the Church of Christ, partakers of those means of salvation which the Lord has entrusted to her. This blessing depends, of course, on our being built on the foundation of the apostles; on our listening to their testimony and maintaining fellowship with them.

The Antiphon chanted while we receive Holy Communion

today may remind us of the ancient custom of receiving the consecrated bread in one's hand. "Put in thy hand, and feel the place of the nails. Cease thy doubting and believe." Adoring, we say with St. Thomas: "My Lord and my God." In this spirit of faith we approach Christmas. When we see the Savior as a weak, helpless child in the crib, we kneel, with St. Thomas, and confess: "My Lord and my God!" In humility I adore thee, hidden Godhead!

Collect: Grant, we pray Thee, Lord, that we may keep in triumph the feast of Thy blessed apostle Thomas. May we be ever heartened by his protection, and maintain his faith with fitting devotion. Amen.